W9-BVQ-174

THE NEW VIGILANTES

Volume 113, Sage Library of Social Research

SAGE LIBRARY OF SOCIAL RESEARCH

1 Caplovitz The Merchants of Harlem
2 Rosenau International Studies & the Social Sciences
3 Ashford Ideology & Participation
4 McGowan/Shapiro The Comparative Study of Foreign Policy
5 Male The Struggle for Power
6 Tanter Modelling & Managing International Conflicts
7 Catanese Planners & Local Politics
8 Prescott Economic Aspects of Public Housing
9 Parkinson Latin America, the Cold War, & the World Powers, 1945-1973
10 Smith Ad Hoc Governments
11 Gallimore et al Culture, Behavior & Education
12 Hallman Neighborhood Government in a Metropolitan Setting
13 Gelles The Violent Home
14 Weaver Conflict & Control in Health Care Administration
15 Schweigler National Consciousness in Divided Germany
16 Carey Sociology & Public Affairs
17 Lehman Coordinating Health Care
18 Bell/Price The First Term
19 Alderfer/Brown Learning from Changing
20 Wells/Marwell Self-Esteem
21 Robins Political Institutionalization & the Integration of Elites
22 Schonfeld Obedience & Revolt
23 McCready/Greeley The Ultimate Values of the American Population
24 Nye Role Structure & Analysis of the Family
25 Wehr/Washburn Peace & World Order Systems
26 Stewart Children in Distress
27 Dedring Recent Advances in Peace & Conflict Research
28 Czudnowski Comparing Political Behavior
29 Douglas Investigative Social Research
30 Stohl War & Domestic Political Violence
31 Williamson Sons or Daughters
32 Levi Law & Politics in the International Society
33 Altheide Creating Reality
34 Lerner The Politics of Decision-Making

35 Converse The Dynamics of Party Support
36 Newman/Price Jails & Drug Treatment
37 Abercrombie The Military Chaplain
38 Gottdiener Planned Sprawl
39 Lineberry Equality & Urban Policy
40 Morgan Deterrence
41 Lefebvre The Structure of Awareness
42 Fontana The Last Frontier
43 Kemper Migration & Adaptation
44 Caplovitz/Sherrow The Religious Drop-Outs
45 Nagel/Neef The Legal Process: Modeling the System
46 Bucher/Stelling Becoming Professional
47 Hiniker Revolutionary Ideology & Chinese Reality
48 Herman Jewish Identity
49 Marsh Protest & Political Consciousness
50 LaRossa Conflict & Power in Marriage
51 Abrahamsson Bureaucracy or Participation
52 Parkinson The Philosophy of International Relations
53 Lerup Building the Unfinished
54 Smith Churchill's German Army
55 Corden Planned Cities
56 Hallman Small & Large Together
57 Inciardi et al Historical Approaches to Crime
58 Levitan/Alderman Warriors at Work
59 Zurcher The Mutable Self
60 Teune/Mlinar The Developmental Logic of Social Systems
61 Garson Group Theories of Politics
62 Medcalf Law & Identity
63 Danziger Making Budgets
64 Damrell Search for Identity
65 Stotland et al Empathy, Fantasy & Helping
66 Aronson Money & Power
67 Wice Criminal Lawyers
68 Hoole Evaluation Research & Development Activities
69 Singelmann From Agriculture to Services
70 Seward The American Family
71 McCleary Dangerous Men
72 Nagel/Neef Policy Analysis: In Social Science Research
73 Rejai/Phillips Leaders of Revolution

74 Inbar Routine Decision-Making
75 Galaskiewicz Exchange Networks & Community Politics
76 Alkin/Daillak/White Using Evaluations
77 Sensat Habermas & Marxism
78 Matthews The Social World of Old Women
79 Swanson/Cohen/Swanson Small Towns & Small Towners
80 Latour/Woolgar Laboratory Life
81 Krieger Hip Capitalism
82 Megargee/Bohn Classifying Criminal Offenders
83 Cook Who Should Be Helped?
84 Gelles Family Violence
85 Katzner Choice & the Quality of Life
86 Caplovitz Making Ends Meet
87 Berk/Berk Labor and Leisure at Home
88 Darling Families Against Society
89 Altheide/Snow Media Logic
90 Roosens Mental Patients in Town Life
91 Savage Founders, Heirs, & Managers
92 Bromley/Shupe "Moonies" in America
93 Littrell Bureaucratic Justice
94 Murray/Cox Beyond Probation
95 Roberts Afro-Arab Fraternity
96 Rutman Planning Useful Evaluations
97 Shimanoff Communication Rules
98 Laguerre Voodoo Heritage
99 Macarov Work and Welfare
100 Bolton The Pregnant Adolescent
101 Rothman Using Research in Organizations
102 Sellin The Penalty of Death
103 Studer/Chubin The Cancer Mission
104 Beardsley Redefining Rigor
105 Small Was War Necessary?
106 Sanders Rape & Woman's Identity
107 Watkins The Practice of Urban Economics
108 Clubb/Flanigan/Zingale Partisan Realignment
109 Gittell Limits to Citizen Participation
110 Finsterbusch Understanding Social Impacts
111 Scanzoni/Szinovacz Family Decision Making
112 Lidz/Walker Crisis as Usual
113 Shupe/Bromley The New Vigilantes

The New Vigilantes

Deprogrammers Anti-Cultists, and the New Religions

Anson D. Shupe, Jr. and David G. Bromley

Foreword by Joseph R. Gusfield

Volume 113
SAGE LIBRARY OF
SOCIAL RESEARCH

 **SAGE PUBLICATIONS**   Beverly Hills   London

Copyright © 1980 by Sage Publications, Inc.

For information address:

SAGE Publications, Inc.
275 South Beverly Drive
Beverly Hills, California 90212

SAGE Publications Ltd
28 Banner Street
London EC1Y 8QE, England

Printed in the United States of America

Library of Congress Cataloging in Publication Data

Shupe, Anson D.
   The new vigilantes.

   (Sage library of social research ; v. 113)
   Bibliography: p.
   Includes index.
   1. Cults—United States. I. Bromley, David G.,
joint author. II. Title. III. Title: Deprogram-
mers, anti-cultists, and the new religions.
BL2530.U5S53   306'.6   80-23276
ISBN 0-8039-1542-X
ISBN 0-8039-1543-8 (pbk.)

FIRST PRINTING

CONTENTS

Chapter	*Page*
Foreword by Joseph R. Gusfield	7
Preface	11
Introduction	13
1. The Anti-Cult Movement in Sociocultural Perspective	25
2. Sources and Dynamics of Strain	37
3. The Anti-Cult Movement Ideology	59
4. The Anti-Cult Associations	87
5. The Deprogrammers	121
6. The Impact of Deprogramming	145
7. The Impact of the Anti-Cult Associations	169
8. Jonestown and the Revitalization of the ACM	207
9. Conclusions	233
References	249
Index	261
About the Authors	269

TO OUR PARENTS

What I have done and will continue to do till I can no longer draw breath, is to fight for an honorable cause, the freeing of the minds of men and women who have been victims of the enslavement and psychological kidnapping perpetrated by thousands of cults now prospering in our country and around the world.

> —Theodore Roosevelt "Ted" Patrick, Jr.,
> deprogrammer, 1976

I am here to protest against child molesters, for as surely as there are those who lure children with lollypops in order to rape their bodies, so, too, are there those who lure children with candy-coated lies in order to rape their minds.

> —Rabbi Maurice Davis to Senator Robert
> Dole, 1979

Let us not forget the anguish of parents is not the only anguish involved here. Let us give equal consideration to the feelings—and rights—of young people who go about in daily dread of being physically seized and subjected to protracted spiritual gang-rape until they yield their most cherished religious commitments.

> —Dean M. Kelley, *The Civil Liberties*
> *Review*, 1977

FOREWORD

Joseph R. Gusfield

Anson Shupe, Jr. and David Bromley have made a unique and sorely needed contribution to the understanding of social movements. This volume and the companion work *"Moonies" in America: Cult, Church and Crusade* (Sage, 1979) should be taken together. The two studies provide valuable research of the interaction between movement and countermovement; a sense of the contribution of movements to public issues and controversies. In their concern for the dual sides of the "cult controversies" Shupe and Bromley advance our insight and knowledge of how movements emerge and change; how they affect opposition and alliance and respond to new events and conditions.

In this short foreword to their excellent study I want to express some thoughts about the implications of their work for the study of social movements. One of the contributions that comes from studying a movement—the Unification Church—and a countermovement—the Anti-Cult Movement—is found in the underlying perspective toward the structure in which movements operate in contemporary life. Conventionally sociologists have thought about movements in the confines of a natural history career and a dissent-status quo paradigm. In this approach movements emerge as challenges to established authorities. They go through a series of definite stages from a fluid association of indefinitely directed partisans to a formal organization of members and leaders. If they succeed, the movement's goals become embodied in institutional acceptance and the movement becomes the new establishment.

That paradigm distorts the flux of public life in America. It assumes that the "status quo" is well understood and exists as a way of behaving about which consensus is easily found. This study indicates the difficulties

7

in any such formulation. Change, newness, and sectarianism are themselves prized and established parts of American life. That very fact of American political life made the attempt of the Anti-Cult Movement to appear as representing established religion in the United States a matter of controversy and argument, not an easy typology of dissenting cults and established institutions. Arguments arose over exactly what conventional theory in social movements literature has assumed to be an agreed-upon matter—what is accepted dissent and what is not. Precisely because change and controversy are constant, the static picture of movements operating within a fixed set of parameters is illusory.

What the cults and the anticultists did was create and confront a public issue. The recruitment of sons and daughters into such groups as the "Moonies," Hare Krishna, or Children of God confronted parents with actions that contradicted the hopes and expectations of future occupational, marital, and educational promise. It seemed bizarre, alienating, and even heretical. Yet, the ideology and legal forms of free choice, of the separation of church and state, and of the value of religious commitments created a real problem. The Anti-Cult Movement provided a rationale for turning the personal conflict of parents into a public issue. The movement sought to provide social controls in what seemed to be a personal and familial problem. In the brainwashing ideology it developed an explanation consonant with both the troubled responses of parents and the general private and public commitment to religions as virtuous per se and to the sanctity of freedom of choice. In deprogramming it provided an immediate activity to "rescue" the seemingly coerced child. Each movement—cultists and anti-cultists—met with both acceptance and rejection in the large society. Each adapted and responded to events and to each other. It is hard, even a decade later, to say that the issues have been resolved.

Here it is important to recognize some aspects of movements that are sometimes lost sight of in the attention given to social movements as organized groups. Characteristically, sociologists have studied movements by conducting research on members and the associations to which they are attached. The impact of resource mobilization theory has accentuated this emphasis on the movement as an organized activity mobilizing a variety of resources at its disposal. There has been a consequent derogation of the import of personal ideas and behavior, of the "hearts and minds" of partisans. This theoretical stance has been helpful in understanding many movements in modern society insofar as they carry on activity in the public and political arena. This is certainly the case in Shupe and Bromley's present study, where the Anti-Cultists attempt to develop social controls through public attention and through activities such as deprogramming which entail confrontations with legal authorities. It is less useful when studying the recruitment, continuation, and defection of young people which initiated the issue.

That aspect of the movement's impact is missing from the approaches which focus on organization and on public action alone. Shupe and Bromley have been unable to put the central figures of the controversy into the picture—the young people whose actions precipitated the movement. They tell us that most of those recruited left the cults after varying lengths of time without any parental or movement action. We do not know whether the cults were more or less successful in recruiting after the Jonestown suicides. We do not know if the movement against the cults created an environment more or less congenial to the cults. We do know, from the earlier work, that the Unification Church made some adaptations in techniques of money-raising and in the internal communal life based on public criticism and even repression. Studying a movement only at the public level overstates the importance of public actions on private behavior and hides the implications for social change in the emergence of movements and countermovements. Is the recruitment of a child into Hare Krishna as troublesome for parents as it was a decade ago, or is it becoming normalized, as the choice of woodcraving as an occupation of an upper-class child has become, if not still troublesome, at least no longer bizarre. The implications of a movement for change are often lost when studies of movements concentrate only on the public arena. Such limitations do not vitiate the splendid accomplishment of this study, however.

One last issue deserves some comment. The dilemma of cults arising in a society committed to free choice and dissent illustrates the problems and complexities of liberalism under challenge. Acceptance of sects and the tolerance of religious choice is easily achieved in principle when the sects are within a recognized and approved spectrum and do not threaten other values and expectations. The personal difficulties of parents are under standable in the cases described here. Yet, in the effort to bring social controls and the state to their aid they create a sharp challenge to the meaning of liberal government. Shupe and Bromley present a picture of attempted repressions and controls that were sometimes successful in being adopted but often ran aground on the shores of legal and political traditions of separation of church and state and of the civil liberties of recruited cult members. Even the awesomeness and public attention of the People's Temple deaths did not lead to legislation or legal repression of new religions and cults in America.

Taken together or separately, these two books by Shupe and Bromley are among the finest studies of American social movements in the past decade. They will become standard parts of sociological literature in the future.

–J.R.G.

PREFACE

This book examines the organized reaction to the rapid proliferation of new religious movements (pejoratively labeled "cults") in the late 1960s and 1970s, a countermovement usually referred to by that minority of persons even aware of its existence as the anti-cult or deprogramming movement. This is the second of two volumes in the *Sage Library of Social Research* dealing with this controversy and therefore may be correctly regarded as the companion to our earlier *"Moonies" in America: Cult, Church, and Crusade,* published in 1979. It is not intended merely as a sequel to that study; rather, whereas the first volume dealt with the formation, expansion, and various fortunes of Reverend Sun Myung Moon's Unificationist Movement in both South Korea and the United States according to the resource mobilization theoretical approach, the present study is less tied to any *specific* theoretical scheme and analyzes a countermovement which had a related but nevertheless distinct set of goals, problems, and developments apart from Moon and his movement.

As was the case with our previous study of the Moon movement, however, in this examination of the anticult movement we purposefully focus our analysis at a sociological (that is, organizational) level as opposed to utilizing psychological, theological, or ethnographic perspectives. This particular emphasis reflects not only our own disciplinary orientation but also a conviction that discussions of the issues raised here have largely been the (unfortunate) preserve of partisans locked within the ethnocentric psychological bias of twentieth-century American society or monopolized by the self-serving accounts of participants in the controversy. As in our first volume of this set, we confront and attempt to dispel a number of myths that sustain both protagonists and antagonists of a social movement. In this sense our goals are twofold: (1) to explain both analytically and concretely the true nature of the conflict surrounding certain religious groups accused of brainwashing and other heinous practices; and (2) to contribute to the sociology of social movements, particularly as our understanding of these involves power relations, and thereby provide a thorough case study that may be of later use for comparative analyses.

We wish to acknowledge our indebtedness to that not unexpectedly large number of individuals who contributed inspiration, information, criticism, or support for this second volume in our multiproject research of social movements. In particular, we owe thanks to John Lofland, who encouraged and constructively criticized our analytic entry into this project; Bruce Busching, whose insights into the dynamics of social repression proved invaluable; Thomas Robbins, who so often was a veritable fount of the latest developments in disciplinary and popular literature on the subject of anticultism and the law; Donna Oliver, who contributed to the development of our ideas about apostasy; and Bob Perkins, Dean of the Graduate School of the University of Texas at Arlington, and Thomas Porter, Dean of Liberal Arts at UTA, who helped secure financial support for our cross-country travels and adventures. We also recognize the indispensable logistical assistance of Lois Williams during compilation of archival data and actual production of the manuscript.

In addition many respondents, informants, and nonpartisan "bystanders" connected to this new religious/deprogramming controversy lent critical assistance. As in our first volume, out of a concern for their reputations and careers within their respective social movements, we directly credit none publicly with providing us with information. Some requested anonymity; others did not but we deemed it our ethical responsibility not to jeopardize their respective social standings by what possibly could be our unpopularly received research conclusions. The methodological aspects of this issue are considered in the introduction.

Last, and of course foremost, we thank our loved ones for the sacrifices of time and alternative activities which they underwent during the researching and writing of this book.

—*Anson D. Shupe, Jr.*
Arlington, Texas

—*David G. Bromley*
Hartford, Connecticut

INTRODUCTION

This monograph examines the loose coalition of groups that arose in response to the innovative religious developments of the 1970s and which became known as the anti-cult movement (hereafter ACM). Our companion volume *"Moonies" in America: Cult, Church, and Crusade* dealt with the best known of these new religious movements, Sun Myung Moon's Unificationist Movement, which became the archnemesis of the ACM. The ACM was a grass-roots phenomenon initiated by the unhappy families of individuals who joined the new religions. As we shall show, because of both the constitutional separation of church and state and guarantees of religious freedom, their opposition to the new religions was not easily translatable into social and political repression. As a result, the ACM emerged as two interdependent but distinct components, each employing separate strategies against their opponents, the "cults." One component, made up of interest groups or family associations, followed the conventional route of lobbying and engaging in other forms of political activism within the context of the formal political structure. The other pursued more vigilante-style, direct action designed to "rescue" the sons and daughters believed by parents to be "lost" to "cults." It was the latter group which captured the popular attention and which won for the entire movement the label of "deprogramming movement." In this book we shall analyze both components of the ACM which we have termed, respectively, *the anti-cult associations* and *the deprogrammers*. Our twofold objective will be to analyze the ACM from an organizational perspective and to delineate the process whereby the ACM sought to initiate the construction and imposition of deviant labels upon the new religions. Because our first book dealt only with the Unificationist Movement and because, as we shall see, this group was designated *the* primary target of the ACM, much of our supporting data and examples will also refer to the conflict between the ACM and the Unificationist Movement specifically.

Conceptual Orientation

In our first volume we utilized the resource mobilization perspective to elucidate the organizational aspects of the development of the Unificationist Movement (hereafter UM). We were interested primarily in how specific components of social movements emerged, "fit together," and supported one another (what we termed "organizational congruence"). Such concerns required an organizational rather than a social-psychological-level approach, and for that reason we utilized the resource mobilization perspective.[1] With it we examined the major organizational resources which any "world-transforming" movement (one which seeks total, permanent, structural change of societies across all institutions) would have to mobilize and/or shape in order to sustain its organization and pursue its goals. *Internally* these resources included ideology, members, financial resources, visibility/publicity, and leadership/organizational structure; *externally* they included the environmental context in which the movement emerged and the societal reaction to it. We briefly recapitulate a description of the UM in these terms in Chapter 1. This capsule summary of the process of resource mobilization, both internal and external, is important because we argue that it was the resultant organizational structure of world-transforming movements such as the UM that fostered the strain and conflict which will be the starting point of analysis in this study.

Here we retain our concern with organization and examine the same resource mobilization variables and processes in the case of the ACM. However, whereas when we previously analyzed the UM we were concerned primarily with the mobilization of key organizational resources to create organizational congruence within the movement itself, in the present study we are more concerned with the ACM's internal mobilization of such resources only as it was a means to the end of imposing deviant labels and sanctions externally on the new religious movements. Although the deviance perspective which underlies much of the analysis in this book does not hinge on locating the ACM in any social movement typology such as that discussed in our previous volume, it is important to note that the ACM is what would be classified as a restorative movement (see Bromley and Shupe, 1979a: 22-24). For our purposes here the significant implication is that the anti-cultists ultimately were concerned with restoring former social relationships and social structures (at least as these were ideally conceptualized) of family, religion, and society that they thought had gone awry. We shall contend that the emergence of the new religions posed a direct threat to the interests and authority of several institutions—most notably the family and religion—and that the "cult"-anti-cult controversy was essentially a struggle to define the boundaries of legitimacy in a generic sense, hence an attempt to locate "cults" inside or outside these boundaries of public morality.

From a deviance perspective, therefore, our analysis begins with the identification of the clash of interests that created strain between the new religions and established institutions. As they gradually emerged, such strains tended to create new symbolic definitions of acts and actors on both sides and ultimately strong pressures for exclusionary actions designed to move the new religions' organizations, leaders, and members into deviant statuses.[2] This process depended upon the formation of alliances between the anti-cultists and a number of conventional institutions which possessed both sanctioning capacities and some stake in the outcome of the conflict. In essence, then, in applying a deviance perspective for understanding the organization and operations of the ACM we have focused on the process of constructing and applying deviant labels which emanated from a struggle between groups with incompatible interests.

Organization and Presentation

With this brief overview of the conceptual framework of this book in mind, we turn to a discussion of the organization and presentation of data in each chapter. We defer until Chapter 9 an integrated discussion of the process of mobilizing resources for purposes of constructing and imposing deviant labels so that we may better refer to the data which are the basis of that formulation. Because it is precisely the emergent nature of these constructions and processes that we wish to emphasize, our argument is better served by first allowing the reader to become familiar with the reflexive pattern of ACM development and its conflict with the new religions as these actually occurred.

In Chapter 1 we simply attempt to provide perspective on the historical/sociocultural context in which the ACM emerged. Specifically, we identify the new religions as successors to the social and political protest movements of the 1960s; discuss the revival of the brainwashing metaphor, which, in its revised form, built upon Korean prisoner-of-war experiences to explain alleged rapid changes in religious affiliation; and recapitulate the historical development and organization of the UM as the quintessential "cult" and chief opponent of the ACM.

In Chapter 2 we locate the sources of strain between the new religions and the ACM, focusing on the family and religious institutions which experienced this strain most severely and directly. We shall contend that it was the threat to these institutions' respective goals and authority structures which provided strain, and we elaborate the dynamics of strain as an emergent process in each case. From a resource mobilization perspective, strain explains the impetus for creating ACM organizations; from a deviance perspective, the strain accounts for the initiation of perception of conflicts of interest and forms the basis for later exclusionary activity.

In Chapter 3 we present the two metaphors around which ACM ideology developed: those of *possession* and *deception* which served to organize the ideologies for a range of both secular and religious opponents to the new religions. From a resource mobilization perspective, we are concerned with how the ACM's ideology (that is, its "set of beliefs about the social world and how it operates, containing statements about the rightness of certain arrangements and what action would be undertaken in light of those statements" [Wilson, 1973: 91-2]) emerged and developed as its proponents attempted to formulate an understanding of the problem they confronted both to guide their own actions and to interpret their actions to others. From a deviance perspective, we are more specifically concerned with how the ideology legitimated the kind of social control the ACM sought to exercise vis-à-vis the new religious organizations, leaders, and members. As much as possible, we present this ideology in the proponents' own language, since the underlying metaphors and rhetorical presentation are central to their efforts to mobilize social control responses. In an attempt to clarify the full social control implications of this ideology, we present it in its full-blown form and, through our use of a combination of sources, undoubtedly create a greater degree of integration and coherence than it in fact possessed.

In Chapters 4 and 5 we examine in considerable detail the development and structure of the two components of the ACM: the anti-cult associations and the deprogrammers. As we shall see, these two components typically served distinct functions within the movement (political lobbying versus direct action, respectively), faced different organizational challenges, but yet maintained a close alliance despite their formal independence of one another. In both cases, from a resource mobilization perspective, we emphasize the unique problems each faced in creating viable, effective organizations. The anti-cult associations faced a series of interrelated problems, such as developing sufficient financial and membership bases, effectively coordinating local groups by a national-level organization, and defining their members' personal grievances to officials in such a way that these could be treated as public issues. The deprogrammers primarily confronted the problem of gaining legal sanction and legitimate occupational status for their erstwhile radical pursuits. Neither group was highly successful despite almost a decade of intensive, ongoing efforts. From a deviance perspective, our concern is principally with the potential of each wing of the movement to mobilize sanctions against the new religions. As we detail in later chapters, what limited success they had in gaining imposition of sanctions was considerably more than they achieved in solving their own basic organizational problems. This observation puts in perspective the overwhelming capacity of established institutions for exercising social repression, for even with only marginal access to power centers the ACM was able to discredit and seriously stymie the new religions.

In Chapters 6 and 7 we assess the impact of both the anti-cult associations and the deprogrammers on new religions. In the case of the anti-cult associations, the families which largely comprised their membership base were decentralized and lacked an independent sanctioning capacity. Therefore, the anti-cult associations mobilized sanctions against the new religions through a series of alliances with other institutions which possessed such capacities. From a resource mobilization perspective, our interest is in the process of this alliance formation; from a deviance perspective, our interest centers on the impact of the sanctions on the new religions which emanated from these alliances. The deprogrammers undertook direct action against these religious groups in the form of abducting their members and establishing the circumstances under which they could recant their faiths. From a resource mobilization perspective, our interest in the deprogrammers centers on the crucial resource of "apostates" (former insiders who could "verify" in personal testimonies the ACM claims and who often were employed as deprogrammers) from the new religions which were provided by deprogrammers to the anti-cult associations. From a deviance perspective, the salience of deprogramming comes through in the impact of the "atrocity stories" which the "apostates" were motivated to recount.

In Chapter 8 we consider a unique historical event (the Jonestown, Guyana, tragedy) which, at least for a time, portended to change the fortunes of the ACM. As we shall show, however, this event surpassed even the ACM's "worst case analysis" in offering confirmation of the claims they had been pressing for so long. That these events did not radically alter the ACM's capacity to mobilize other institutions to levy sanctions against the new religions casts in bold relief the futility of any hopes that their crusade might ultimately and fully achieve its stated goals.

Methodology

Over the four-year period of researching the anti-cult movement, we employed a variety of qualitative and quantitative methods. Such an eclectic approach was necessary due to the various types of data sought and the problems entailed in obtaining each. Needless to say, informational parameters became more "slippery" when dealing with a social movement whose members are more intent on achieving their urgent goals than in record-keeping for the convenience of outside observers. Briefly, we summarize our five primary sources of data: (1) formal interviews, (2) participant observation, (3) organizational files and correspondence, (4) organizational publications, and (5) other social science research/outside publications.

FORMAL INTERVIEWS

Beginning in fall 1976 and continuing into mid-1980, interviews by telephone, mail-out questionnaires, and traditional face-to-face methods were conducted with national, regional, and local spokespersons of organizations in the anti-cult movement. The former two survey methods were adopted due to pragmatic realities of distance and cost (our respondents and informants were located in virtually every corner of the continental United States). Many were repeatedly interviewed in our efforts to keep abreast of organizational changes, mergers, strategies, and so forth. Names and addresses were obtained by snowball sampling, and introductions were arranged; problems of rapport were resolved through personal endorsements by other anti-cultists and sheer persistence. We possessed one great initial advantage, in that the first national coordinating office of groups in this movement (the National Ad Hoc Committee Engaged in Freeing Minds) was fortuitously located during 1976 in Grand Prairie, Texas, a city adjacent to Arlington and our university. Interviews with CEFM's volunteer staff persons helped convince them and others to whom they freely referred us as to the basically objective goals of our research. Dissemination of a professional paper describing the composition of the movement's organization, ideology, and functions, which members of the movement perceived as essentially fair and neutral, also helped dispel suspicions as to our motives (see Shupe et al., 1977a). Copies of this basically descriptive (ethnographic-historical) paper were sent in 1977 to dozens of anti-cult leaders and representatives, and their comments and impressions were solicited. A number responded either to suggest minor qualifications or to validate our interpretation of the movement's origins and growth.

PARTICIPANT OBSERVATION

Due to the dispersal of the anti-cult movement's various component organizations across the United States, chances to engage in participant observation were limited. One national convention of anti-cultists which the authors planned to attend was scheduled to be held at Georgetown University in Washington, D.C., but was abruptly canceled by the administration for reasons not totally clear to us; other such meetings were held without publicity, and we did not always learn of them until after their occurrence. We were not always provided with advance information for some anti-cult gatherings for very good reasons (from the movement's proponents' standpoints). Our failure to "go native" and adopt a partisan stance toward the movement's goals, plus anti-cultists' knowledge that we were simultaneously researching Sun Myung Moon's Unificationist Movement, no doubt preserved for us a marginal status. (The methodological problems and implications of researching two mutually opposed social movements at the same time are discussed at length in Bromley and Shupe, 1980b, and Shupe and Bromley, 1980a.) Nevertheless, we were able to take advantage of a number of opportunities for participant observation.

The first of these was the aforementioned location of the National Ad Hoc Committee Engaged in Freeing Minds near our university. Both of the authors and two graduate assistant colleagues (Roger Spielmann and Sam Stigall) were able to make repeated visits to CEFM's "headquarters"—a Dallas businessman's home in Grand Prairie, Texas. As a "trade-off" for the time being interviewed and discussing developments in the anti-cult movement, and as a means of discerning both the specific activities of the organization and the "feel" of working in such a movement, our colleagues worked at sorting and filing requests for information on various new religions. These observations, plus those gleaned during the authors' own visits to CEFM "headquarters," were an important source of insight into the movement's resources and world view.

The second opportunity for participant observation occurred at a pivotal two-day "secret" meeting of national anti-cult movement spokespersons in mid-1977 in the Dallas-Fort Worth Metroplex. This was a key strategy meeting for the anti-cult movement following its experiments at centralization in 1976 and 1977 (see Chapter 4), the results of which would determine the shape of the movement for the next several years. It was attended by various anti-cult luminaries, to whom one of the authors spoke in general terms about his research; fielded blunt questions as to his personal diagnosis of the movement's strengths, weaknesses, and possible future alternatives for growth; held discussions with professionals present who were sympathetic to the anti-cult movement; and met with individual organizations' representatives.

The third form of observation was visiting and closely monitoring a local manifestation of a national trend: the American Jewish Committee's differences with the American Civil Liberties Union over such groups as the Unification Church, the Hare Krishna, and the Jews for Jesus in regards to their status in American religious pluralism. The Dallas chapter's subcommittee on interfaith affairs met on a number of occasions in private homes to discuss the production of a special "educational" film to be integrated with a speaker and testimonies of "ex-cult" members under the endorsement of a Dallas interfaith council.

Fourth, one of the authors attended a program designed to inform home economics teachers in various Texas high schools, colleges, and universities about the "cult menace." This occurred in fall 1979 in Fort Worth, Texas, and yielded a good sense of not only the general level of naivete about "cults" among many persons but also the shock effect caused by suddenly thrusting before an audience the standard litany of atrocity stories concerning these religions as served up by credible parents and professionals.

Fifth, activists in the anti-cult movement, including several regional directors and other knowledgeable informants, provided vicarious participation by periodically briefing the authors on current developments. In this way we stayed abreast of changes which we personally could not observe. Information gathered in this way included the movement's ongoing response to new religions' attempts to improve their own public images, court battles, accounts of proceedings at anti-cult meetings that we were unable to attend, and what could best be characterized as the ongoing gossip of personalities and rumors about the movement.

ORGANIZATIONAL FILES AND CORRESPONDENCE

Anti-cult informants with whom we established strong rapport and honest dialogues openly provided us with memos, rough drafts of upcoming resolutions and petitions, and interorganizational correspondence from the movement. In addition, participant observation and subsequent discussions at CEFM "headquarters" permitted us to obtain invaluable information on the frequency, types, and dimensions of anti-cult written communications. Furthermore, we were occasionally given permission to read letters and/or hear tape-recorded messages from offspring in new religions to their parents. Particularly when they had been unsuccessfully deprogrammed at some point, such cases permitted us rare and sensitive glimpses into the conflicts and dynamics of such situations.

ORGANIZATIONAL PUBLICATIONS

Publications of the ACM by and large fit most closely into that category which librarians refer to as "fugitive publications": they were not copyrighted, bound, or printed in such a way as to lend themselves to permanent archival retrieval. Often they were hastily reprinted, copied, xeroxed, or photocopied by some other means for fast dissemination rather than for long-term storage. In some cases these pamphlets, newsletters, and "reports" were anonymously authored.[3] The publications were of four general types.

(1) Mimeographed or printed newsletters were mailed to subscribers at fairly regular intervals (such as monthly or bimonthly); these were issued by each separate organizational headquarters and, if a given group was large enough, by seperate branches.

(2) Over time, anti-cult groups developed small libraries of pamphlets detailing specific religious groups or discussing controversial issues (such as First Amendment rights versus claims of brainwashing); these were circulated from group to group and often distributed in information packets or "kits."

(3) We obtained organizational memos and news releases, some of which came attached with newsletters to all subscribers and some of which were "leaked" to us personally by informants who trusted our motives and discretion.

(4) There was also a miscellaneous category, such as reprints of newspaper articles and copies of apostates' testimonies and affidavits. Also included were various other printed or packaged materials, such as videotaped interviews of spokesmen and—obtained through sympathizers in at least one major television network—prints of documentaries critical of the Unificationist Movement and other groups.

Finally, there were also a number of materials concerning the anti-cult movement, either from it or about it (for example, courtroom affidavits) which we could not have obtained directly from its members. In some cases our earlier research on the new religions—in particular, the Unificationist Movement—had put us in contact with such materials in their files, a procedure which we earlier used to our advantage when anti-cult files provided us data on the new religions (Bromley and Shupe, 1979a).

OTHER SOCIAL SCIENCE RESEARCH AND PUBLICATIONS

Research that specifically addressed itself to the anti-cult movement was extremely limited. Aside from our own published research, only a handful of pertinent sources existed, principally: Harper (1979), Lofland (1977: epilogue), Enroth (1977b), APRL (1977), and Stoner and Parke (1977). As will be evident in later chapters, we also studied newspaper and other treatments of both the new religions and stories told by spokespersons of the anti-cult movement. We performed separate thematic and semantic content analyses on articles indexed in *The Reader's Guide to Periodic Literature* and in the New York *Times* for the entire decade. We also performed a detailed content analysis on a sample of almost 200 nationally published newspaper atrocity stories about new religions in terms of their construction, presentation, and functions (details of which can be found in Bromley et al., 1979, 1980). As will be evident in Chapter 3, an extensive body of "anti-new religions" books and pamphlets published during the 1970s was utilized in our thematic analysis of the varieties of anti-cult ideology. In order to gain historical perspective, we drew on the even larger corpus of such literature available from the first half of this century and the nineteenth century (for example, anti-Christian Science/Johovah's Witnesses/Mormons/Catholics—for an essay dealing with the fruits of this perspective, see Bromley and Shupe, 1980c).

ADDITIONAL REMARKS

Additionally, we mention four issues relevant to our methodology and this volume. First, we deal here only with the experience of the American anti-cult movement. Such movements appear also to have surfaced in other countries such as Japan, West Germany, France, and Great Britain,[4] but because we have little data on them or do not wish to engage in the complexities of cross-cultural analysis, we have resisted looking beyond the American case.

Second, in writing our account of the anti-cult movement we were forced to deal with the issue of anonymity of respondents and informants.

In the text we referred to some specific interviews with identified respondents. At other points we were deliberately ambiguous as to our sources of information. During the course of research, some informants set the prior condition to cooperation that we not use their names out of fear of embarrassment or reprisals, either to themselves or to their offspring who might still be members of new religions, by those groups they opposed. While we may or may not have thought such precautions necessary, we have respected these informants' wishes. In those cases where we have identified names and personalities connected with the movement, they belonged to persons who were publicly identified in the movement's own newsletters, press annoucements, and publications, or who offered the mass media interviews.

Third, we did not attend any coercive deprogrammings during our research, not for want of opportunities to do so, but primarily out of our own ethical reservations about participating in or even being associated with such acts. This did not seriously compromise our research, however. In addition to our interviews with persons who had been through coercive deprogrammings (representing both sides of this controversy), a copious popular and professional literature (not to mention media accounts) existed which described the elements of deprogramming (see, for example, Melton, 1980; Anthony, 1979; Conway and Siegelman, 1978; APRL, 1977; and Patrick and Dulack, 1976). *Virtually all observers/participants concurred on the details of the sequence of events if not on their interpretation.* (A similar situation existed for the recruitment/socialization processes employed by the Unificationist Movement's west coast Booneville Ranch, about which various social scientists, ex-Moonies, and journalists were in close agreement as to specific events and actions but disagreed as to their meaning.) As will be evident in later chapters, we have drawn freely from all sources, sympathetic and hostile, related to deprogramming and invested our own efforts in not only recapitulating the observations of many others but in linking these interpretations to organizational aspects of the anti-cult movement.

Finally, whatever other of our personal biases become apparent to readers, we have not shared the anti-cultists' simplistic view that there existed in the 1970s in American society a definable, homogeneous (in terms of lifestyle, recruitment/socialization practices, organizational style, or belief) coterie of exploitative religious groups that can be called with any precision "cults." The latter became a "buzz-word" used indiscriminately (as we shall see) to refer to a general religious and cultural climate of diverse innovations, dissimilar in styles and beliefs, which included many groups and organized practices not ordinarily associated with organized religion. Because the word "cult" conjures up pejorative stereo-types that became the focal points of uncritical prejudice and attempts at actual repression, we have refrained from using it alone except in quotes to separate ourselves from its typical usage by advocates of anti-cultism. Instead, we employ the term "new religions," minus quotes, throughout the text because of its more neutral connotation.

NOTES

1. The "resource mobilization" perspective, as developed in a growing literature, emphasizes both societal supports and constraints of social movements, stressing such factors as the variety of resources which movements must mobilize, the linkage of a given movement to other groups and institutions, the dependence of movements on external support for success, and the tactics used by authorities (and others) to control or coopt movements. We make no attempt to summarize the perspective here but refer readers to some of the more recent, definitive statements of it (McCarthy and Zald, 1973, 1974, 1977; Gamson, 1975; Zald and Ash, 1973; Zald and Berger, 1978).

2. The differential emphasis on external impact which we have given to the two movements in large measure derived from their relative stages of development and also from our admittedly value-laden judgments of their respective potentials for achieving their stated goals. The UM was at a relatively early stage of its development, and—at least from our social deterministic frame of reference—possessed virtually no "realistic" potential for substantially altering the structure of the society in which it emerged. Conversely, the ACM had, in our judgment, reached its zenith by the late 1970s. As we shall see, the ACM, particularly in its interest group component, despite a greater potential for achieving impact, never successfully resolved basic organizational problems; further, even apparently fortuitous events which might have been expected to boost substantially ACM fortunes (such as Jonestown) failed to provide the movement with sufficient impetus to move beyond its precarious existence.

3. We are currently in the process of duplicating these and locating them in an institute library in order to make such materials available to sociologists and scholars of American religious history. In addition, an annotated bibliographic history of the anti-cult movement can be found in Shupe et al. (forthcoming).

4. For example, a small literature developing around the vicissitudes of the British anti-cult movement can be found in Barker (1980) and Beckford (1978a, 1978b, 1979, 1980).

Chapter 1

THE ANTI-CULT MOVEMENT IN SOCIOCULTURAL PERSPECTIVE

The 1970s witnessed the rise of both new religious movements and organized opposition to them in the form of a loose network of regional organizations which we have termed the anti-cult movement (ACM). In this chapter we shall briefly consider three specific matters which help to place the emergence of the ACM in sociocultural perspective: (1) the environmental context in which the ACM and UM developed, (2) the adoption of *brainwashing* as an appropriate metaphorical explanation for the kinds of changes youthful members of new religious movements were allegedly exhibiting, and (3) the history and organization of the UM as an archetypal "cult" in this controversy.

Environmental Context

The United States in the 1970s underwent a broad, highly visible revival of religiosity which, at least on a symbolic level, seemed to indicate a disenchantment with secular/political institutions and movements. Bellah (1976: 339) argued that America during the 1960s had encountered a "crisis of meaning" in which "the inability of utilitarian individualism to

provide a meaningful pattern of personal and social existance" became
increasingly apparent. Bell (1976: 28-30) concurred and prophetically
concluded that increased religiosity was a likely result:

> What holds one to reality, if one's secular system of meanings proves
> to be an illusion? I will risk an unfashionable answer—the return in
> Western society to some conception of religion.

Evidence of this resurgence of religiosity can be found in the increased
church attendance noted throughout the decade, the perceptions of
increased influence of churches in American life, and a growing conviction
that religious morality should not be divorced from political decision-
making. For example, the percentage of adults reporting that they had
attended church in the previous week climbed from a low point of 40
percent in 1971 to 44 percent in 1977 (Christian Science Monitor, Jan. 19,
1977). Likewise, those holding the opinion that churches had influence in
American life showed a turnabout. In 1970 only 14 percent of adults
polled nationally viewed the church as gaining influence, while by 1977 44
percent of those surveyed were willing to agree with that statement. In
addition, religiously based political activity increased. President Jimmy
Carter, for example, made his own religious commitment a major basis of
appeal in his first presidential campaign. Prayer in public schools and
abortion became significant political issues, particularly in state and local
elections. There were also a number of conservative denominations and
individuals at the end of the decade attempting to exert broader and more
direct influence on the political process. These included the Baptist Joint
Committee on Public Affairs of the Southern Baptist Convention, which
openly admitted to its lobbying activities in Washington, D.C. (see Fort
Worth Star-Telegram, Sept. 23, 1979, Dec. 22, 1979), and media evangelist
James Robinson, who aggressively courted political influence and publicly
avowed the goal of establishing a political party grounded in fundamentalist Christian morality (see Fort Worth Star-Telegram, Jan. 26, 1980).

Much of this religious revival took place in conservative rather than
mainline denominations (for example, Kelley, 1972). Indeed, the latter
denominations, such as the Methodists, Presbyterians, and Episcopalians,
continued to lose members throughout the 1970s despite continuous
increases in the number of individuals reporting weekly church attendance.
By contrast, media estimates of those claiming to have had a "born again"
experience ranged as high as fifty million Americans. One stimulus to the
visibility of this revival was the large number of luminaries and public
figures who lent their names and support to evangelical activities: Presi-

dent Jimmy Carter, Senator Mark Hatfield, Representative John Anderson, Governor John Carroll, entertainers Paul Stookey, Pat Boone, and Donna Summer, athletes Archie Griffin, Stan Smith, and Billy "White Shoes" Johnson, and billionaire Nelson Hunt were prominently associated with the evangelistic movement. In addition, a number of more notorious individuals also were swept up in the religious fervor and publicly dedicated their lives to Christ, including former Black Panther Eldridge Cleaver (who was later to declare his admiration and support for Reverend Sun Myung Moon), former Watergate defendant Charles Colson, Tex Watson, one-time member of the Charles Manson "Family," and Larry Flynt, editor of *Hustler* magazine. At the same time, several prominent political activists joined new religious groups. For example, ex-Yippie Jerry Rubin became a member of the human potential movement, and Rennie Davis, a Chicago Seven defendant/anti-war activist of the sixties, became a disciple of the teenage Perfect Master Maharaj Ji.

Yet, it would be a mistake to overestimate the impact of these trends. *Hustler's* scatalogical treatment of female genitalia, for example, did not significantly change after Larry Flynt's conversion. Likewise, the reaffirmation of Christian faith by millions of Americans should not be confused, as ebullient evangelists were often tempted to do, with major changes in behavior. This point was illustrated by a follow-up survey (Time, Jan. 23, 1978: 78) of those attending a Billy Graham crusade in 1976 which revealed that 54 percent of those who "came forward" to witness their faith in Christ were simply rededicating themselves, and that of 8400 pledge cards filled out by those attending, only 15 percent ended up as church members several months later. A similar evaluation of Bill Bright's evangelical campaign concluded that only three percent of those who made a "decision for Christ" over the phone subsequently joined a church.

During the 1960s, youthful protest movements such as civil rights, black power, anti-war, and campus protest reflected the dominant secular/political orientation toward the definition and solution of social problems. For a variety of reasons discussed elsewhere (Bromley and Shupe, 1979a; Foss and Larkin, 1979; Bellah, 1976; Needleman, 1972), these political movements which had so occupied youthful protest activities and public attention during that decade had dissipated by the beginning of the 1970s. At roughly the same time as their demise a number of new religious movements appeared which incorporated various countercultural themes of the previous decade. For example, the Jesus movement and its more controversial communal offshoot, the Children of God, began in California in 1968, the Hare Krishna sect was established in New York City in 1965, and Transcendental Meditation arrived in the United States during the late 1960s, as did the Sikh sect Happy-Healthy-Holy. Scientology (which had experienced popularity during the 1950s as Dianetics) enjoyed a resurgence toward the end of the decade, the India-based Divine Light Mission arrived in the United States in 1971, and, finally the UM, which actually had its missionaries in this country since 1959, only became visible with South Korean founder Sun Myung Moon's immigration to America in late 1971. Each of these groups experienced fairly rapid growth of members and revenues, especially during the first half of the 1970s.

According to Wuthnow's (1976: 279-285) poll of 1000 persons 16 or older in the San Francisco Bay Area, members of most of these groups were youthful (in their late teens or early twenties), although there were such exceptions as Jews for Jesus, which tended to attract older individuals. Movements such as Transcendental Meditation, Hare Krishna, and Scientology attracted persons interested in radical political change, while others, such as Jews for Jesus and Children of God, were more conservative in orientation. The former type of movement seemed to manifest a certain continuity with the political movements of the 1960s in their search for alternative values and lifestyles, while the latter type sought to confirm and reassert more traditional versions. All of the movements included in Wuthnow's survey attracted better-educated individuals, but there still was substantial variation, with groups such as Transcendental Meditation and the Hare Krishna scoring highest and the Children of God scoring lowest. Although only a tiny minority of individuals actually became members of any of these groups, the latter did achieve high visibility among those in the Bay Area's young adult population. Wuthnow found, for example, that

> nearly four out of every five persons claim to know a little about at least one of these [thirteen] movements, over half claim to know something about at least three of them. . . . More than half of the population is currently attracted to at least one of them and about a third is attracted to at least two of them. . . . One out of every five persons claims to have taken part in at least one of these groups. Eleven percent . . . said they had taken part in other groups similar to them.

It should be stressed that the ACM as a national movement was contingent upon the simultaneous emergence of the array of diverse new religious movements which we have just described. It is important to emphasize this point, since most of the new religions had a maximum of only a few thousand members each; thus, no one of them provided a sufficiently large or visible presence to create the amount of alarm which the ACM needed to coalesce and survive on a national level. As we shall indicate in later chapters, small local pockets of opposition to such groups as the Children of God and the People's Temple existed without producing a national countermovement. It was the discovery of common interests and experiences among families of young adults in a variety of disparate new religions scattered across the United States which facilitated formulation of the loose network of local groups into a major component of the ACM. In this sense the increased religiosity in American society spawned both the new religious movements *and* their opponents. As we pointed out, much of the increase in church attendance during the 1970s occurred in fundamentalist circles. Yet, interestingly enough, this same increase in conservative religiosity also provided the membership base for more sectarian groups such as the Children of God and the UM, groups which evoked the greatest hostility, *and* for the fundamentalist Christian groups which were their most hostile critics.

The Brainwashing Metaphor

One major cultural theme which was appropriated by ACM activists in the midst of this religious ferment and incorporated into ACM ideology was what has been termed the "brainwashing metaphor" (Robbins 1979a; Robbins et al., 1977). The notion of "free will," of course, had long been a central cultural component in western conceptions of man, inseparable from fundamental assumptions underlying religion, philosophy, and law. However, a number of trends, including the rapid development of social and behavioral science, had gradually eroded belief in the existence and inviolability of free will since the early nineteenth century. In the period since World War II in particular, American society had been confronted with a series of disturbing events which further muddied the waters surrounding the concept of free will. The notion that individuals could be *brainwashed* (that is, that an individual's free will could be subverted by manipulative coercive means, rendering him compliant or submissive to the will of outside agents and implanting in him not only a new set of attitudes and beliefs but even a different personality) emanated from studies of POWs returning from the Korean war and refugees from Communist China (see the classic treatments of this subject by Hunter, 1953, 1962; Lifton, 1957, 1963; Sargent, 1957). A series of similar incidents during and after the Vietnam conflict (for example, the capture and torture of the crew of the *USS Pueblo's* crew by North Korea) and popularized treatments of brainwashing, such as the motion pictures *The*

Manchurian Candidate and *The Ipcress File,* reinforced this assumption.

Events more closely juxtaposed to the emergence of the ACM also seem to have influenced its adoption of the brainwashing metaphor for explaining "cult" members' behaviors. In particular, the Tate-LaBianca murders associated with the Charles Manson "Family," the Patty Hearst kidnapping episode, and violence associated with the Synanon drug rehabilitation organization all served as dramatic illustrations of the extent to which people presumably could be manipulated for anti-social purposes. In each case there was substantial public fear and confusion about the social and psychological dynamics of this process. In the Hearst case, for example, the public seemed divided between those who believed that Patty Hearst was acting voluntarily in bank robberies and in eluding the police and those who accepted the interpretation that she had been brainwashed into blind obedience to her captors. Similarly, the extent to which she was legally liable for the actions following her kidnapping was hotly disputed, and ultimately she was released from prison prior to the completion of her sentence, partly because the issue of her motivations and free will seemed so irresolvable.

Thus, when youthful recruits of the new religions allegedly began to manifest striking changes in demeanor, attitudes, and even personality, parents began to formulate explanations for those changes which drew on this imagery. At first, the psychiatric evidence collected after the Korean conflict was heavily cited; later, the testimonies of psychologists and psychiatrists as well as the accounts of apostates from the new religions were used as evidence to demonstrate that manipulative coercive procedures akin to brainwashing had been employed to effect these "undesirable" behavioral and attitudinal changes. This is not to imply that the idea that individuals' free wills could be stolen or displaced was a new innovation. Far from it. As we shall develop extensively in Chapter 3, the metaphor of demonic possession had long existed from pre-Christian eras to explain apparently radical alterations in individual behavior and personality. What the brainwashing metaphor did was to provide a secular equivalent to this archaic religious theme, reshaping it into a form more acceptable to twentieth-century rational man and documented with "scientific" evidence which would account for such radical individual changes in a fashion more consistent with dominant paradigms of human behavior.

The UM as the Archetypal "Cult"

Throughout this volume we shall document our arguments with data from the conflict between the ACM and the UM. We have singled out the

UM for several specific reasons. First, it is the new religious movement with which we are most familiar. Indeed, this study is intended as a sequel to our previous research dealing with the UM (see Bromley and Shupe, 1979a). Second, no other new religious movement sought visibility and sociopolitical influence to the extent that the UM did, and therefore it attained more notoriety than other such groups. Third, as we shall document in Chapter 4, the ACM specifically designated the UM as its primary target and arch nemesis, not only because it was considered by ACM members to incorporate more of those objectionable "cult" characteristics than any other single group, but also because successful repression of the UM potentially could serve as a precedent for attacking other marginal religions. In the remainder of this chapter we present essential characteristics of the UM as a millenarian social movement in order to illuminate the sources of conflict between the ACM and the UM. Readers are referred to our previous work on the UM for more extensive analysis of that movement.

HISTORY

The UM began as one among a series of religiously based social movements in post-World War II Korea which scholars have termed *Shinhung Jonngyo* (Newly Risen Religions). Its founder, Sun Myung Moon, was born in 1920 in rural Pyungan Bukedo province of northwestern Korea and raised in a family which converted to a Pentecostal brand of Presbyterianism when he was ten years old. At the age of 16, on Easter Sunday morning, 1936, Moon claimed to have received a vision in which Jesus Christ announced to him that he, Moon, had been chosen by God to attempt the complete restoration of the physical Kingdom of God on earth. Among other things, a radically different interpretation of world and postbiblical history and an unique promise of the imminent future were bequeathed to Moon. However, Moon did not act publicly on his revelation until he began preaching in 1946. From the time of his vision to the founding of the UM in 1955, Moon claims to have alternately prayed, studied, and meditated. After some study in Japan and following that country's defeat in World War II, Moon returned to Korea and began his ministry at Pyongyang.

Surviving persecution from both communist invaders and South Korean regimes (often aided by allegedly invidious western missionaries), the UM went on to prosper. Moon's millenarian message of sacrifice and hope for the future had popular appeal, and the UM's aggressive recruitment efforts began to build its ranks. By the end of its first decade in existence, the UM numbered its membership in the tens of thousands. Its

communal lifestyle, which included employment in a diverse array of
movement-owned industries (such as arms manufacturing, titanium
factories, and pharmaceutical production), also brought Moon himself
great personal wealth and the UM a substantial financial base. Moon's
staunch anti-communism won him powerful friends in the South Korean
government. At the same time, the movement began to standardize Moon's
revelations and spiritual message as followers wrote it down, resulting in
the UM's scripture, the *Divine Principle*. Even by the late 1950s, the
movement had prospered to the extent that it could begin missionary
work overseas.

The first UM missionaries arrived on the west coat of the United States
in 1959 and for the next dozen years struggled to gain more than a
foothold in American culture. The adventures of the first UM outposts and
their earliest converts have been described (albeit with pseudonyms) in
Lofland's (1966, 1977) classic monograph, *Doomsday Cult*. Essentially,
the movement languished in obscurity and impotence until Reverend
Moon deliberately shifted the focus of his international "restoration"
mission from Asia to the United States in late 1971. Thereafter, the
movement, under his direct supervision, embarked on an accelerated
schedule of increasing recruitment, maximizing the effectiveness of fund-
raising, and generating publicity in American society. In this way the
incipient American branch of a Korean religious sect which numbered
barely two dozen in the early 1960s and only several hundred at most by
the early 1970s grew to include several thousand full-time members by the
mid- to late 1970s as well as millions of dollars worth of assets across the
nation.

IDEOLOGY

Unification theology offered a millenarian systhesis of the fundamentalist Christianity exported to Korea by western missionaries and
indigenous Neo-Confucian philosophy. Fundamentally, its tenets revolved
around the estrangement of mankind from God, beginning with Eve's
literal sexual seduction by the archangel Lucifer and the disobedience of
both she and Adam in the Garden of Eden, and the painful, laborious
process—detailed in the historical chronology of the *Divine Principle*—of
restoring God's intended kingdom on earth. This was the Fall of Man,
from which all succeeding generations of mankind genealogically were
descended with Satan as spiritual parent. Jesus Christ (to be the second
"Adam" in this restoration process) represented one in a sequence of

potential messiahs who, after lengthy periods of "providential" preparation (that is, paying indemnity to Satan), attempted restoration. Although Jesus accomplished the spiritual goal of his mission and achieved salvation for humanity, he was rejected by the ancient Jews and prematurely crucified before he could accomplish his full mission, which was not only to establish spiritual salvation for humanity, but also to lay the foundation of the physical kingdom of God on earth by creating God-centered relationships through marrying a "perfect woman" and beginning a model God-centered family.

Contrary to the orthodox Christian doctrine of the Trinity, Christhood was defined as an achieved status, one to which numerous historical personages had unsuccessfully aspired, and the need therefore remained for yet another messiah to come and complete Jesus' unfulfilled mission. Reverend Moon proclaimed, by the authority of divine revelation, that a critical opportunity for full restoration, the Second Advent (or Coming) of the messiah (the Third Adam), would present itself in the latter half of the twentieth century. However, there was the definite possibility that mankind might again fail to make use of the opportunities which God had lovingly prepared, as it once did by rejecting Jesus. Thus, the crucial mission of the UM was to disseminate the message of the brotherhood of all mankind as revealed by Sun Myung Moon in the *Divine Principle* and to work to prepare the earthly conditions necessary for complete physical restoration. Should this current opportunity be lost, mankind would be required to pay indemnity, or reparations, through strife and suffering for millenia. In this way the UM confronted a task of colossal scope, one which it was required by the rigorous timetable of the *Divine Principle* to attain in a relatively short period of years.

Later additions to Moon's theology, not included in the original versions of the *Divine Principle*, occurred when Moon shifted the focus of his ministry from the Orient to the United States. These additions incorporated a number of more explicitly political themes. Moon claimed that the events recounted in Genesis had direct consequences for the modern age. Along with what he termed the *vertical* fall of mankind from God when Lucifer seduced Eve, there also occurred a *horizontal* fall when Eve seduced Adam to hide her sin and subsequently Cain slew his brother Abel. The horizontal fall represented the estrangement of one human being from another and divided the world spiritually into two opposed camps: the satanic or Cain-positioned, and the righteous or Abel-positioned. In the twentieth century this opposition came to be represented on a physical level as the struggle between atheistic communism and God-fearing democracies. America was assigned the divinely ordained role of "archangel" that would help complete restoration by serving and protecting South Korea, the "New Israel" from which the messianic Lord of the Second Advent was to emerge. In this way biblical events were explicitly translated into religiously mandated political obligations for the United States and other nations. Moon's ministry to this country therefore focused on educating American leaders and citizens in the requirement of the "archangel" role, calling for recognition of its duty to integrate its secular/political actions with its mandated moral purposes.

CHARISMA

Since the UM's cosmic timetable revealed that these modern times were propitious for another attempt to restore the Kingdom of God on earth, that the messiah had already been born, and that he was already meeting conditions God had established for him to assume his role, there was considerable anticipation among UM members that Moon was indeed this messiah. While this issue was not fully resolved in the minds of all UM members (the messiahship being an achieved, not an ascribed, status), virtually all UM members believed that Moon was, at the very least, the most important prophet in biblical history, serving a modern John the Baptist role. In this vein he assumed the stature of a classical charismatic leader, as Weber (1964: 398) defined him, with extraordinary powers and psychic rapport. On the basis of repeated spiritual revelations from God, Moon claimed the authority to chart a radically new course for the movement and the lives of its members. For example, it was his inspiration which led to the foundation of numerous UM projects and enterprises such as the much publicized fishing fleet/canning operations and a New York daily newspaper. On an individual level, he frequently selected individuals for specific positions within the movement and even their mates when he "blessed" them in spectacular wedding ceremonies. Moreover, his own suffering and personal sacrifices during the Korean war, and his heroic struggles with Satan, were the exemplary model by which other UM members measured their own spirituality and individual growth. For these reasons, Moon, because of his spiritual status, possessed within the movement the ultimate moral authority to make virtually any claim on individual members, thus radically reorienting members' former priorities and allegiances.

ORGANIZATION

On a macro level, the UM consisted of a number of quasi-bureaucratic organizations designed to achieve movement goals or serve functions parallel to those of their institutional counterparts in the "fallen" world. These included *The News World,* the movement's New York daily newspaper dedicated to presenting news in a "compassionate" way so as to be a "force for unity" (that is, stressing family stability, human rights, and racial harmony) in the world; the Freedom Leadership Foundation, an organization focusing its efforts on combating worldwide communism; the International Cultural Foundation, the task of which was to promote the "search for absolute values" and the unity of science; the Collegiate Association for the Research of Principles, a collegiate UM affiliate organized to encourage students (primarily at major state universities) to discuss the message and values contained in the *Divine Principle* as a means of recruitment; and the Unification Theological Seminary, an institution established to provide graduate seminary training for future UM leaders. At the same time, there were several shorter-lived, ad hoc committees and task forces designed to handle specific tasks (for example, Young Americans for a Just Peace and National Prayer and Fast for the Watergate Crisis Committee). These groups were typically created and dissolved spontaneously and, like some of the more established components of the UM, were regarded by hostile critics as UM "fronts." At the same time, despite the apparent organizational integration of the movement on a national level, there remained considerable local autonomy and even factionalism. Contrary to ACM attempts to portray the movement as monolithic both doctrinally and organizationally, there was considerable disagreement and even conflict among various wings of the movement.

On a micro level, the UM was organized in communal fashion. Essentially, at this level the UM consisted of small, often mobile fund-raising and witnessing teams or more permanent churches/centers. The lifestyle of these communal groups was consuming and totalistic, similar to those of many researched utopian groups (see Kanter, 1972). Thus, in characteristic communal fashion members gave up all but minimal personal possessions upon joining, eschewed individual careers outside the movement, and devoted literally all their time and energies to sustaining the communal group. They observed strict rules of celibacy until personally married by Moon; related to each other as family members (in this fictive kinship system Moon and his wife were designated "True Parents" and UM members as brothers and sisters); emphasized affective relations and spiritual growth while simultaneously seeking to repress rationality, individuality, and ego; limited their contacts with outsiders to fairly ritualized situations such as fund-raising and proselytization; and, finally, found their mate and careers within the ranks of the movement.

The UM as a social movement was highly visible and aggressive in its world-transforming goals. Thus, Moon actively promulgated his ideology in a series of highly publicized, lavish speaking tours and rallies across the nation to which both prominent luminaries and the general public were invited. Moon also assiduously cultivated relationships with national public officials, including former President Nixon and members of Congress. Both of these strategies were aimed at, in the words of UM members, "making Reverend Moon and the Unification Church household words." Further, the UM' mobile fund-raising and recruitment teams lent the movement high visibility at the grass-roots level across the country. The movement therefore was difficult to ignore as it constantly flung itself into the public eye and asserted its existance.

Summary

In this chapter we have described some important aspects of the sociocultural environment of the United States and of the UM organization which provide a background for understanding the emergence and direction of the ACM. We have argued that the emergence of both the new religions and of the ACM can be located in part in the resurgence of religiosity in the United States during the early 1970s. This revival was fundamentalist Christian in character and hence provided recruits for some of the more sectarian new religions as well as increased membership and activity in those groups which were most hostile to conservative and radical new religions. We also have contended that the adoption of the brainwashing metaphor can be understood in terms of a series of events dating back at least to World War II and probably earlier which challenged conventional assumptions about free will. Finally, we have briefly outlined several salient dimensions of the UM as an archetypal cult to which we will make reference in succeeding chapters as we explain the dynamics of ACM development and strategies.

Chapter 2

SOURCES AND DYNAMICS OF STRAIN

In this chapter we shall consider the sources and dynamics of strain between the new religions of the 1970s and the two primary institutions with which they came into conflict: the familial and the religious. Particularly in our analysis of the family-new religions conflict, we shall base our argument specifically on the family-UM conflict, since (as we noted earlier) the UM was the ACM's chief antagonist and incorporated most of the characteristics against which families reacted so vehemently. The nature of the UM's challenge to the two institutions differed, however. In the case of the family, the primary threat was to the family's goal of preparing offspring for participation in the economic order. UM membership took individuals out of conventional social networks and career paths and led to the inculcation of individual qualities inconsistent with a competitive, economic achievement orientation. The family's authority structure also was threatened as both the UM's leader, Reverend Sun Myung Moon, and its communal organization supplanted the family as a reference group and source of emotional nurturance. However, because much of the family's authority was directed toward socialization for career mobility and families were already in the process of relinquishing control over their maturing offspring, the familial authority structure in itself was not the basic issue. In many cases this strain emerged gradually as parents sought to dissuade their offspring from their chosen course and resorted to increasingly stronger arguments and sanctions; simultaneously, the converts' involvements and commitments to the new religions progressively deepened, rendering parental support less necessary and parental sanctions less effective. Of course, parental contact with the ACM often led to more rapid escalation of this reaction, but here we have chosen to present a single case in reflexive detail to illustrate and emphasize strain as an emergent process.

The challenge to the religious institution was not uniform, since churches' interests varied enormously. The most serious direct challenge by the new religions was presented to the fundamentalist churches' authority structures. For these groups, biblical literalism (particularly with respect to the doctrine of the Trinity, salvation by faith and not works alone, and biblical history) served to regulate the day-to-day behavior of believers and preserve the church's authority vis-à-vis its members. Thus, theological reformulations did not merely represent ideological disputes; rather, they constituted a real threat to the social order of congregations. Mainline denominations generally sought and possessed less daily influence over their members; therefore radical theological reformulations were far less threatening to them. On the other hand, established denominations' goals included accommodation with the established political/economic order, and this the new religions *did* potentially threaten. However, because the new religions did not possess either great size or power, the threat was not of great magnitude; therefore, mainline churches often responded only with exclusionary tactics designed to deny the new religions a place in the purportedly "open" system of American religious pluralism. Not surprisingly, in the case of the religious institution, the emergence of strain occurred more quickly and predictably than it did with the family. Established churches had experienced numerous sectarian challenges historically and hence were relatively well prepared for the latest set of "new religions."

Familial Institution

SOURCES OF STRAIN

Of the two sources of strain between the UM and the American family, the threat posed to the family's goal of preparing sons and daughters for participation in the economic order was clearly more important than the challenges to the authority structure of the family, although the two were not completely separable. Much of the socialization process within families was devoted to producing offspring capable of achieving socially and economically successful careers/lifestyles. In order to fulfill this goal parents attempted to bring up children in such a way that they would be able to play highly specialized roles, possess self-interested motivation, be free from ideological constraints, and hold instrumental (as opposed to affective) role orientations. As Greeley (1972: 227) put it, a child was "expected to honor autonomy, self-expression, self-realization, mobility, sexuality, and family. He is expected to be competitive, risk-taking, eager to learn." Parents therefore specifically sought to develop their children's educational opportunities; individual skills, personal initiatives and autonomy; self-interest as the criterion for career and marital choices; and calculative, rational decision-making capabilities. These attributes were fostered by parents in such specific (if mundane) ways as rewarding scholastic achievement, encouraging competitiveness in academic and athletic activities, providing money and possessions as a means of instilling a sense of personal ownership, and encouraging children to mingle with a diverse circle of friends and acquaintances in a wide variety of groups and social settings.

Membership in groups such as the UM, by contrast, involved assuming a very diffuse role requiring few specialized skills. Members' communal organization was designed to suppress self-interested motivation by forbidding accumulation of more than nominal personal possessions, limiting individually controlled wealth, and discouraging even distinctive clothing or grooming practices which might accentuate individuality. Particularly among novitiates, a great deal of time and energy was devoted to learning to "free" themselves from the "constraints" of ego and possessions, placing the good of the group above their own personal needs and desires, and pursuing spiritual rather than material ends. Further, UM members were expected to reject the calculated reciprocity characteristic of instrumentally based role relationships for what they termed "heartistic" relationships. The latter referred to affectively based relations predicated on the UM's fictive kinship system in which other members were literally treated as one's "brothers" and "sisters." All of these requisites of communal life received strong support both from peers and from UM ideology which located the source of most of mankind's most serious, persistent problems in selfishness and pursuit of individual goals. Thus, communal solidarity, rather than developing the requisites for conventional careers, was the preeminent UM concern, and the UM's socialization process offered virtually no preparation for integration into the contemporary American economic system.

Since the vast majority of UM converts were at the transition point between adolescence and full adulthood (that is, 18-24 years old and in the process of culminating their educational preparation), and—at least by their parents' estimation had previously demonstrated precisely those qualities conducive to achieving success in conventional terms, their apparently sudden change of direction and complete abrogation of all that they and their parents had worked so hard to achieve left the latter stunned and then angry. Indeed, for many parents, these changes in orientation were incomprehensible, and they felt that their children had become virtual strangers to them, as the following statements illustrate:

Our son join a cult? Impossible! I would have said before it happened. Here was a young man who had been an excellent student from prep school through college. He was a religious youth, though not a zealot. He held strong moral views, had lots of friends, a good home, and an older brother he was close to [Readers Digest, 1976: 129-33].

Try to imagine what it would be like to have their son or daughter take a trip across country after graduating from college, planning to return home at the end of a stated time, to resume the life and career for which they had been preparing . . . and then to receive a phone call from an unspecified place three thousand miles away, from someone who sounds only vaguely like the son (or daughter) they knew so well only a few months before, but whose voice is the voice of a ventriloquist's dummy, who speaks to them only in the stilted phrases of a religious pamphlet, who seems to have no recollection of the twenty-one years of mutual caring and struggling and tears and laughter that makes a family [CEFM, 1976a: Vol. II, 9].

Our twenty-two year-old daughter Anne was a devout practicing Catholic who dreamed for years of being a public health nurse in Appalachia. She even visited the town in which she would be trained after her graduation. Her dreams and ours were shattered suddenly last January, 1974 when Anne came home unexpectedly and announced she was quitting nursing college and joining the Unification Church [CEFM, 1976a: Vol. II, 39].

Richard was three days into his senior semester as a Pre-Med student, University of Texas, Austin. He had a 3.989 grade-point average. The cult got him almost on the spot. At this time he has no ambitions, no aims. This is the young man who was to be an MD and President of the United States by the age of Fourty [sic] [CEFM, 1976a: Vol. II, 18].

The other source of strain between the UM and the familial institution emanated from the authority structure of the family itself. Although parents socialized their offspring to assume autonomous adult roles, they anticipated that adult independence was not inconsistent with continued loyalty to the family unit and even expected that titular leadership of the family would remain in their hands. However, the UM's communal-style organization required full-time involvement and, particularly for the first few years of membership, continuous geographical mobility on witnessing and fund-raising teams. Members' new and increasingly consuming commitments rendered frequent visits or even contact with parents difficult to sustain, and anguished parents interpreted this lapse in communications (somewhat correctly) as evidence of reduced loyalty to the family unit. For example, distraught parents voiced the following complaints during a public ACM meeting in 1976:

> How can parents cut through the invisible barrier that isolates their children from free and open contact with their families? How can parents combat an atmosphere that combines isolation, curtailment of letter writing or telephone calls, fear, and a breakdown of trust in parents [CEFM, 1976a: Vol. I, 17]?

> We are not able to contact her directly. . . . We never know where she is. . . . The result is that even were we in the same locale we would not see her [CEFM, 1976a: Vol. I, 37].

> After the few letters, our only contact with her were collect phone calls from scattered areas. In almost three years she has been allowed to come home twice [CEFM, 1976a: Vol. I, 35].

It was not merely parents' isolation from their offspring which troubled them, however. Even more disconcerting to parents was the perception that their very roles *as parents* and their titular family leadership were being appropriated by Moon and his wife. Indeed, within the UM's fictive kinship system, Moon and his wife were designated as "true parents" and clearly differentiated from members' "biological parents." These designations took on more than symbolic significance, however, as a result of the charismatic status accorded to Moon by members.

Their "recognition" of Moon's superior moral status in essence ceded to him the authority to make extraordinary claims upon them personally, and they in turn assumed the status of disciples, open and submissive to Moon's moral leadership.

UM members' allocation of the right to greater moral authority over their actions to "true parents" than "biological parents" had profound implications for the former's expectations of retaining titular family leadership. On one level it simply was galling to parents that their sons and daughters would unquestioningly abandon alcohol, drugs, cigarettes, long hair and sexual freedom for Moon when even advice from parents on such matters had evoked hostility. However, much more threatening was the prospect that offspring would cede to Moon the authority to make very basic decisions which parents rightfully should at least be made in consultation with them. Initial membership in the UM led to a number of usually unilateral decisions by offspring that were disturbing enough to parents—giving up possessions, moving into a UM center, taking on a new identity, indefinitely postponing or even eschewing former career and marital plans, attenuating relationships with outsiders, and devoting all their time and energy to the movement. At this stage parents were likely to feel threatened when important symbolic occasions were ignored because the new UM member was simply "too busy" with work for Moon. One mother expressed her chagrin:

> She didn't even send her father a birthday card. . . . She said she didn't even consider us her real parents, only her physical parents. Moon and his wife were real parents [The Home News (New Brunswick, N.J.), Oct. 12, 1975].

Subsequently, however, even more fundamental (and, from parents' perspectives, irrevocable) commitments were made as members were required to marry within the movement, mates were approved or selected by elders within the movement, and any children of such marriages were raised (often apart from the parents) within the movement. Such commitments deepened parental anxieties and hostilities. Said one mother of her daughter:

> She has given up her freedom and is willing to go wherever Moon sends her, to marry whomever he chooses, to do whatever he asks, even if he considers violence necessary to thwart communism [CEFM, 1976a: Vol. II, 35].

The ultimate horror, of course, for parents was that they, along with all other outsiders, might be reduced to the status of expendable nonbelievers. Parents elicited such confessions as the one below from their children once the latter had renounced UM membership:

I remember seeing them cry. . . . But I recall no feeling. They were aliens to be converted to the church [The Sun (Colorado Springs, Colo.), Nov. 23, 1975].

He would have killed us. He admitted it. It's an honor, Richard said. You'll be rewarded for it [Sun Messenger (Cleveland Heights, Oh.), Oct. 16, 1975].

DYNAMICS OF STRAIN

In order to clarify the emergent nature of this crisis we shall briefly recapitulate one case out of a number from our research which we believe is typical of the dynamics of strain between UM members and their families. We rely heavily on personal correspondence made available to us and have altered certain details in order to preserve the anonymity of our informants.

Parents' initial response to their offspring's announcement of UM membership was often a mixture of disbelief, horror, and panic. Since a substantial proportion of UM members joined the UM while traveling or working or studying away from home (see Bromley and Shupe, 1979b), family discussion of these choices was difficult and frequently limited to long-distance phone calls or exchanges of letters. In this case a young woman named Deborah had just graduated from a prestigious, east coast liberal arts college and won a fellowship for graduate study at a well-known European university. Upon arriving in Europe, she began sightseeing before beginning classes. She met a group of UM fund-raisers and attended a three day workshop. Writing home, she reported that "their doctrine is remarkably comprehensive and thoroughly logical. I had a feeling that what I was hearing was really true. Whether I will join this movement is, nonetheless, an open question."

Within a few weeks, however, she had decided to join the UM. In the interim her mother, anticipating this outcome, had made contact with a local ACM group. In exchanges of letters (which required nearly a week for delivery) Deborah's mother sent local press clippings and warnings from ACM groups about the UM as well as her own admonitions that Moon was a "religious demagogue" and that Deborah's involvement with the UM was "foolish" and "tragic." Nonetheless, shortly thereafter Deborah announced that she had given up her scholarship and undertaken UM missionary work "for an indefinite period of time." Parental expressions of concern and pleas to reconsider hastily made decisions were typically countered by their children's reassurances that the UM was the most wonderful and fulfilling group they had ever encountered. Indeed, Deborah sought to allay her parents' fears, referring to her decision as an act of "self-affirmation." She admitted that "the article you sent me raised doubts in my mind about Rev. Moon, who I have never met and of whom I know only a little." But her own confirmatory experiences with the "idealism," "sacrificial quality," "truth," and "sense of urgency" among members of the movement were much more influential than her parents' warnings. She asked her parents to "make a small sacrifice. Please suspend your preconceptions of the movement." Recognizing that her parents were responding primarily to ACM depictions of the UM, she wrote,

> Even as I write now, I can't help but think that I am hopelessly outgunned in this deadly serious polemical confrontation, what with the powerful [local media] on the other side. . . . I am reduced to making a plea: please keep in mind that many things in this world are not as they seem. How about an emotional plea: are you going to believe me or the . . . media establishment? How about it, Mom, me or CBS news?

She closed, "I know in my heart I have nothing to apologize for and yet I'm so sorry about all this." Yet, another tone gradually began to emerge as indicated in Deborah's request that her parents suspend judgment temporarily on the UM followed by this statement: "If you will do this it will make me much more at ease and make it much easier to write to you."

Once it became apparent to parents that UM membership was not a transitory or ephemeral phase, they began attempting to apply greater pressure on what they now perceived to be their errant, misguided offspring. For example, as time went on Deborah's letters indicated deepening commitment. She wrote, "I'm so proud to be in this movement, so proud of the young people who are making this thing go. I don't know what to say. I've had many spiritual experiences now, so no matter what happens to us and to me personally, I've got a foundation of faith to fall back on." She concluded that letter by saying, "I am extremely proud to be your daughter and to inherit your personality, but every day it becomes clearer to me that I wasn't created simply for myself." The reciprocal reaction of parental pressure took a number of forms. Deborah's mother continued sending anti-cult literature, her father pressed her on a number of occasions about repayment of debts she had incurred (and abdicated responsibility for), and her parents arranged a lucrative occupational opportunity in her field as an alternative to UM membership. Further, her parents arranged for close family friends to fly to Europe to persuade her of the error of her ways. While she acknowledged the friend's "extraordinary persuasive skill," she also was upset by how little faith they manifested in "God to lead and direct me in the right direction and . . . in me to distinguish between a man of God and a false prophet." She concluded ominously, "It is also clear how little faith you have. That hurts and angers me."

At this juncture parents frequently begin to realize that the normative and economic means of influencing their offspring upon which they had come to rely (that is, economic dependence, parental authority, familial loyalty, and shared goals) no longer were effective. Further, many parents become convinced that their offspring are not responsible for or in control of their own behavior. How else could what was from their point of view such a rapid, radical deviation from a course so carefully planned and sacrificed for be explained? And how else could their offsprings' resistance to the obvious "truth" about the "charlatan" Moon and the economically exploitive, politically subversive" UM be explained? In the case at hand, Deborah's parents concluded, after the attempts by family friends to persuade her to return, that she was no longer responsive to rational appeal. They turned to deprogramming. Her mother, along with a nationally known UM apostate, traveled to Europe where Deborah was lured into a hotel room and held for several days while the deprogrammer attempted to "break through" the "cult-imposed" thought patterns "holding" Deborah.

In Deborah's case the deprogramming was bungled badly, although she allowed later that it did have "a certain impact on my thinking" and that she was "undecided about the content of my allegedly idolatrous faith." Nevertheless, the deprogramming attempt seemed in other respects to increase her commitment to the UM. She noted, "I was treated as a mental patient from the very beginning, without recourse to fair rules of evidence or argumentation." Further, she observed, "In contrast to the gentleness and warmth I had experienced within the church, I found my accusers bullyish and even divided against one another. I would have laughed, but the air was too full of anger, fear, and an undeniable concern for me." She finally decided to confront church leaders with the deprogrammers' allegations but concluded that "in the meantime I am a very much befuddled wretch."

The increasingly overt nature of the conflict in itself increased the mistrust and distance between parents and offspring, but neither side really had an interest in terminating contact. On the one hand, the parents continued to hope their appeals would eventually get through: Communications in angry conflict were better than no communication at all. Indeed, in this case Deborah actually requested ACM materials and reported reading them. Many UM members hoped that their parents would eventually come to understand and accept their commitments. Thus, Deborah continued to write home with some frequency reasserting her love for her parents and including statements such as, "Don't think I don't appreciate all the trouble you are going to on my account. I just wish I could show my appreciation without violating my principles."

Yet, despite these attempts to keep up appearances the conflict was difficult to contain. It was impossible to constantly overlook the basic clashes of interest. For example, Deborah's parents began to question whether they were being forthrightly informed of her whereabouts and activities. At the same time, Deborah's mother had become increasingly active in the ACM without Deborah's knowledge. For her part, Deborah began to question her parents' good faith and wonder if a visit home might result in a second attempt at deprogramming. Deborah's mother wrote to friends that she thought that "Moon's minions have turned Deborah into a robot programmed to do *anything* decreed by Moon." In another letter she continued, "After all it is abnormal for kids like Deborah to be out 'begging' on the street with their puny wares and wilted flowers." In these letters she asked recipients to "please keep this in confidence . . . because . . . I do want to get Deborah out one of these days."

Exchanges at some points became increasingly frank and hostile and also less frequent as both sides became resigned to the other's intransigence. For instance, Deborah's mother's resignation was apparent in a letter to a friend: "I don't plan to write Deborah on controversial issues. It wouldn't do any good, anyway. They will just withhold the letter if it is too negative. Or brainwash her a little bit more about Satan's influence through her mother." Deborah's recognition, too, became apparent: "Mom, I love you very much, as you know. I wish we could somehow bridge the distance between us, but I don't know how. My love and admiration for my parents is unchangeable. My commitment to the Unification Church is total. What's a poor Georgia girl to do?" Her mother responded with greater frankness than at any other time:

> You asked what you could do to bridge the distance between us. One way would be to come home for a visit and try to look at your movement from afar. You could always go back if you wished. . . . Deborah, I have had to make my peace with what you are doing. Otherwise I would be in a mental institution. You will simply have to forgive us for not "understanding" what you are doing, just as we have forgiven you for giving up your education and career.

Some months later the conflict finally became overt. Deborah began to reject her parents' contentions that they were only interested in her welfare and located their opposition to her activities in their own pride and selfishness. She wrote:

> You claim that you and Dad would not try to stop me from participating in the movement. . . . That's actually not quite honest, is it? Two years ago you thought it was a good idea to kidnap and "debrainwash" me. Have you changed your tune? I don't think so. . . . What a comedown it was for me to abandon my scholarship without asking your permission. My daughter the distinguished student. My daughter the AP correspondent. My daughter the world traveller. But could you admit, "My daughter the brainwashed cult follower?" Wouldn't your friends feel sorry for you?

The wounds healed slightly when Deborah made a trip home for a short visit, but the reunion was marred by continuing dissention over her UM membership. After several years in the UM she enrolled in the Unification Theological Seminary, an event that had both positive and negative implications from her parents' perspective. On one hand, she was now off the streets and back in the United States. On the other hand, communication was no more frequent and the seminary appointment indicated deepening commitment to the movement. The small healing of family wounds, however, was quickly ruptured again when Deborah announced her marriage to an Oriental UM member selected by church elders. In fact, the relationship was extremely difficult for Deborah's parents to assimilate. In addition to its arranged quality, the pair were married in a secular ceremony so that the groom could legally remain in the United States. However, the newlyweds were immediately separated by the church as they had not yet completed their mandatory probationary period of three years' celibacy. Deborah's parents refused to accept the marriage and, of course, Deborah could not agree to visits without her new husband. Events had reached an impasse.

Religious Institution

SOURCES OF STRAIN

In understanding the threats posed by the UM to the authority structure and interests of the religious institution it is important to first observe the caveat that religious belief systems are inherently nonempirical in nature. Given their lack of an empirical referent, such belief systems depend upon consistency rather than objective verifiability (that is, reliability rather than validity in a methodological sense) for their status as knowledge. Because many of the normative prescriptions and proscriptions incorporated into or associated with theological systems are universalistic in nature (claimed to apply to all people, in all places, at all times) so as to maximize their authority, it is imperative that they retain the appearance of immutability. Religious belief systems are, therefore, subject to two major types of challenge: to the content of the beliefs or doctrines themselves and to the essentially subjective spiritual experiences associated with the beliefs and their expression. Variability on either dimension would erode theological immutability. Churches historically have attempted to contain these two sources of threat by drawing boundaries around the range of legitimate theological doctrine and spiritual experience. The more closely theological doctrines serve as guides for daily behavior, of course, the more importance their authoritative character assumed. It was for this reason that fundamentalist churches experienced a greater threat from UM doctrinal innovations than did mainline denominations. Most of the documentation which follows was drawn from fundamentalist literature precisely because fundamentalists reacted overtly and with the most hostility to the UM and other new religions.

The doctrine permutations and combinations in religious belief systems are virtually limitless, as the history of sectarian innovations in Christianity has amply demonstrated. Over time, therefore, many churches have established criteria whereby potential theological revisions can be evaluated and judgments of heresy invoked. It was not surprising, then, that fundamentalist Christians attacked the new religions for doctrinal deviations from an orthodoxy equated with "truth." Sparks (1977: 19), for example, defined orthodoxy as "straight, right, safe, correct and true beliefs about God" and heresy as "departure from the accepted norm of belief." Breese (1979b: 10-11) was more eloquent:

> [Christianity is] the highest mountaintop beyond which it is downhill no matter which way one goes. There is nothing greater, nothing higher, and certainly nothing more magnificent than the mountaintop of divine revelation in Scripture and Jesus.

His depiction of heresy was equally graphic:

> Beyond rationality is insanity, beyond medicine is poison, beyond sex is perversion, beyond fascination is addiction, beyond love is

lust, beyond reality is fantasy. Just so, beyond Christianity is death, hopelessness, darkness and heresy.

Berry (1976: 18) offered a classic rebuke of the UM for its presumptuous theological innovation:

> The Unification Church is based on the philosophies and concepts of man rather than on the Scripture. Because God has all power and knowledge, He had the ability and wisdom necessary to communicate His revelation to man as He wanted it to be understood. There is no need to think that one has to compose an intricate scheme to make the Scriptures understandable. God has not always told us all we care to know about some things, but if He has remained silent, it is best that we be content to leave the reasoning to Him rather than to make our own opinions binding on others.

Sparks (1977: 22-25) attempted to specify the common qualities of such heretical doctrines: (1) Parts of the Scripture are accepted while other parts are denied; (2) rejection of Jesus Christ as simultaneously man and God; (3) denial of the Trinity (the Father, Son and Holy Spirit as three distinct and equal persons who together make up one God); (4) rejection of man as saved through accepting the atonement of Christ's death on the cross as payment for his sins and coming into communion with God through the new birth; and (5) maintenance of other practices and beliefs inconsistent with biblical injunctions such as "fixing an exact date for Christ's return," "controlling the minds of adherents," and "domination of the group by one man who is considered the sole authority and interpreter of God's truth." The intensity of fundamentalists' feelings about such doctrinal heresy was reflected in the virulence of some of their condemnations. Consider, for example, the following invectives of Sparks (1977: 177):

> The blunt truth of the matter is that the Children of God is a bastard orphan heresy. It is a bastard because it admits its mother to be a whore; an orphan because it pronounces its whore-mother dead; and a heresy because it had departed from the true teachings of the Scripture as those teachings have been passed down through the historic Church.

Not only could the Christian faithful be led astray by heretical doctrines, but they could also be deceived by "counterfeit" spiritual experiences. This powerful influence of unreliable, subjective confirmatory experience with a "false" spiritual guru, pseudo-Christian doctrine, or minister-interpreted mystical/meditative episodes could, fundamentalists feared, lead Christians to mistake the superficially similar qualities of a "cultic" religion for its true Christian counterpart. Fundamentalist Christian writings were replete with dire warnings of the chimera of mystical experiences provided by such eastern originating groups as the UM and the Hare Krishna. Clements claimed (1975: 36-37).

> A man can get hooked on certain experiences and thereby miss out on true human fulfillment. A Christian may ask if mysticism cannot be just this kind of egocentric exploration of man's spiritual capacity rather than a proper fulfillment of it, a type of spiritual masturbation in which desires and feelings ought to be turned outward to the distract, person Creator God and Father of Jesus Christ have been introverted and debased.

In order to distinguish between "real" and "counterfeit" religious experiences Christians were cautioned to employ biblical doctrine as the basis for evaluating such experiences and to build their faith upon both doctrine and personal experiences. Thus, Clements (1975: 52) instructed:

> The Word without the Spirit is sterile and puzzling to man. If it produces anything, it is only intellectual Christianity like that of the Deists. On the other hand, the Spirit without the Word can be no more than an incoherent mysticism that is practically indistinguishable from dangerous intuitions wrought by evil spirits.

Or as Sparks (1977: 21) confidently asserted, "We know that when the Spirit guides, the result will be in accord with the Scriptures."

The UM and other new religions posed three interrelated but distinct challenges to the authority structure and goals of the religious institution: (1) a reformulation of the orthodox interpretation of the Trinity, (2) a redefinition of biblical history, and (3) an emphasis on works rather than grace as the basis for salvation. Each of these eroded doctrinal consensus and raised the specter of spiritual experiences outside the purview of church control. Further, in each case the fundamentalist groups experienced the threat to their interests more directly than others.

Disputing the orthodox interpretation of the Trinity represented one of the major challenges to the authority structure of fundamentalist Christian denominations. From a sociological perspective, the source of God's ultimate moral authority in Christianity is found in the reduction of man's moral status (through the doctrine of original sin) along with the elevation of God's moral status through attribution of perfection on numerous dimensions (for example, omniscience, omnipotence, and omnipresence). The moral imbalance thus created was so great that God was due total obedience from man. Given the enormous moral distance between man and God, Jesus was introduced as the bridge (the "way-shower" and "redeemer") between the physical and spiritual worlds. Jesus, the god/man, was the founder of the Christian Church, the direct human link with deity, and the referent for invocation of divinely ordained normative prescriptions. Thus, Jesus constituted a charismatic leader in the classic sense, an individual who was able to exercise diffuse and intense influence over the normative orientations of other actors (see Etzioni, 1961: 203; Katz, 1975). Jesus' unique status had implications both for the formal authority structure of the churches and for the behavioral orientations of individual members vis-à-vis those churches. On the one hand, Jesus as the Son of God was the link through which religious leaders claimed authority; any redefinition or reorientation of the messianic role thus constituted a direct challenge to the formal, explicit sources of churches' authority. On the other hand, Jesus was the authority through which individual church members oriented their own behaviors. Particularly in fundamentalist churches, regulation of alcohol and drug use, sexual behavior, and husband-wife role definitions, for example, were based upon religious norms. Again, any redefinition of the messanic role had the potential for undermining the authority upon which individuals based the kind of social relationships they wished to have and for which alternative sources of symbolic legitimation may have been unavailable.

Christianity was rendered particularly vulnerable to such theological innovations as a result of Jesus' human qualities and the prediction of the messiah's return, and thus individuals claiming to be the messiah could not be lightly dismissed. UM doctrine posed precisely such a sectarian challenge. According to Moon's *Divine Principle,* Jesus was merely the latest in a series of messianic figures who sought to restore fallen man to God, and, like others before him, Jesus was not successful in this effort (although Jesus did succeed in achieving "spiritual" as opposed to "physical," and thus partial, restoration). Three elements of this formulation were especially offensive to Christian denominations. First, because Jesus failed, his ultimate moral authority was diminished. Second, the messianic role was defined as an achieved role; hence, any individual with the proper credentials (spiritual qualities *and* accomplishments) became a candidate for this role. This formulation, of course, removed the unique, ascribed kinship-based role definition of Jesus as the only Son of God and created the possibility of claiming messianic authority on the basis of achievements rather than the spiritual authority vested in and transmitted through the church. Third, because Jesus failed, there remained the possibility (and, indeed, the necessity) for a new messiah to finish the divinely mandated task of restoration. Not surprisingly, Moon's own biographical characteristics and life trajectory closely matched the criteria by which he claimed new messianic candidates were to be judged.

Moon in this sense had created and in himself constituted an alternative source of spiritual authority. His Unification Church literally sought to unify (supplant) existing churches based upon the new spiritual authority offered by the biblical reformulation presented in the *Divine Principle* and Moon's status as the new messiah. The visible evidence of this challenge came in the form of a reformulated Bible, a new church which denied the spiritual authority of its established Christian counterparts, and individual members who reoriented their lives and priorities as individuals would only for an individual with ultimate moral authority. It was to these challenges that Christian churches—and fundamentalist groups in particular—reacted with vehemence and anger.

Fundamentalist Christians uncompromisingly rejected the notion that any living human being and certainly any individual outside of the orthodox Christian church could be the messiah. Fundamentalists' writings were in fact preoccupied with biblically based warnings of "deceivers" who would seek to lead the unwary Christian faithful astray. Further, Christians were supplied with biblically derived lists of qualities which were designed to serve as tests of messianic status and expose fraudulent "cult" leaders for what they really were (Bjornstad, 1976: 75-95; Martin, 1979: 177-178; IFF, 1978b; Nederhood, 1979). These "tests" were actually lists of unsavory traits that allegedly typified all "cult" leaders (as opposed to "true religious leaders") and included greed and financial exploitation, excessive boldness and arrogance, sexual promiscuity/immorality, messianic presumptions, megalomania/delusions of grandeur, vindictiveness, and authoritarianism. Contrasting "cult" leaders with Jesus, Sparks (1977: 263) noted: "Jesus Christ is unmatched in all history. . . . While men like Sun Myung Moon and Maharaj Ji get rich quick off their people, Jesus Christ died for His. While Witness Lee instructs his followers to crush their own souls by dying on their own crosses, Jesus Christ *has taken our place in death."* In short, the true messiah was sacrificial, the pseudo-messianic pretenders greedy and self-serving.

A second and related source of strain emanated from the UM's attempts to redefine the temporal structure shared by established Christian denominations. Christian churches constructed the past and the future in such a way as to locate themselves along a historic course which began with creation and would end with the erection of the Kingdom of God on earth. This formulation had two important consequences. First, established churches were defined as the legitimate heirs to the legacy of Jesus Christ and the only pathway to the Kingdom of God. Thus, legitimacy was accorded the present by virtue of its relationship to the past and future. Second, at the same time, ultimate charismatic authority was carefully segregated from the present and located in the past or future. Since the churches were the legitimate heirs to Christ, charismatic leadership was available to them in routinized form. However, the revolutionary implications of the messiah's return, his condemnation of a corrupted world, and a radical restructuring (or even disbanding) of human institutions were all simply relegated to the indeterminate future. To have done otherwise would have required an organizational structure for churches which would have involved mobilization of greater social control over members than the latter would permit and one which was incompatible with the political accommodation based on mutual support and noninterference worked out with the state.

The UM challenged the churches' positions by reconstructing biblical history and prophecies. According to its reinterpretation, the fall of man through Eve's physical seduction by Lucifer left all future human generations literally satanic in origin, a source to which humankind's myriad contemporary failings and problems were traced. Thus, rather than being heirs to a sanctified spiritual tradition, Christianity and non-Christian contemporaries alike bore the stigma and corrupting influence of their satanic heritage. With respect to the future, the *Divine Principle* prophesied that the redemption of humankind was at hand if only the opportunity was seized. This dual reinterpretation of the temporal schema contained in Christian theology discredited contemporary churches as bearers of a corrupt tradition and dramatically increased the salience of current religious behavior since redemption was potentially imminent. UM theology therefore challenged the basis of church-state accommodation (and established denominations were therefore compelled to disavow it) and threatened the basis on which the church exercises influence over their members.

Fundamentalist Christians took a hard line with respect to all such reformulations of biblical history. They insisted that God's word had been received without error in full and final form. As Breese (1979: 25-26) expressed:

[God] has revealed himself fully and finally to us in Jesus Christ as revealed in the Bible. . . . [This is] God's final and complete revelation, and this revelation can be supplanted by no other. . . . [The cults claim] God has spoken and recorded words . . . *since* He gave us the New Testaments Scriptures. . . . [The Scripture places] a dreadful curse upon anyone who presumes to present a new verbal revelation from God.

The third source of strain between the UM and the churches grew out of the former's emphasis on salvation through works and the latter's assertion that salvation was attainable only through God's grace. The churches' doctrine that faith in Jesus Christ as the only savior was the sole path to spiritual salvation had the effect of firmly locating spiritual salvation under the jurisdiction of the church. While it was possible that individuals might "give themselves up to Christ" and still remain outside the church, this was unlikely, and such individuals certainly posed no threat to the churches' authority. Even more importantly, the doctrine of salvation through grace served to divorce salvation from individuals' secular activities. As long as one acknowledged Christ (and hence tacitly the church), salvation was assured. This symbolic formulation was consistent with the limited social control churches sought vis-à-vis their members and their quest for monopolization of spiritual authority. Further, since the effects of one's spiritual status were detached from one's secular behavior, religious norms were less intrusive on economic and political behavior. Again, this doctrine permitted an accommodation with the political institution so that the church was relatively free from regulation as long as it did not challenge the political and economic priorities of dominant interest groups within the society.

The UM, of course, threatened these arrangements by its emphasis on works as the basis of salvation. According to the *Divine Principle,* man's fall necessitated the payment of indemnity as a precondition for mankind's full and final restoration to God. UM members therefore were continuously engaged in theologically legitimated activities which were believed to help members purify themselves and to set the conditions necessary for the world's physical restoration. Such apparently secular activities as fund-raising, for example, were endowed with a virtually sacramental status; the capacity to gain donations was taken as an index of a member's spiritual growth (their ability to love others brought donations which could be put to God's work), and the money so collected was defined as "restored to God's (rather than Satan's) purposes. Indeed, virtually all of members' daily activities were endowed with spiritual relevance and were evaluated in terms of their contribution to restoration.

Further, the UM's communal organization and separation from the larger society as a response to the corruption of the latter took individuals out of conventional career networks. The fact that spiritual works became the individual's preeminent concern created the potential for conflict with the political and economic institutions, since members were no longer influenced by the kinds of incentives controlled by the dominant institutions. Churches therefore were threatened by a doctrine of works, not only because of the implications for church authority but also because of the prospect of upsetting accommodation with the state. In fact, Moon's theology went so far as to identify a specific role for the United States as the archangel in the cosmic struggle against the Satanic forces of Godless communism. The archangel role specified the military protection of new Israel (South Korea) as well as western democracies in general. Needless to say, this doctrine explicitly projected the religious institution back into the political domain from which it had so carefully and painfully been extricated in America over several centuries.

Evangelical critics attacked this sectarian emphasis on works. Sparks (1977: 26), for example, stated:

> We must never fall into an attitude that we have earned everything we have. Our very existence depends upon the grace and goodness of God.... [Cults] think they have earned what they have because they have supposedly kept their rules and regulations which were laid down by self-appointed leaders.

Likewise, Yamamoto (1977: 106) criticized "cults" in general and the UM in particular for stressing works: "The telltale mark of many cults is that this system of salvation is established on works and not on grace." Breese (1975: 33) put it baldly:

> [The New Testament positively establishes] the basis of salvation to be in the finished work of Jesus Christ alone and our faith in that

work. By contrast, Scripture teaches that all other forms of salvation, based on human efforts, are cursed by God. . . . No message is more viciously attacked by cult promoters. . . . Those who would promote slavish religious systems are infuriated at the gracious offer of Jesus Christ to bring His life to the sin-darkened soul and to do it without any form of payment.

THE EMERGENCE OF STRAIN

As we have already noted, the churches were better prepared to meet the UM's challenge than was the family because an organization was already in place and because earlier waves of sectarian challengers had provided occasions for preparing for the current challenge. By the time the UM had begun to grow in size and visibility in the United States in the early 1970s, Moon had already encountered conflict with Christian churches both in Korea and in California. In 1948 Moon was imprisoned in Korea, apparently as a result of a letter-writing campaign by Christian ministers. The Korean Council of Churches, representing major Christian denominations, denounced the UM and refused it membership (Bromley and Shupe, 1979a: 48-49). There were also some clashes with individual churches early in the 1960s when the movement was transplanted to California (Bromley and Shupe, 1979a: 94-95), but the movement was so tiny and invisible at this point that the conflict drew no public attention.

UM leaders therefore were cognizant that the movement's theology and organizational style would evoke opposition. Nevertheless, driven by its world-transforming goals, the UM pushed ahead with a series of activities which brought it into direct confrontation with established Christian denominations. Beginning in 1971, Moon arrived in the United States on a semipermanent basis and began a series of national tours in which he propounded UM theology and his vision of America's role in the struggle against communism. In the course of these tours the UM portrayed itself as a Christian group; sought to coopt social and political luminaries through invitations to banquets accompanying Moon's speeches, solicitation of special holidays, and honorary titles for Moon in various cities and states around the country; and took advantage of every opportunity for favorable media coverage. Because of the UM's aggressive strategy, churches felt compelled to answer the challenge, and initially it was fundamentalist groups which protested the UM's self-portrayal as Christian. Organized protests greeted Moon's entourage at each stop on the tours; and press coverage began to shift from the favorable tenor accompanying a visiting dignitary to the neutrality accorded a party to an as yet unresolved dispute.

However, the UM's actions did not end with rhetorical presentations of its theology. The UM also sought formal legitimation through acceptance into the National Council of Churches and the New York Council of Churches, accreditation of its seminary, and joint activities in religious and charitable activities with other churches. These latter efforts resulted in a more extensive reaction against the UM. Not only were requests for affiliation with established denominations which would have accorded legitimacy to the UM denied, but a steady flow of Christian publications sought to warn Christians of the "counterfeit," ' heretical nature of the UM.

Certainly the most damaging event was Moon's entanglement in the Watergate crisis (see Bromley and Shupe, 1979a: 159-61). In 1973 Moon claimed that God had spoken to him in a vision, saying Americans must forgive President Nixon. In essence, Moon asserted, because it was God's will for Nixon to remain in office, the American people did not have the authority to remove him. Moon went so far as to organize a rally in front of the White House on behalf of the beleaguered president. This blatant intrusion by a religious leader into partisan politics was rejected by both the political and religious institutions. The controversy, however, gave the UM more national publicity than it had previously received and was a real watershed in its relations with the media. The UM's high visibility caused reporters to dig for background on the movement, and old conflicts and charges came to light. From that time on, the media coverage took an increasingly negative, hostile tone. It thus became relatively easy for established churches to deny the UM access to the legitimacy it so avidly sought: They had merely to refer to the litany of charges lodged against the UM over a period of several decades. In Chapter 8 we shall consider the impact of these exclusionary practices in detail.

Summary

Chapter 2 examined the sources and dynamics of strain between new religions such as the UM and the two primary institutions with which they came into conflict: the familial and the religious. Considering each institution separately, we examined first how the major threat of communally organized "cults" was to endanger the family's goal of preparing offspring to participate in the economic order by removing them indefinitely from conventional career-training trajectories. A second type of strain was located in the threat to the family's authority structure caused by off-spring substituting "cult" leaders for biological parents as titular authority figures and accepting the consequences thereof, from mandated daily lifestyles to such far-reaching decisions as mate selection. Strains resulting from the estrangement of offspring and parents were in many cases not "overnight," abrupt discontinuities; rather, strain was often produced through a gradual emergent process. In particular, we presented in some detail a case study to illustrate the dialectic of evolving polarization in parents' and offsprings' respective interpretations of the latter's decision to join a specific "cult."

Examining strain developed in the religious institution by the meeting of new religious movements with older, more orothodox Judeo-Christian groups, we found that fundamentalist Christian churches (as compared with mainline denominations) experienced the most perception of imminent threat. We noted that part of this strain was rooted in the fundamental nature of religious truth as knowledge; that is, because it is empirically nonverifiable, confidence in validity results from the consensual reinforcement of believers. Fundamentalist churches, with their heavy reliance on biblical literalism for daily control of members' behaviors, felt the strain most acutely as a number of sectarian groups such as the UM and the Children of God rejected this consensus and postulated alternative "literal" interpretations of the Bible or dispensed with it altogether. The radical reformulations of a group claiming Christian identity such as the UM (for example, denial of the doctrine of the Trinity or an emphasis on works over grace) therefore posed a serious challenge. Yet, churches and denominations, more so than families, were experienced in coping with "heresy" and "doctrinal error," and for that reason the religious institution was better able to weather and even stay the "cult" challenge.

Chapter 3

THE ANTI-CULT MOVEMENT IDEOLOGY

As we documented in Chapter 2, the institutions most directly threatened by the UM and other new religions were the familial and religious ones. The nature of the threats varied in each case, however. For the family, the primary threat was to its interests in preparing offspring for placement in the economic/occupational structure; the challenge to the familial authority structure, although indisputably present, was nevertheless secondary in importance. In the case of the religious institution, it was clearly the fundamentalist churches which experienced the greatest threat, chiefly to their authority structures, from the new religions. For this reason, we shall consider only the fundamentalist response to new religions in our examination of the religious institution's overall reaction. Indeed, as we shall show later, the mainline denominations were not highly visible or vocal in the conflict over new religions and on occasions even offered support for such movements' civil rights.

The conflict between the new religions and the familial and religious institutions incorporated two distinctive ideological *models*, one essentially secular/rational in character and the other religious/theological. In both cases the ideologies constructed by ACM members constituted attempts by the respective institutions to defend their interests and authority structures in symbolic terms that were consistent with their organizations and relationships with other institutions. For each institution, however, a range of *metaphors* were available which implied very different levels of threats and potentials for the invocation of social control. We have dichotomized those options for purposes of discussion into what we refer to as the "possession" and "deception" metaphors. The distinctions between the two metaphors can be clearly seen when they are compared on a number of specific characteristics, as shown in Table 3.1.

The possession metaphor presumed the existence of an absolute inherent evil force whose periodic disruption of human affairs was only dimly understood by most persons. By contrast, under the deception metaphor, pathological sociocultural conditions were thought to pave the way for malevolent forces to intrude into everyday life.

Possession implies direct physical control of human beings by this irresistable, anti-social force. In the religious model Satan or demons literally invade the body and personality of the victim, thus using him or her for speech and action, whereas in the secular model control of the victim is achieved through such means as drugging, hypnosis, and brainwashing. By comparison, the deception metaphor depicted a less coercive, indirect control that that gained by taking advantage of human weakness. The religious model specifies pride and spiritual naivete as typical sources of human weakness, while the secular model pose idealism and lust for power as characteristic, exploitable human frailties.

The overwhelming nature of this evil force, in both religious and secular models, renders all humans vulnerable and defenseless. Invasion, whether through demonic possession or through techniques such as the purported "spot hypnosis" power attributed to UM members, occurred without the victim's awareness or opportunity for resistance. Alternately, in the deception metaphor, human beings were presumed to have a greater capacity to resist the encroachment of evil, and indeed some persons were considered relatively invulnerable. For example, those thoroughly grounded in "truth" of revealed Christianity and/or forewarned and educated about the dangers of "cults" were largely immune to seductive blandishments. The two metaphors also differed with respect to the ultimate effects for victims. Both secular and religious versions of the possession metaphor posited literal destruction of demonically possessed or brainwashed victims. Attempts to document the deleterious effects of such invasions by proponents of either religious or secular versions of this metaphor resulted in strikingly parallel lists of "stigmata" (characteristic, identifiable traits of possession.) Individuals who were simply innocent victims of deception,

TABLE 3.1 A Systematic Comparison of Possession and Deception Metaphors

DIMENSIONS	POSSESSION	DECEPTION
Source of influence	Absolute, inherent evil	Pathological socio-cultural conditions
Methods of control	Direct, overwhelming physical control	Indirect control through exploitation of human weakness
Vulnerability	Total	Limited
Effects on victim	Destruction of individuality	Distortion of individuality
Imagery[a]	Zombie	Zealot
Danger to others	Extreme	Moderate
Solution	Exorcism/deprogramming	Witnessing/rational dialogue

[a] We wish to acknowledge our indebtedness to Bruce C. Busching of James Madison University for initially suggesting the zombie/zealot distinction and for contributing to the conceptualization of its implications. For further discussion, see Bromley et al. (1980).

on the other hand, suffered harmful but not irreparable effects from their seduction. Some of victims' human qualities became exaggerated or distorted, but their essential humanity was retained.

In the possession metaphor individuals were portrayed as zombies—that is, cold, lifeless, automatons controlled by either the demonic force (as in the religious model) or by the Svengalian "cult" leader (in the secular model). By contrast, the deception metaphor depicted individuals as zealots: passionate, exuberant, or even fanatical but misguided advocates of an illegitimate crusade, whether secular or religious.

The zombies in both models, having lost their will and individuality, obviously were much more dangerous than either type of zealot; the latter merely channel their passionate zeal in an inappropriate direction. Zombies were capable of "infecting" others as they themselves become infected, while zealots' threat was contingent on the weakness of their potential victims.

As a consequence, the solution for neutralizing possession in either model involved radically repressive forms of control as compared with the milder educational/correctional approach flowing out of assumptions in the deception metaphor. In the religious model this radical social control involved the casting out of demons as exemplified in classical exorcism rites; in the secular model the equivalent process was termed deprogramming that is, a reversal of the presumed brainwashing process. With respect to the deception metaphor, both religious and secular models relied upon basically the same process of discussion/argumentation, "witnessing" in the religious model and "rational dialogue" in the secular model.

Both of these ideologies emerged as the conflict between the UM and familial and religious institutions gradually unfolded. However, the religious model was more fully developed than the secular because the religious institution had been persistently confronted by sectarian challengers throughout history. Nevertheless, the fundamentalist tracts which attacked the heretical doctrines of the new religious in fact constructed greater consensus on theological doctrines than had existed prior to the challenge posed by the new religions. In many respects what was presented as a defense of orthodoxy was in reality the very search for and creation of it. Individual families, by contrast, possessed neither an organization or an ideology, and only gradually and painfully did they search through the repertoire of cultural imagery to locate and shape a conceptual scheme in terms of which actions to further their interests could be legitimated. Thus, our presentation here of the full-blown ideological themes should be understood as the product of the conflict process, and it should be reiterated that none of the protagonists entered this controversy already armed with an intact, well-developed ideology.

The Religious Model

THE POSSESSION METAPHOR

Although the imagery of direct satanic possession was by and large not part of the "cult"-anti-cult struggle, this was not because the presence of devils or demons was a totally discarded notion for most Americans. Indeed, as Glock and Stark (1965) and Nunn et al. (1978) have demonstrated, a surprisingly high proportion of national opinion samples have agreed with the statement that "the Devil exists." In fact, Nunn et al.'s (1978: 132) comparison of 1964 and 1973 national opinion poll results indicated that while 65% agreed with that statement in 1964, fully 71 percent agreed in 1973. Such findings are lent further support by fundamentalist Christian literature (for which there is a substantial popular market) that asserts the presence and activity of demons in daily life (Grant, 1973; Orr, 1972).

Thus, the reason for the absence of direct demonic possession imagery as a means of explaining "cult" members' behaviors is not entirely its cultural rejection, although it certainly must be granted that the underlying possession metaphor does clash with the secular/rational ideology of modern political/economic institutions. Rather, we would contend that allegations of direct possession would invite or even mandate a kind of social control incompatible with the position of churches vis-à-vis both their parishioners and the dominant societal institutions. In short, this imagery was inconsistent with the kind of control the churches sought to levy. Nevertheless, this model deserves discussion both to serve as a contrast to the religious deception model and to demonstrate the striking parallelism with the secular brainwashing model.

Possession has been defined as "evil spirits" or similar entities taking "control of the senses so that a person possessed is not responsible for what he does or says under these conditions" (Keller, 1974: 262). In its most extreme form possession is demonic; that is, a demon or demons or Satan himself directly invade and occupy an individual body in order to use it as a vessel for speech and action. During much of human history, demonic possession was considered to constitute an extreme danger to all humans because it was brought about by a virtually irresistable force and because it struck randomly and unpredictably. Speculation about the causes of possession and why, in the face of universal vulnerability, some persons rather than others became victims ranged from their having dabbled with occult practices to predestination, but ultimately the matter remained an "unresolved puzzle" (Martin, 1976: 29). Individuals who were possessed were regarded as extremely dangerous to themselves and others and therefore were to be approached only in highly ritualized fashion. Finally, to the nonpossessed observers, victims of possession were considered abhorrent and repulsive, having lost their essential individuality and humanity. In essence, possessed individuals became zombie-like—their former personalities disappeared, consistently or during periodic seizures, to be replaced by the new disturbing personality of the possessing demonic force. In Oesterreich's (1966: 17) words: "It is as if another soul had entered into the body and thenceforward subsisted there, in place or side by side with the normal subject."

Possession was believed to be accompanied by distinctive physical, psychological, and behavioral signs by which possessed states could be recognized and confirmed. For example, characteristics attributed to possessed persons by Oesterreich's (1966: 17-25) classic work on the subject included (1) changes in physical appearance of the individual, particularly in facial features, posture, and gait; (2) radical distortions of vocal qualities (for example, from feminine to masculine); (3) the speech of the possessed individual reflecting the new personality of the possessor; (4) extraordinary physical strength and flexibility (for example, the capacity for contortions and extreme violence); (5) nervous agitation and movement; and (6) desperate rage when confronted with sacred symbols, religious implements, and beliefs. Among other characteristics, according to Robbins (1974: 203-206), were a yellow or ashen palor over the entire body and "extraordinary emaciation, impotency of vigor and extreme langour." (A similar list of physical manifestations, with biblically based references, can be found in Langford, 1977: 165.)

The only remedy available for possession was exorcism, a highly ritualistic ceremony most often performed by a priest or specially ordained official which brought the forces of good into direct confrontation with the evil possessing spirit(s). Even this remedy was not infallible, however, and some individuals were lost who could not be recovered. Whenever possible, previous victims of possession were employed as exorcists or assistants because of their unique experience with possession and empathy with the possessed victims (Robbins, 1974: 201). The ritual itself was conducted using standardized rites such as the Roman Catholic Church's *Rituale Romanum* (a rite based on ancient tradition and finalized in the seventeenth century) which involved a sequence of alternating prayers, scripture readings, and invocations to the demon to leave. The process of exorcism, which might last from a matter of hours to days, has been divided by Martin (1977: 19-27) into six stages: (1) *Presence*—establishing the existence and locus of the possessing evil; (2) *Pretense*—attempts by the possessing entity to disguise its presence and identity; (3) *Breakpoint*—the possessing entity begins to refer to the possessed in the third person, thus acknowledging his invasion; (4) *Voice*—the possessing entity attempts to confuse the exorcist with a babel of incomprehensible, alien speech; (5) *Clash* the "singular battle of wills between the exorcist and the Evil Spirit"; and (6) *Expulsion*—the entity is driven out and the victim's former natural personality instantaneously reemerges (often accompanied by some amnestic reaction to the possession experience). At the end of this exorcism process, if it proved successful, the individual was returned to his or her previous normal identity.

DECEPTION METAPHOR

In the deception metaphor used by most religious critics of the new religions in twentieth-century America, a satanic power active in human affairs was still presumed to exist. For example, Yamamoto (1977: 125) of the fundamentalist Spiritual Counterfeit Project in Berkeley, California, claimed: "These past years the Evil One has been exerting his influence in every segment of our society. . . . His aim is to erect a super-spiritual structure through which he can rule." However, this power's intrusion into the everyday world was assumed to be indirect. Langford, (1977: 121) with regard to the UM, was quite specific on this point:

It is not necessary for Satan or his angels to possess a man in order to use him for their ends. Anyone who leaves the way of life in Jesus Christ is open to influence and control by the powers of evil. At the very minimum we are accurate in saying that this is true of Sun Myung Moon and the Unification Church.

The influence of Satan might be explicit or implicit, but it was further assumed that this influence was expressed through "cult" leaders and members who were themselves regarded as having been duped by virtue of their human weaknesses. Breese (1979b: 124) wrote: "Clever individuals with a smattering of religious knowledge are emboldened by their own pride and motivated by Satan to press for their own piece of influence in today's religious scene." Likewise, Yamamoto (1977: 125) maintained that Reverend Moon was himself an unwitting victim of satanic deception:

> Unquestionably he was a spiritually sensitive young man.... Per-
> haps Moon was approached by Satan or one of his associates pre-
> tending to be Christ and who appealed to Moon's natural and human
> desire for glory and power.

As a result of his unrecognized deception, Moon then became an uncon-
scious purveyor of satanic works, leading his naive followers astray. This
imagery was explicit in monograph titles such as *They Followed the Piper*
and *The Puppet Master*. Indeed, Yamamoto (1977: 129) succinctly drew
out the implications of this metaphor, concluding, "Moon himself is more
deceived than those whom he deceives. Moon is not the puppet master,
Moon is the master puppet. Satan is the puppet master." Others, such as
Bjornstad (1976: 94) and Clements (1975: 58), suggested indirect control
of "cults" by Satan himself.

Although satanic influence was perceived to be indirect, nonetheless,
world events were still cast in terms of a struggle between the forces of
good and evil. In this contest satanic direction was the hidden "prime
mover" behind the expansion of various new religions, a favorite theme in
much of the popular evangelical literature. Writing within the framework
of chiliastic expectations of Armageddon, Levitt (1976: 108) noted:

> The antichrist's unity of the world will be a dictatorship based on a
> personality cult, not unlike the Unification Church. For the short
> period of seven years the world will be duped into following a false
> "messiah" motivated by Satan himself.

The vulnerability of individuals to this indirect satanic influence was
conceptualized as lower than in the direct possession model. A given false
theology was seen as appealing, but seduction was mediated both by
individual weaknesses which "predisposed" individuals to join "cults" in
search of truth of security and by manipulation of their weaknesses by
"cult" leaders. Among the traits predisposing individuals to be susceptible,
according to Yamamoto (1977: 50) and Sparks (1977: 17-18) were (1) a
need for authority figures; (2) alienation/rebellion toward family, church,
and society; (3) recent emotional trauma and/or emotional desperation;
(4) attraction to an idealistic/absolutist philosophy; (5) spiritual hunger
emanating from membership in "dead" churches; (6) recent conversion to
Christ not yet accompanied by an adequate understanding of scriptures;
and (7) mere curiosity and/or boredom.

According to proponents of the deception metaphor, individuals were perceived to be in less danger than advocates of the possession model would have considered them to be, and their essential humanity was seen as remaining intact. Indeed, it was their very humanity and their focusing on human needs and aspirations which led them to commit themselves to false belief systems in the first place. Such individuals were not regarded as abhorrent or repulsive but rather might even be attractice to others by virture of their zealousness and sincerity. While victims of deception were seen as wasting their own lives and energies and even contributing to the spread of satanic influence, they also were not perceived as more dangerous to themselves or others than other non-Christians. On this theme Yamamoto (1977: 101) stated:

Is a person in the Unification Church pursuing his own desires any worse off than a [non-Christian] person in the world pursuing his own desires? Many people in the Unification Church are happy, contented and fulfilled Whether a person is conformed to Moon's desires or to his parents' desires makes no difference, for the ultimate meaning of life is in the crucified Savior and being conformed to his desires.

Ultimately, the danger they posed to themselves, or to others they might influence, was the lowered probability of spiritual salvation—that is, to their own souls.

Since the deception metaphor presumed that "cult" followers were simply normal persons gone astray, or at worst weak or gullible individuals who had been deceived, there were fewer observable characteristics or traits which distinguished them from others. As Zealots, they manifested exuberant emotionalism, single-minded commitment to their causes, and dogmatic conviction of the rightness of their beliefs. As Yamamoto (1977: 59-60) observed of UM members, most were young adults, with conservative, clean-cut appearances (short hair, modest dress, no make-up). "Their most striking characteristic, however, is their smiles. . . . They will insist they are offering you a way of life and not a religion."

That acceptance of a false set of beliefs underpinned misdirected "cult" members' religious crusades was evidenced by evangelical depictions of the "cults' " recruitment/socialization practices as well as the measures advocated to deal with their religious zealotry. Although some of these writers made reference to "brainwashing" and "mind control," their loose usage of those terms differed considerably from either the religious possession or secular brainwashing metaphors. Bjornstad (1977: 39), for example, described the "conversion" process as follows:

> It is psychological coercion which is used in Unification centers. The first step is isolation, where one is removed from the usual cultural support system of his or her pattern of behavior. To prevent one from leaving this new environment they use psychology. . . . We love you very much (This is called "love bombing."). . . . The second step is willingness, which is usually already accomplished because the person freely comes to the center. From here on it is only a matter of producing thought control or brainwashing in a controlled social environment, one in which the initiate conforms to the group's perception of reality.

Bjornstad (1977: 40-41) went on to comment that Unification socialization practices represented more than indoctrination and conversion, but added the qualification that "this is not to say that every person involved in the Unification Church is brainwashed." Indeed, he acknowledged that "some accept the theology because they agree with it." Thus, a general process of intense indoctrination which Bjornstad and others termed brainwashing was used to "reinforce" and "bring about acceptance" of doctrines. In the same vein Langford (1977: 6) reconstructed a typical recruitment experience for a UM member named Denise:

> Once a young person is contacted on the street, a college campus, or through a casual friendship, he or she is invited to attend a week-end retreat at one of Moon's ranches. . . . After she arrived a subtle program of indoctrination and mind-bending began. . . . Denise at first worked twelve hours a day. . . . She was soon going to class at regular intervals to hear Moon's teachings repeated again and again. She was allowed only five hours of sleep each night, and her diet consisted primarily of starches. . . . Eventually Denise became so exhausted physicaly that she couldn't think straight. She was undergoing a spiritual re-forming she knew nothing about. . . . She was encouraged consistently by their smiles, handclasps and hugs. . . . Denise and others discovered that the breakdown in resistance is hastened as group members aim at basic human requirements such as the need for love, the need to belong, and the need to be involved in something useful.

Almost identical presentations were incorporated in MacCollum (1978: 8-9), Yamamoto (1977: 59-60), and Sparks (1977: 16-17).

Since individuals were presumed to be misguided rather than literally possessed by evil themselves, Evangelicals advocated confronting cultists with the "truth," and therefore they explicitly rejected deprogramming. *This is a salient fact which highlights the ideological divisions running deep throughout the ACM and generally unrecognized by most observers of it.* For example, Yamamoto (1977: 101-102) directly repudiated deprogramming. He asserted, "A Christian must respect the right of another person to accept Christ or reject him." He reaffirmed this point when he noted that UM socialization techniques were effective because of a "void" in a potential convert's life. Because of this most important spiritual problem, deprogramming offered, at best, symptomatic treatment. "If this underlying, personal need is not recognized or dealt with, even the most technically 'effective' deprogramming will be ultimately useless." From this perspective of the evangelical critic, the real issue was whether one accepted the "truth" (Jesus Christ as the Savior of humanity), a choice which in the end had to be made freely. Thus, attempting to coerce misguided zealots lacked both meaning and relevance in a spiritual sense, as Yamamoto (1977: 103) pointed out when he charged, "Deprogramming . . . is an attempt to take the act of grace into human hands, to manipulate the mechanics of grace to a predetermined result." Indeed, it is noteworthy in one of the most uncompromisingly virulent fundamentalist attacks, Breese's *Know the Marks of Cults* (1979b), there was never a consideration (nor even a mention) of deprogramming as a viable option in handling the "cult" problem. In fact, Breese stressed (p. 96), "So important to the writers of Scripture is the preservation of Christian freedom that we are not only advised that we possess it, but we are carefully warned never to lose it.

While "cult" zealots were clearly not as dangerous as those directly possessed by Satan, nevertheless most evangelists advocated some wariness and preparation for even the more experienced and dedicated Christians before taking on "cult" missionaries in debate or confrontation. For example, Christians were warned not to attend "cult" meetings, not to "swap spiritual experiences" and not to "quote isolated biblical texts" because that was to meet cultists on their own ground. Rather, Christians were advised to present patiently their biblical "truth," to "treat devotees as human beings made in the image of God and keep the historical Christ central to your witness" (Clements, 1975: 59-62; Breese, 1979a: 27; Yamamoto, 1977: 98). One writer (McBeth, 1977: 26) advised the less experienced (teenagers) against any attempt to conduct such witnessing:

> Should Christian young people confront Moonies and seek to win
> them back? In most cases, probably not. As in seeking to save a
> drowning victim, unless the rescuer is a trained life-guard, there is a
> better-than-even chance that the victim and rescuer will perish
> together. With this in mind, the minister to youth in a Fort Worth
> church cautioned teenage Christians, "If you are stopped by a
> Moonie, don't walk; run until you are safely away.

The Secular Model

BRAINWASHING METAPHOR

The various definitions of brainwashing, as the term was used in the
1970s and 1980s by ACM supporters, all stressed a radical, "unnatural"
personality transformation. For example, Verdier (1977: 11), a clinical
psychologist, defined brainwashing as "the process of causing a person to
undergo a radical alteration of beliefs and attitudes." Similarly, Galper (in
Aversa, 1976), also a clinical psychologist, defined brainwashing as the
implanting of "definite attitudes and beliefs into the person by creating
stress and psychological pressure." As in the possession metaphor, the
most extreme examples of brainwashed individuals were thought to have
lost their free will and to have been directly controlled by malevolent
forces. Conway and Siegelman (1978: 13), in discussion of the phenomenon of "snapping" (their term for sudden loss of free will and freedom of
thought to some form of external or automatic control), came close to
recapitulation of the possession metaphor when they wrote of self-reports
of dramatic personality change: "It appears as if the individual's entire
personality has 'snapped,' that there is a new person inside the old one,
someone completely different and unrecognizable."

This change was posited to be complete in every respect. Thus, the
latter authors (1978: 189) recounted an anecdote by a former member of
the Hare Krishna who claimed that the "cult"-imposed personality of the
Krishna rendered him unrecognizable even to the family dog:

> "Our dog wouldn't have anything to do with me for days after I
> joined the cult," he told us. "He would growl at me and then bark as
> if I were a stranger. It wasn't because of smells or my looks or
> anything. When I first came back home I still had my hair but it
> didn't make any difference. Then when I came back after I left the

cult, I didn't have any hair at all, but he recognized me just the same and we were pals again."

In effect, the alleged transformation could be so total because, Verdier (1976: 1) contended, "All of an individual's personal convictions and moral principles can be contravened through the process of brainwashing." Contrary to the possession metaphor, the locus of evil in the brainwashing metaphor was found not in the incarnate personality of Satan himself but rather in inherently evil, anti-social, anti-democratic ideologies and systems such as Nazism and Communism. This was in no small part due to the legacy of post-Korean popular literature on brainwashing and mind control which was permeated with a hostile anti-totalitarian Cold War perspective (see, for example, Lifton, 1957, 1963; Hunter, 1953, 1962; Sargent, 1957; Meerloo, 1956).[1] Thus, Verdier (1977: 13) stated in his elaboration of brainwashing: "An uncomfortable reality has at last come home to the American public: brainwashing, which once seemed exclusively a Communist technique, is here in America and used by cults." Merritt (1975: 3), a psychiatric social worker and founder of the anti-cult association Return to Personal Choice, Inc., likewise observed: "The only comparisons that can be made with these new religious groups to help explain them, is [sic] to that of the Hitler Youth and the techniques used by the Chinese during what they call 're-education.' "

While in the possession metaphor a cosmic struggle between God and Satan was understood to exist at all times and therefore self-evidently explained Satan's motivation in capturing human souls, the motives of "cult" leaders who allegedly brainwash individuals required greater explication. In general, some combination of pathological, political, and economic motives almost always attributed to the latter. Arch-deprogrammer Ted Patrick (Patrick and Dulack, 1976: 228-229), for instance, citing Reverend Moon's various industrial ventures in South Korea and his alleged exploitation of American youth in fund-raising, proclaimed: "Moon doesn't have anything to do with religion. It's a business operation, plain and simple." Patrick further contended that "cult" leaders' arrogant quests for power, like those of Hitler and other classic authoritarian leaders, were obvious: "He's said over and over again that he wants to rule the world."

As in the possession metaphor, virtually everyone was considered vulnerable by the brainwashing metaphor's proponents, and precisely who would be victimized was difficult to predict. Indeed, the lack of predictability accentuated the danger. Thus, Patrick (Patrick and Dulack, 1976: 69) stated: "The cults strike at random. They will approach anyone

anywhere with regard to the person's age, background, sex or occupation."
As he pointedly responded in an interview (Siegelman and Conway, 1979:
88) to a question about vulnerability to mind control techniques, "Every-
body is vulnerable to them." Authors Conway and Siegelman (1978: 184)
concurred: "Everyone, without exception, is susceptible to snapping."
Yet, while everyone was a potential victim, nevertheless certain individuals
were regarded as prime targets. According to Patrick (Siegelman and
Conway, 1979: 163-164), the majority of "cult" recruits were young,
white, middle-class, Catholic or Jewish, intelligent, idealistic, sensitive, and
basically naive individuals who were "easy prey for religious shysters who
seek to exploit them."

These brainwashed individuals themselves became perceived as dangerous as they employed their brainwashing capabilities (somehow transferred
to them in the process of losing their own free will) to gain control over
other innocents in a fashion reminiscent of vampires.[2] Patrick and Dulack
(1976: 50) stated: "Most of the leadership of the cults in America are
themselves robots, zombies, incapable of rapid thought, decisive action or
instantaneous improvisation." Further, like others possessed by evil forces,
brainwashed individuals allegedly became repulsive in their appearance and
demeanor. For example, Patrick and Dulack (1976: 10) described a UM
member whom Patrick sought to deprogram as follows:

> He put himself into a kind of trance in which time seems to cease. In
> fact three hours go by, during which he does not speak, and does not
> move, ankles crossed, hands folded, spine arched, in a position of
> intense militancy, a curious smile distorting his features, like a
> grimace, or the drawing back of the lips from a corpse's teeth when
> rigor mortis sets in.

As in the case of the possession metaphor, and also in the folklore of
European/American witchcraft (see, Shupe and Bromley, 1980b), during
the 1970s a series of stigmata by which brainwashed individuals could
allegedly be identified gradually developed in the ACM. Among the more
widely listed stigmata were glassy eyes and dilated pupils ("the thousand-
mile stare"), hyperactivity and extreme nervousness, overall physical
debilitation (gaunt facial appearance, hollow eyes), body odor (sometimes
called "Moonie odor," purportedly due to neglect of daily hygiene), facial
skin rash (sometimes called "Moonie rash," purportedly due to a vitamin
A deficiency in diet), hunched or bent frame, fixed permanent smile
("with the mouth only"), monotonic and inflection-free voice levels and/
or higher pitch and tone, and other linguistic aberrations, such as

extremely truncated vocabulary lacking the "richness of imagery" and "mindless parroting of cult doctrine" (Conway and Siegelman, 1978: 159). Stoner and Parke (1977: 147) mentioned, in addition to most of the above "marks of the beast," a Hare Krishna woman who reported that many of the sect's married women ceased menstruating upon marriage in the group (presumably before pregnancy). Clark (1979: 280) also mentioned cessation of menstrual periods in "cult" female members as well as the slowing of beard growth in males. Conway and Siegelman (1978: 159-160) listed other stigmata attributed to "cult" members, including a reduction in peripheral vision (its origins unexplained) and even, in one case, an eerie ray emanating from a "cult" member's eyes: "One mother in the Midwest swore to us—observers confirmed—that during a confrontation with her daughter, who was in a Christian cult, she actually saw a beam of red light shoot out of the girl's eyes." These authors went on to describe voice changes in "cult" members closely resembling those of victims of demonic possession:

> Quite often, their voices changed markedly. The pitch rises and the tone becomes more shrill, an alteration which many believe to be a reflection of mounting tension within the individual. Entire speech patterns may change dramatically as well, and posture and mannerisms may be transformed beyond recognition.

In the possession metaphor the mysterious quality of the possession process derives from its preternatural, other-worldly locus; in the brain washing counterpart the locus of the process was foreign, secular evil (that is anti-democratic Communism). However, there was substantial room for disagreement as to how precisely mind control (or "mentacide," as it was called) was achieved. Verdier (1977: 1), for example, began his monograph by acknowledging the paucity of information on the subject before developing a physiologically based theory of brainwashing. Patrick (in Siegelman and Conway, 1979: 62-64) outlined a series of stages through which recruits were purportedly brainwashed."

> Their technique is to get your attention and your trust, they can create a kind of on-the-spot hypnosis . . . Cult recruiters take advantage of this to place suggestions in your mind. . . . Days later you may feel a strong urge drawing you to look into the cult. Your mind has already been opened to suggestion.

Second, once they "get" a person into the cult, "they use a combination of fear, guilt, hatred, deception, poor diet and fatigue." Third, after the cult has physically and psychologically broken the individual down, "they program you with repetition until you have no desires and no emotions left. You feel no pain, no joy, no nothing. They destroy everything about you." Finally: "In order to keep a person in that frame of mind, they make it impossible for him to ever think or act on his own, and they do that with self-hypnosis, auto-suggestion." Claimed Patrick in a sweeping characterization of all "new" religious movements, "they *all* use the same set of techniques to turn their members into zombies."

In addition to offering a similar broad generalization concerning "cult" methods of indoctrination, Conway and Siegelman accepted wholesale Patrick's "on-the-spot hypnosis" scenario as the explanation of how individuals initially became involved in such groups. Once a person had entered, however tentatively, presumably he was subjected to the ubiquitous grueling physical and psychological pressures, including insufficient sleep, poor diet (particularly lack of protein), and intense emotional experiences. After that, they maintained,

> under the cumulative pressures of this sweeping physical, emotional, and intellectual blitz, self-control and personal beliefs give way. Isolated from the world and surrounded by exotic trappings, the converts absorb the cults' altered ways of thought and daily life. . . . While their attention is diverted to contrived spiritual conflicts and further weakened by lack of food and sleep, the new cult members slide into a state of mind in which they are no longer capable of thinking for themselves . . . a state of explosive over-stimulation or emotional collapse [1978: 57].

The individual, then, according to Conway and Siegelman (1978: 135), literally reached a point where the will was released ("a depth charge of emotional response") and "it is this act of capitulation that sets of the explosion we call snapping" when "an individual's personality may come apart." At this time, they claimed, the recruit's brain was not simply open to new ideas and information but rather to a whole new restructuring. Finally, if the individual were to return to his familiar surroundings immediately following the snapping experience, the effects might dissipate in a short time. Otherwise, the recruit would enter a state of "not thinking," incapable of voluntarily disengaging himself from or leaving a "cult" (1978: 170). The long-range effects of such a change could be subtle but nevertheless subversive and complete. Ultimately, in a manner reminiscent of the vintage 1950s horror movie *Invasion of the Body Snatchers,* "the telling signs of his altered state may disappear. Then, the transformation complete, he is, to all but those who knew him before, quite undetectably a new person altogether" (1978: 160).

The "programming" or brainwashing process which we have just described was believed to culminate in a situation where the "cult" member was no longer acting of his or her own free will and therefore was incapable of voluntarily disengaging from a "cult" (see Conway and Siegelman, 1978: 36). That is, the person's free will had been totally subverted, as in the possession metaphor, and forcible removal of the individual was the only recourse left to desperate families and friends. In this way what at first appeared to be a violation of individuals' constitutional rights and personal integrity was interpreted by those engaged in conducting deprogrammings as a necessary, if unpleasant, and beneficial act. Freedom of religion was disassociated from First Amendment considerations, since recruits had only been involved in "pseudoconversion" (West, 1975: 2), and deprogramming became construed as "undoing" rather than "doing." Patrick apologetically expressed this sentiment when he proclaimed (Patrick and Dulack, 1976: 71):

All I want and all I do is to return to them their ability to think for themselves, to exercise their free will, which the cults have put into cold storage. I thaw them out, and once they're free of the cult, with very few exceptions they begin again to lead productive lives.

At the outset of a deprogramming, as in the rite of exorcism, the individual was presumed to be totally under the control of a separate entity—in this case of the "cult" through its doctrines and agents. In this vein Patrick (1976: 11) told parents on one occasion: "You're not dealing with your son at this point. You're dealing with a zombie. You have to do whatever is necessary to get him back."

Elsewhere in his book he stated his conception of the mind as "a battle with the cap screwed on tight" and that his primary goal was to counteract the deleterious, incapacitating effects of cult involvement by starting the person thinking again. In actuality the heart of the deprogramming process was a direct attempt to discredit, through argumentation, the particular "new" religion of the person's involvement and its leaders and to convince the person that he or she had been seduced, duped, and brainwashed. In the case of the UM, as with other groups located in the Judeo-Christian tradition (such as the Children of God and The Way), he would attempt to show scripturally how the group was "false" and its charismatic leader Reverend Moon was at the very least a charlatan and latter-day Simon Magus, if not in fact the anti-Christ of Revelations. He would produce copious files of newspaper clippings and magazine articles criticizing the group, particularly calling attention to its foreign political connections and Moon's politically tinged speeches as well as to the large financial empire allegedly at Moon's control. He would show videotapes of former Moonies repeating such charges of Moon's self-aggrandizement, often in empathetic terms that an individual could find appealing. Like his counterparts in exorcism, Patrick would even bring in exvictims to assist in the deprogramming, giving their testimonies and pleading with the deprogrammee to consider what his involvement meant to other loved ones, all this performed in an emotional "hot-house" that usually included parents, siblings, and even clergymen. Attempts to play on the free-flowing emotions of family members, as when parents would burst into tears before their offspring, were also frequent. While the primary strategy was argument, wearing the deprogrammee down through restricted movement, closely guarded and rationed sleeping periods, ideological and counterideological harangues, outright brow-beating, threatened and even occasional physical violence (see Shupe et al., 1977b), and the psychologically draining uncertainty resulting from a possibly extended "captivity" played an important part in the deprogramming "therapy."

The "cult"-dominated individual was portrayed as initially highly resistant to these "benevolent" efforts, even violently so in some cases, again a direct parallel with the possession metaphor. The individual might resist through withdrawal, self-hypnosis, chanting, and sometimes even violence. For example, Patrick (1976: 72) recounted that Pam Collins "was sporadically violent, slapping her mother in the face at one point." One newspaper account of a deprogramming clearly illustrated the brainwashing process:

And he fought it all the way, blocking his ears so he couldn't hear what they were saying, hypnotizing himself. Chanting these things over and over. He wouldn't listen to any suggestions. When I came back I saw a change. He was beginning to be a little more receptive. That was after about five hours. We were in that room 14 hours. All that time nothing to eat of anything. Just constant, constant, constant fighting fire with fire. Richard recalled "I ripped the mike out of their tape recorder and ripped out the phone because they wouldn't let me call Berkeley" [The Sun Messenger (Cleveland Heights, Oh.), Oct. 16, 1975].

The deprogramming session, like the exorcism, was portrayed as a virtual siege, a desperate *rite de passage* during which the time the "cult" victim and his "therapist" must be closed off in isolation from the world. Thus, doors were barred and locked, windows were nailed shut, furniture and objects were removed which could serve as weapons, provisions for days and even weeks were stored, and deprogrammers and family slept near the "victim."

Gradually, however, after hours or even days, the individual would eventually weaken (according to the assumptions of the metaphor) and begin to argue with the deprogrammer, in the process almost imperceptibly drifting into a receptive state. Finally would come the moment when the individual "snapped," and, as in the moment of truth when priest confronted demon, his or her "true personality" broke free from the mental fetters imposed by the "cult." This critical point in the deprogramming was always dramatically portrayed in emotionally charged imagery. Patrick (Siegelman and Conway, 1979: 70-71) described it:

"Then there'll be a minute, a second, when the mind *snaps back* and he comes out of it. The only way I can describe it is that its like turning on the light in a dark room or bring a person back from the dead. It's a beautiful thing, the whole personality changes, it's like seeing a person change from a werewolf into a man."

Equally overladen with similes, he gave this description (Patrick and Dulack, 1976: 73):

Suddenly, late that night, she broke. The moment when that happens is always unmistakable. It's like an emotional dam bursting. Pam began to weep, and she embraced her parents and kissed them.

Typically, immediately after the crisis "snapping" point, there was an emotional, teary outpouring of gratitude from the deprogrammed individual to the family and particularly to the deprogrammers. Such a finale was in indispensable element in any description of a deprogramming (Patrick and Dulack, 1976: 101):

Wes threw himself at his father again, only this time not to strangle him but to embrace him. He kissed his father and they hugged each other, and he apologized over and over for what he'd done, what he'd said, how awful he'd behaved.

Although, after such a reconciliation, the deprogramming itself was now complete, the individual still faced a period of weeks or even months of potential relapse or "floating"—a time in which he or she was still vulnerable to suggestion and could possibly "slip back" into the given "cult" under certain conditions. Patrick attributed most of his "failures" to insufficient surveillance of successfully deprogrammed persons during this period. Patrick (Siegelman and Conway, 1979: 76) compared the "floating" period with a car, unused for a long time, whose battery had completely run down, been jumpstarted, and then required further driving to bring the battery up to normal service. He stated:

> If you have been incapable of thinking and making decisions for so many days, weeks, months or years, once you get the mind working again you've got to keep it working until the person gets in the habit of thinking and making his own decisions.

Patrick claimed a virtually perfect success record when proper deprogramming procedures were followed, contending that fewer than 30 of the 1600 persons he claimed to have deprogrammed ever returned to "cults" (and then because they were not properly supervised during their "floating" states).

DECEPTION METAPHOR

The deception metaphor in the secular model utilizes the perspective which sociologists have termed social pathology (Rubington and Weinberg, 1971: 15-45; Mills, 1942). Each of the major spokespersons who wrote from this perspective implicitly or explicitly made reference to sociocultural conditions which were deemed pathological in the sense that these conditions inhibited normal social adjustment. For example, Ungerleider (1979: 4) hinted at such a state of affairs when he described "cults" as "comfortable refuges from the achievement-oriented intellectual stresses that are placed on so many young people today by their families." Thus, he interpreted young adults' joining "cults" as coping attempts to deal with problematic personal and social conditions. As he put it, "What has impressed me is the social seeking, the dissatisfaction that these bright searching people were trying to move away from, and the vague ideal they were pursuing. They could not find it in school or in work." Stoner and Parke (1977: 68-69) were more explicit in locating the joining of "cults" in a general cultural malaise that included disillusionment with affluent materialism, patriotism, and occupational competition:

> [T]he cults cannot be blamed for the cultural conditions that make today's young people especially vulnerable. Society must accept this responsibility. . . . The family, school, mainline churches, and the

government have contributed to the void by not constructively ministering to the needs of the young.

Such "pop" sociological analyses were invoked almost ritualistically following even psychiatric discussion of individual "cult" members:

> We are living in a era of frenetic change. In our own frenzied devotion to mobility, growth, material acquisition, and technological advances we have undermined the traditional social structures of our society. . . . The proverbial generation gap is now a genuine entity, with youths no longer able to emulate their parents as easily as in the past [Levine and Salter, 1976: 417-418]

Young adults in their late teens and early twenties, caught in transition from adolescence to occupational and domestic careers, were regarded as the most vulnerable or susceptible to the appeals of "new" religions. According to Ungerleider (1979: 7):

> In a broad sense it is the vulnerability of adolescents that makes them susceptible to these groups' entreaties. But all adolescents are emotionally disturbed, yet all do not join. There is probably a whole constellation of factors at work here—bright young people seeking answers, disenchanted with the world, overburdened by the stress of achievement and competition, looking for protection from their often ambivalent sexual feelings, and probing drug experimentation—all not uncommon in young people today.

Commenting on the "cults' " predilection for recruiting college-age youth, Stoner and Parke (1977: 26) concurred:

> If the young people who are the prime targets of cult recruiters don't understand themselves, the cult seems to understand them and their vulnerabilities very well. It is by building on the natural hopes of the young—for a better world, for a better life sometime in the future that the disciples of contemporary gurus and messiahs hope to recruit others to their way of life.

Clearly, however, within the potential pool of young adult recruits who came into contact with "cults" only a small number actually joined. The search for distinguishing characteristics comprised a major effort for proponents of the secular deception metaphor. Psychiatrists and psychologists examined samples of "new" religions' members but found few, if any, significant differences between members past or present and nonmembers (Ungerleider and Wellisch, 1979a, 1979b; Galanter et al., 1978; Levine nd Salter, 1976). Journalists Stoner and Parke (1977: 68), on the other hand, recognized the differential appeal of "cults" but could do little to delineate the types of persons to which they were appealing. They concluded: "In our efforts to profile the cult member, we hurtled into blind alleys each time we groped for a simple solution or pat generalization."

Proponents of the secular deception metaphor, in contrast to those of the brainwashing metaphor, portrayed members of the "new" religions both as being in less danger themselves and as being less dangerous to others. As we pointed out in previous quotes, such persons were believed to be the victims of their own misdirected idealism and personal inadequacies but *not* dehumanized (as Patrick and others would have them). Thus, Ungerleider (1979: 16) said:

> On the whole, I think psychologically the joiner of a cult is less healthy than the person who has the wherewithal to wrestle with his own feelings of inadequacy, dependence, anger, and sexuality. The latter person, I think by and large, will be better off than those who try to deny these conflicts, pretend they do not exist, or try to pray them away.

Ungerleider went on to state that those who remained members in a "cult" on a permanent basis did not achieve "the complete ego formation that comes from external pressure." Yet, despite the view that such persons were possibly less healthy than non-"cult" members who did not turn to "new" religions, Ungerleider did not perceive them to be psychologically damaged. Indeed, his own research cited earlier found no evidence of psychiatric impairment. Fundamentally, Ungerleider seemed to claim that the "cult" experience could only be defined as destructive or constructive in terms of a specific individual's needs and not (as did brainwashing metaphor advocates) through any blanket condemnation of all "cults." He concluded (1979: 15-16): "For many persons, the benefits obtained in terms of temporary control of their impulses and external controls is worth that price. For many others it is not." He even maintained that a person who joined a religious movement, made its work his life, and eventually rose through its hierarchy to an elite position probably gained "a better experience than those who never experience this phenomenon at all." Levine and Salter (1976: 418) went even further; they concluded that "these religions, as fatuous and as reprehensible as most people may find them, are improving the personal lives of many of their members."

Galanter et al. (1978: 10) also were relatively positive in their evaluation of the consequences of joining a new religion: "Conversion apparently provided considerable and sustained relief from neurotic distress."

Ungerleider therefore explicitly rejected Conway and Siegelman's (1978) negative interpretation of the "snapping" experience, referring to it as the "a-ha phenomenon, the sudden illusion, the finding of what one has been looking for" rather than as the point at which one surrenders or loses free will and psychological integrity. Like Ungerleider, Levine and Salter (1976: 414) concluded in their study of members from various "cults" that "psychiatric diagnoses could not be applied to the majority of cases. . . . It would be fallacious to label all of these religious followers as more emotionally disturbed than their peers." Nor did they believe that membership in a "cult" was necessarily a dangerous experience for individuals. They acknowledged (1976: 417):

> Of those who do join the fringe religions, most will not be markedly changed, or harmed, any more than if they had joined any other intense belief system and cult, be it political, for example, Communist, chemical (drug scene) . . . or therapeutic (primal groups).

The predominant imagery of those authors we have clustered under the secular deception metaphor was one of zealotry rather than of zombiism. Stoner and Parke perceived the majority of "cult" members whom they encountered in their research as zealous in the same way many sectarian Christians are zealous. In fact, they asserted (1977: 30): "We have yet to meet a cult member, or former cultist, who has convinced us that he was hypnotized into a new religion." They regarded "cult" members as examples of simply misdirected idealism which had previously been expressed by joining groups such as the Peace Corps. However, they acknowledged that these conventional alternatives had fallen into disfavor during the 1970s and went on to conclude that "Their [youths'] energy and enthusiasm need constructive channeling."

From the perspective of deception metaphor advocates the indoctrination or "programming" process which "cult" recruits presumably underwent was of a much less extreme and coercive nature than that assumed by brainwashing metaphor advocates. Rather than recruits having their former attitudes, personalities, and free wills totally eradicated or subverted, they were subjected to rather strong encounter group pressures stopping short of actual coercion, and then kept within the "cult" through a combination of peer pressure and persistent arousal of feelings of guilt and obligation.

In the brainwashing metaphor free will and individuality were removed entirely from the recruit; in the deception metaphor free will and individuality were merely rechanneled, perhaps assuming less priority in determining a person's behavior, for the group's purposes.

With respect to the indoctrination process, those employing the deception metaphor were usually in close agreement on details. Ungerleider (1979: 11-12) referred to the most important element as "coercive or group persuasion" (noting also that its practice varied widely among groups) and stated:

> The potential candidate goes to a dinner and hears no shouting. In fact, he sings with the group and feels very good. Then he is invited for a weekend or a week to an "indoctrination center," where group pressure apparently is exerted. Not in a physical sense, but just strong pressure to remain, to participate. The effort may be accompanied by encouragement to stay up late, some sleep deprivation, chanting of phrases, and singing a lot. There have been reports of people being refused access to telephones, to automobiles, and the ability to leave, but not usually on actual physical restraint. I think most people underestimate the power of group pressures of these types.

Stoner and Parke (1977: 154-160) divided the process into three stages. In the first stage the recruit was literally overwhelmed with a combination of separate tactics designed to mislead and disorient him and to wear down his critical resistance, all with the aim of producing thoughtless obedience and role internalization. These tactics included outright deception as to the group's purpose and identity, strong group pressure during indoctrination sessions to conform and participate in a frenetic sequence of activities (which they claimed produced the *equivalent* of actual imprisonment), a lavishing of flattery and attention, a deliberate arousal of strong emotions (particularly guilt and fear), isolation of recruits not only from outside distractions but also from each other, an exotic unfamiliar diet insufficient in various respects, and a one-sided rosy view of the "cult's" communal lifestyle. The first stage, by creating suggestibility through fatigue and pressure, prepares a recruit for the second stage: implanting new beliefs. In this stage inhibitions and otherwise normal skepticism, now critically eroded, can be by-passed and basic idealistic orientations can be redirected. In the third stage, albeit the least developed of the sequence, the recruit's consciousness is altered and his mind controlled by the "cult"—by members who have themselves undergone the identical process and have become true "believers."

Whereas proponents of the brainwashing metaphor assumed that, once taken into a "cult," individuals would continue to remain in servitude as automatons indefinitely unless forcibly removed, the deception metaphor's advocates contended that the observed diminution of individuality in regimented "cultic" lifestyles was voluntarily maintained. Ungerleider (1979: 12), for example, saw supression of the ego and individuality as something consciously and deliberately surrendered by, rather than usurped or stolen from, members:

> They felt good. They felt they had not experienced those good feelings before and they were willing to pay their price of regimentation, lack of intellectual stimulation, and acceptance of the authoritarianism of the major figure in the group.

Consistent with their argument about the quasi-voluntary decision-making process by which individuals entered new religions, and with their perception of limited danger to these persons, advocates of the deception metaphor express ambivalence about both the efficacy and need for deprogramming. While they were sometimes sympathetic with the motives of the deprogrammers, they nevertheless recognized that deprogrammings could do more harm than good and were not necessarily the best means of bringing about a reconciliation of family members. In general, they recommended a noncoercive strategy of patience, moderation, and open communication. Just as many young adults had joined "cults" for idealistic reasons, so they were likely to become disenchanted at some point for the same reason and leave. As Ungerleider (1979: 17-18) put it,

> Ambivalence about remaining in the group is typical of many of these young people. They don't know how to get out and they may send very subtle messages to the parents, generally saying, "Come get me." That is why all parents should try and have their young people visit with them for a few days. Keep the communication open.

Should parents wish to take action, what frequently was called for was a "re-evaluation," a term coined by Rabbi Maurice Davis to refer to open dialogues between family members on "neutral turf," and not a coercive deprogramming. Such a "re-evaluation" involved frank discussion with give

and take on both sides rather than the one-sided harangues characteristic
of deprogramming sessions. Deprogrammings were viewed as illegitimate
attempts to assert parental dominance without regard to the integrity of
the young adult. Unlike brainwashing metaphor defenders such as Conway
and Siegelman, who staunchly maintained that deprogramming was univer-
sally imperative, deception model advocates such as Stoner and Parke
more readily conceded that many persons simply walked away from
"cults" after a period of exuberance, withdrawing a mandate of authority
which they had freely given in the first place. As Stoner and Parke (1977:
xi) commented:

> We found ourselves . . . arguing that young people have the right to
> decide what to do with their own lives even if such decisions include
> membership in offbeat and restrictive religious groups.

Further, deprogramming could have some decidedly negative consequences.
Ungerleider (1979: 18) cautioned that a member "must not substitute
deprogramming or drugs or dependence on psychiatrists or family for the
former dependence on the cult experience." Likewise, Stoner and Parke
(1977: 270), noting that deprogrammings could fail and did backfire,
warned: "These failed deprogrammings did little to weaken the religious
convictions of the young people they were designed to 'rescue.' They may,
in fact, have further alienated them from their already distant parents."
They also observed that (p. 24), despite sympathy for the plight of parents
and a faith in the benevolent motives of most deprogrammers, often the
latter, particularly ex-"cult" members, were poorly prepared to "interfere
with the lives and dabble in the sanity of other young people." These
authors flatly stated of many ex-"cult" members who had turned deprogrammers: "Vindication, for their own deception by the cults, may be
their sole motivation." As a consequence Stoner and Parke strongly
endorsed "re-evaluations" over deprogrammings.

Summary

Our analysis of ACM ideology has presented its salient elements in
terms of two distinctive ideological models, one secular/rational, the other
religious/theological. Each model, in turn, was composed of two parallel
variations based on what we have termed *possession* and *deception* metaphors. In each case we presented fairly extensive examples from ACM
literature so that readers might see that our typology was not artificial,

forced, or arbitrary. Many persons (including some ACM members) were not aware of the diversity in ACM beliefs, nor that a significant (religious) wing of the movement operated on the assumption that the new religions represented something more sinister than merely entrepreneurial empire-building by megalomaniac leaders, nor that there were striking sometimes shocking parallels between the twentieth-century brainwashing argument, heavily laced as it was with the jargon of behavioral science, and an archaic belief in demon possession. Whereas in the religious model the demonic possession metaphor was not explicitly a part of modern ACM ideology, its once dominant influence remained as the proponents of the deception metaphor suggested that the new religions were at least satanically inspired. The secular model's brainwashing metaphor was a direct parallel to the religious concept of possession, heavily grounded in the scientific and popular literature on coercive attitude change written since World War II rather than in a personified "evil force." The secular deception version incorporated more sociocultural elements, such as the general cultural malaise that formed a background condition to the naive idealism of enthusiastic young adults. In either model the use of the possession metaphor in constructing zombie imagery posited a more serious threat represented by the new religions and called for greater exclusionary labels and actions than did the zealot imagery generated by the deception metaphor. Each model was the response of a specific institution (familial or religious) attempting to defend its interests and authority structures in symbolic terms consistent with its organization and relations to other institutions. That alliances, as we shall see, could be pragmatically struck among persons and groups holding distinctly different versions of ACM ideology should not obscure those very dissimilar underlying metaphors and assumptions upon which each based entry into anti-cult activities.

NOTES

1. The term "brainwashing" is itself a popular corruption of the literal English translation of Chinese characters meaning "to cleanse the mind." The latter phrase was used by Communist Chinese officials in widespread group dynamic attempts during the 1950s to eradicate medieval Confucian and other contrasocialist sentiments. The translated term originally used by Lifton (1957) was "thought reform" and perhaps could have been better translated as "correction of thoughts." The popular term "brainwashing" has lent itself to that uniquely human process in which a metaphor is reified into an alleged concrete phenomenon; that is, the "washing

clean" of former thoughts, beliefs, and memories to produce a zombie-like tabula rasa mind.

2. Cox (1978b: 10-11), in an insightful article on "Myths Sanctioning Religious Persecution," referred to "the myth of the evil eye, or the myth of the vampire." Under this rationale, individuals could be persecuted who were "seen simultaneously as both the agents of unusual demonic or psychic powers and also the victims." He suggested the analogy of vampires, since the latter were "partly victims and partly predators."

Chapter 4

THE ANTI-CULT ASSOCIATIONS

In the two preceding chapters we analyzed the sources of strain between the UM and the familial and religious institutions of American society and linked the former to the structures and contents of their respective ideologies. Here we shall examine the formation and development of anti-cult associations from an organizational perspective. These associations were comprised almost exclusively of parents and other relatives of members of the new religions whose fundamental objective always was "recovery" of their errant offspring, thereby reestablishing the previously valued patterns of family authority. While established churches offered various forms of support to anti-cult associations (such as church space for meetings, publicity, and moral support), there was little formal relationship between the two. Since the churches were primarily concerned with the implications of heresy for their own power structures, and since formalized procedures were already established for identifying and rejecting heresy, there was little need for them to form new anti-cult organizations or to join in those of the families. (The organized religions' response will be considered more fully in Chapter 7.)

Two previous attempts to analyze the structure and/or origins of the ACM have awarded the credit for creation and guidance of the anti-cult associations solely to Ted Patrick, commonly regarded as the "father" of deprogramming (see Chapter 5). However, one of these analyses was Patrick's own apologetic, heavily romanticized account of his exploits (see Patrick and Dulack, 1976) while the other (APRL, 1977: 18b) represented a simplistic effort to perceive and create a personalized coordinated movement where decentralized plurality, rather than monolithic centralization, existed. In actuality, as we shall show, the anti-cult associations component of the ACM did not begin as a cohesive, centralized social movement, but rather had its origins in a number of spontaneous and independent grass-roots reactions to the new religions.

Development of the Anti-Cult Associations

ORGANIZATIONAL ORIGINS

In the late 1960s the Children of God, a radical sectarian wing of the Jesus Movement, emerged as the first and most active of the communally organized new religions; thus, it is no coincidence that the earliest ACM opposition was directed at that group. Because the UM and other new religions which subsequently became highly visible at that time had not yet achieved their later notoriety, parents lacked any referent or context in terms they could use to understand their offspring's sudden "conversions." As a result, when their offspring unexpectedly disappeared or suddenly announced their new-found commitment to the Children of God, parents reacted with a combination of bewilderment and shock. Indeed, they typically had so little information about the beliefs and lifestyle of the sectarian group that the literal horror which later set in did not even initially manifest itself. In some cases offspring simply disappeared for extended periods of time after announcing their conversions; often, when parents managed to locate them, they seemed disturbingly indifferent to parental distress and completely unreceptive to their families' pleas to reconsider their decisions.

Usually, the first avenue of recourse pursued by parents was *local*—they contacted the police, district attorney, or some other law enforcement official in their city or county. However, parents quickly found this option offered little solace. If the offspring had simply dropped out of sight or moved much beyond the local area, police were usually unsuccessful in locating them; if the young person had joined a Children of God commune or traveling group but (as often was the case) was legally an adult, the latter's declaration that he or she was with the group by his or her own free will effectively removed the matter from police jurisdiction. The fact that the group was openly religious and specifically professed itself Christian gave local officials further cause for hesitation. Alternately, the police (who themselves were uninformed about the growing "cult controversy') might treat parental complaints as evidence of a simple family squabble. Hultquist (1977: 25-26) recounted how a policeman impatiently broke up a confrontation between her family and a Children of God troupe which her teenage daughter had joined:

> I told him of the phone call we got in the middle of the night, and told him we just wanted to talk to our daughter and find out what was going on. Rev. Craven told him that this group of people took kids away and kept them from their parents, and brainwashed them, and most kids need psychiatric help when they get away from the group. The policeman looked at Rev. Craven as if he were mad. "I see," he said dryly, He shook his head, "I don't understand you religious people fighting over kids. . . . She's of legal age. . . . You have no business meddling in her life, anyway. You couldn't tell her what to do even if she does come back here."

A historical incident recapitulating this model process and seminal to the founding of the first anti-cult association occurred in 1971. At that time William Rambur, a retired naval officer-turned-school teacher and his wife, residing in Chula Vista, California, learned that their 22-year-old daughter (then a registered nurse) had abruptly abandoned home, a fiancee, and her career to join a transient "family" of the Children of God. Eventually locating her in a north Texas COG commune, theRamburs found—by their own account—a confused, frightened young woman who seemed ambivalent both toward returning with her parents as well as remaining within the community of her new faith and who appeared highly suggestible to demands of COG leaders. When her parents were unable to remove her physically from the commune and efforts to enlist police assistance were unsuccessful, the Ramburs then drove to nearby Dallas where they held a press conference to denounce the Children of God. Soon after that series of incidents COG presented them with a libel suit for $1.1 million. This threat of suit, the subsequent total disappearance of their daughter, and the continued inability of local law enforcement officials to aid them left the couple not only stunned and angered but also, upon their return to California, determined to warn other parents of their experiences (personal interviews, 1976; see also CFF, 1974a; CEFM, 1976a: Vol. I).

Sometime that same year Ted Patrick,[1] who later initiated the practice of deprogramming, had his own encounters with the Children of God (see Chapter 5). In 1972, with Patrick's encouragement and help, the Ramburs and other angry like-minded families met in San Diego and founded the first formal anti-cult association in the United States, "The Parents' Committee to Free Our Sons and Daughters From the Children of God Organization," later shortened to "Free the Children of God" and the acronym FREECOG. The families that formed FREECOG, like those which established later anti-cult groups, made initial contact with each other largely through such serendipitous processes as chance reading of local newspaper reports and informal referrals by sympathetic public officials or clergy themselves previously contacted by other parents. Early meetings among parents of COG members who discovered and shared their common problems and concerns led to the formation of FREECOG, which provided a basis for sustaining their contacts with each other. Once established (as Shupe et al., 1980, noted), this group quickly took on a number of duties.

First and foremost of its functions was *solidarity*. FREECOG provided the opportunity for emotionally distraught families to express their anxieties, vent their anger and frustration, and maintain some hope for restoring their former family patterns, all before a sympathetic and supportive audience of peers. Despite the fact that the California-based FREECOG had envisioned a nationwide attack on the Children of God and even selected a Detroit businessman as FREECOG's first president (personal interviews, 1976; CFF, 1974a), it remained largely a collection of San Diego-area parents. Because solidarity reinforced by periodic face-to-face contact was such an important function to group members, the organization could not transcend its largely local orientation despite its pretentions to become a force of national scope.

A second function was that of providing an *information dissemination* service which emerged as the Children of God continued to gain members and as, becoming aware of FREECOG's existence, parents of these new COG members sought the same kind of information (such as the "cult's" beliefs, structure, and geographical movements) which the founders of FREECOG themselves had once sought. While never having intended to offer this service, FREECOG leaders nevertheless felt unable to deny requests for assistance and soon were literally inundated with calls and queries for information about the Children of God and other groups as well. Third, FREECOG also served a related role as *referral agent* by putting parents in contact with other parents in their locale as well as with deprogrammers and ex-COG members who specialized in tracking down and (if necessary) detaining the sect's members for deprogramming (a process described in the following chapter). This was a particularly vital function in the early days of the ACM when the identities of deprogrammers were less visible than they were to become later and the term "deprogramming" was virtually unknown.

FREECOG performed a fourth function when it served as a forum in which parents could share successes and failures in their attempts to oppose COG and rescue their children and/or discuss new options for united action. Additionally, like many other local groups of concerned citizens, FREECOG mobilized a variety of skills and expertise. Individuals with various legal, medical/psychiatric, educational, and political talents were able to contribute to the group's quest for a viable strategy of action. For example, local political activists frequently were able to designate officials most amenable to providing help to the group, and lawyers were able to offer specific advice on the legal implications of various strategies proposed in group meetings.

The formation of FREECOG had two significant but unanticipated consequences. First, establishing an anti-cult group, irrespective of its narrow focus, served as a veritable beacon for a multitude of parents whose offspring had joined various other exotic, unconventional religious groups and who suffered the same confusion and fear. Given their own specific personal concerns, the leaders of FREECOG had initially resisted involvement with families seeking information on sons or daughters who had joined other "cults" such as the Divine Light Mission, the Hare Krishna, and the UM. Over time, however, the similarities they perceived in the stories they were told by exasperated parents became disturbing and difficult to ignore. Families contacted FREECOG with tales of "overnight" conversions to unconventional religions, estrangement of youths from their biological families that seemed deliberately encouraged by various groups, and accounts of exploitation of young converts by charismatic leaders ranging from sexual abuse to virtual slave labor. Gradually, the leaders of FREECOG came to the conclusion that the Children of God represented only one example of a broader religious phenomenon sweeping the nation.

Second, as the now emerging anti-cult movement began to expand the scope of its services and the targets of its opposition, it was also forced to confront the limitations and constraints under which it was operating as a largely local interest group. Indeed, the early discussions among members of FREECOG revealed few viable strategies that the organization, as it was then constituted, could implement to combat "cults." FREECOG began to recognize that national organization and interest-group-style political pressure were necessary if substantive impact was to be achieved, since the broader array of groups to which it began to turn its attention were not limited to any one geographic area but rather operated across the continent. This realization came about as politically naive parents often abruptly learned the futility of simply petitioning local public officials for redress of their personal grievances in the hope that the latter would provide prompt effective action. As a consequence, the decision was made to broaden FREECOG's scope of activities, and, in view of FREECOG's newly expanded objectives, to rename the organization the Volunteer Parents of America. VPA was spearheaded by Henrietta Crampton, a Redondo Beach, California, housewife whose daughter had entered the controversial Love Israel sect. Communicating by letters, telephone, and cheaply reproduced newsletters, VPA struggled for a short time to present a united front opposed to a vaguely defined coterie of marginal religious groups which increasingly came to be referred to simply as "cults."

VPA, however, was short lived, its weakness (particularly its purely local orientation—regionally centered in Southern California—and influence) soon readily apparent to the anti-cultists. As William Rambur, (CFF, 1974a) recalled,

> it wasn't long before we realized that to be totally effective we must have an effective central administrative arrangement. Realizing that none of us were able, for various reasons, to administer such a large organization, it would be necessary to hire an administrative staff. We also needed other services such as public relations, fund raising, publications, films, etc.

In light of these shortcomings, in 1974 the Ramburs organized another national meeting of interested families, this time held in Denver, Colorado, and founded the Citizens Freedom Foundation with William Rambur as its president. The national composition of its initial board of directors reflected again the intent to establish a nationwide countermovement: Of its ten members, two directors were from Ontario, Canada; four were from California; two were from Ohio; and one each were from Rhode Island and Virginia (CFF, 1974a). While the CFF never achieved the status of national coordinating body for the ACM during the 1970s, it unquestionably emerged as the preeminent anti-cult association in the western United States, claiming 1500 members by summer 1975 (CFF, 1975b). Perhaps because of the emergence and/or location of so many new religious movements in California,[2] and perhaps also because of that state's dense population in certain urban areas, even the local chapters of CFF dwarfed many other individual anti-cult associations elsewhere in the country. For example, one CFF chapter headed by former VPA chairperson Henrietta Crampton in Redondo Beach claimed (in 1976) approximately 200 members, many of whom met twice monthly to discuss strategies and exchange information (personal correspondence, 1976).

In the next several years, after frequent repetitions of experiences similar to the Ramburs, influential and/or articulate individuals either began their own ad hoc anti-cult associations or sought out existing ones. From 1974 to 1976 grass-roots groups with such patently expressive names as the Citizens Engaged in Reuniting Families, Inc. (Scarsdale, New York), Love Our Children, Inc. (Omaha, Nebraska), Return to Personal Choice, Inc. (San Diego, California), and Citizens Organized for the Public Awareness of Cults, Inc. (Greensboro, North Carolina) spontaneously emerged across the continental United States. Many others of more limited means and goals, their number undetermined, appear to have surfaced, merged, or dissolved, often unaware of their counterparts elsewhere until their paths crossed in media reports or by chance encounters.

Their leadership was primarily composed of persons possessing high economic and educational resources *and/or* access to persons with political influence. William Rambur, as we mentioned earlier, was a public school teacher. George M. Slaughter III, who was to become director of the first national-level anti-cult association (discussed below), was a financially successful businessman in the Dallas-Fort Worth Metroplex. Among the 18 key individuals involved in organizing the first "Dole hearing" in 1976 in Washington, D.C. (discussed below) were six persons with the title "Doctor" (an assistant director of guidance services at a New York State community college, a professor of pharmacology at the University of Kentucky, a dean of the school of education at a New York university, a doctor of divinity, and two others for whom background information was unavailable); a rabbi, an assistant director/psychiatric social worker of a children's clinic at Boston University; a retired colonel in the military; an east-coast state commissioner of insurance; several others of apparently considerable financial means; and the mother of former New York Senator James Buckley's godson (an ex-member of the Unification Church), herself the wife of a prominent San Francisco attorney (see CEFM, 1976a: Vol.

1). While we would make no claim that the general membership composition of the ACM approximated such high status individuals, a crucial core
of leaders that precipitated organizational structures and initiated important actions quite obviously manifested upper-middle-class characteristics.

DYNAMICS OF EXERTING INFLUENCE AT THE LOCAL LEVEL

The dynamics of their respective appeals, exchanges, and confrontations with authorities at both local and national levels followed a fairly
standard course. Disconcerted by the defection of their offspring from
conventional family patterns, parents initially contacted local authorities.
At that time they presented their problem in the way they thought would
best mobilize official action by locating it within familiar categories; that
is, they reported their offspring as runaways, missing persons, or even
kidnapped. While we are aware of some cases when local sheriffs or similar
law enforcement officials would act swiftly (and probably illegally) to
recover adult offspring, in many instances parents learned to their dismay
that town, city, and state bureaucracies were unable to help. The latter, in
other words, could not respond to the offsprings' defections in terms of
such categories as kidnapping or runaways, and parents were unable to
produce the evidence that would bring the defections under the officials'
jurisdiction. "Kidnapped" or "runaway" individuals, upon being chased
down, often turned out to be, from their own statements, legal adults and
voluntarily residing away from home. That their defections involved religious conversion further removed the matter from official domains.

Faced with such a lack of response, parents (1) attempted to redefine
their problem to fit existing categories of official jurisdiction (for example, claiming that these groups were pseudoreligions operated by a few
malevolent leaders for personal gain and therefore beyond the First
Amendment protection guaranteed to "legitimate" religions), and/or (2)
shaped new categories into which offsprings' defections could be placed
(for example, that apparently voluntary conversions were really the result
of combinations of hypnosis and "mind control" that represented a
threatening new form of mental illness). As we have seen, a psychological
literature on brainwashing and an archaic cultural tradition of spiritual
possession existed to be tapped by such parents. Out of these attempts in
the early 1970s to reinterpret the defections of offspring in ways that
could plausibly allow officials to act in ways consistent with their own
bureaucratic/legal constraints emerged the "brainwashing" imagery of the
ACM (discussed in the previous chapter) that was to play such a crucial

role in legitimating the actions of both the anti-cult associations and the deprogrammers.

Yet, even with elaborate redefinitions and reinterpretations of their offsprings' actions as well as of those official categories into which "cults" could be fit, parents could mobilize little action. The extent of local official response was invariably limited to polite sympathy accompanied by the explanation that whatever the anti-cultists' own interpretations as to the "true" religious status of these "cults" and their offsprings' conversions, such important matters could not be decided at the local level. One anti-cult memo deplored this seeming impotence of official community leaders to provide meaningful response to parental grievances:

> We had received almost no help from anyone we had gone to whether political professional or religious. We had been told that they understood our concern. That was the end of it [LOCI, 1976].

Frequently, anti-cultists' frustration turned to outrage. In 1974, CFF president William Rambur wrote in CFF's newsletter:

> It is inconceivable that individuals can commit crimes such as these under the protection of the Constitution, and a continuance of this interpretation will render the Constitution totally ineffective. The protection of the criminal at the expense of the victim must cease [CFF, 1974b].

Thus, it was at the national level, in executive and legislative circles (so families were told), that officials could best interpret the subleties of constitutional protection of both families and religious groups and officially define the domain of religious freedom. Parents did, either on their own or through anti-cult associations, contact congresspersons and federal officials. By the mid-1970s, they had honed their claims into fairly consistent arguments, solicited sympathetic professional witnesses to support their views, and "learned the ropes" of making contact with busy officials often preoccupied with a vast array of responsibilities and decision-making. They had learned to deal with bureaucratic buck-passing, to anticipate the standard reservations voiced by bureaucrats against meddling in the affairs of sectarian religious bodies, and to present their case not as one concerned with particularistic domestic tragedies but rather as a social problem menacing the entire American public. In short, they had constructed a "public" in the sense in which C. Wright Mills (1959) used the term: translating personal troubles into public issues.

DYNAMICS OF EXERTING INFLUENCE
AT THE NATIONAL LEVEL

Yet, at the federal level, in addition to the resistance of "cult" organizations, they encountered a new set of problems in the form of organized opposition from various other interest groups—in particular, civil liberties watchdogs such as the American Civil Liberties Union and the National Council of Churches—which maintained ongoing vigilance against attempts to alter church-state relations. In a larger sense anti-cult representatives and parents became one interested voice among many competing for attention from the federal bureaucracy. Thus, what had begun in the early 1970s as straightforward attempts to have authorities mobilize social control and recover offspring from deviant religious groups while dealing punitively with the latter necessarily evolved into an intense lobbying effort which raised profound questions about the limits of religious freedom, family rights, and even personal liberty. To be sure, the national level was where such issues were appropriately discussed, but despite the anti-cultists' naive confidence that simply informing congresspersons and officials of alleged abuses by "cults" would result in automatic redress, the federal government moved no less ponderously and reluctantly to consider their complaints than had the local agencies. When they succeeded in gaining an audience or forum for airing grievances, anti-cultists achieved some measure of symbolic victory in further discrediting a number of controversial religious groups. Meaningful action from the national government, however, remained elusive.

This ability of the anti-cult associations to learn the mechanics of bureaucratic procedure—that is, how to enter the world of officialdom and make contact with bureaucrats—and their subsequent failure to effect significant substantive results from those contacts is well illustrated by the 1976 "Dole hearings." During the first half of the decade a network of communications among the major regional ACM groups (such as CFF) grew up and quickly established those groups' common interests. By early 1976 sufficient collective sentiment had been amassed among ACM spokespersons and groups to organize what became an important milestone in the movement's development: the first public forum of ACM complaints in Washington, D.C. Responding to a petition which he claimed contained 14,000 signatures (orchestrated by ACM parents), Senator Robert Dole (Kansas) arranged an "unofficial" public meeting in Washington, D.C. on February 18, 1976 between various senators, representatives, and federal bureaucrats and 352 parents and ex-"cult" members from 32 states (CEFM, 1976a: Vol. I; Dole, 1976).[3] The petition had been the result of a cooperative effort by various anti-cult associations across the nation coordinated through a special ad hoc committee under the direction of Citizens Engaged in Reuniting Families and chaired by CERF president-elect George Swope, a Baptist minister and community college social science professor. The agenda was set by this special committee in a meeting with Dole on February 17 and emerged as strongly critical of various marginal religions—in particular Sun Myung Moon's UM. The latter was, by common agreement of the anti-cult representatives, not only the largest and most threatening of such groups (and therefore offering a clear precedent for attack) but also the single group embodying those characteristics about which all ACM members had complaints (see CERF, 1976; also included in APRL, 1977). Thus, ten anti-cult spokespersons, including clergymen, parents, and ex-UM members, were selected to present grievances and to ask specific questions of Dole's panel, focusing specifically on the UM. Since the panel met only for a single two-hour session, each presentation was strictly limited. Other participants were requested to submit one-page "testimonial letters" and affidavits which, together with the transcripts of the two-hour session, were later printed and distributed by ACM leaders as *A Special Report. The Unification Church: Its Activities and Practices* (CEFM, 1976a: Vol. I, 1, Vol. II).

ACM members were clearly enthused by this opportunity to bring their complaints to the attention of high governmental officials. In retrospect, however, they just as clearly did not share the same interpretation of the event as did the congresspersons and bureaucrats. ACM spokespersons, since their earliest days of organized activities, had persisted in believing that as citizens they had only to bring their allegations to the attention of officials in order to stimulate outrage and evoke remedial action. The government's hesitation to act, they reasoned, had been the result of a lack of documented testimony and poor communication. On this assumption they spent the entire two hours parading angry ex-Moonies, exasperated parents, solemn clergymen, and various professionals delivering omnious warnings before the Dole panel. Yet, in the best tradition of "commission politics" (Lipsky and Olson, 1968), the bureaucrats, aware of the larger issues at stake and the equivocal nature of most of the anecdotal evidence, realized beforehand that there would be little of any consequence that they could do to help the ACM. Informal moral support was as far as they could officially provide under the circumstances; thus, for Dole's panel participants, the hearing was largely an exercise in "cooling out" some rather unhappy constituents. While the spokespersons of the anti-cult movement saw the hearing as a prelude and significant first step in the repression of "cults," the officials viewed it rather as the climax to dealing with the problem of parental discontent.

This admittedly cynical interpretation emerges from a retrospective reading of how the officials handled the meeting. At the outset, Dole carefully delineated the informal, unofficial, nonbinding character of the hearing (CEFM, 1967a: Vol. I, 6):

> I want to emphasize that . . . it is not a Congressional hearing; it is not any kind of investigation; it is not a public speech-making forum; and above all it is not a debate between opposing points of view.

Soon after, he reiterated this disclaimer:

> I would remind everyone one more time that we are not taking any testimony and no one is under oath. Moreover, nothing that is said or done is to be interpreted as a prejudgment or stamp of approval by the legislative branch on anything.

Dole also carefully laid the groundwork for directing specific complaints into bureaucratic channels:

> [I]nquiries will be referred to the relevant agency for a more complete, written response. Obviously, there are some areas that simply do not lend themselves to open discussion. Moreover, there are others that might require extensive deliberation before a meaningful reply can be offered.

ACM participants did not perceive the sequence of events in that way. Time after time, they questioned such officials as the representatives from the Department of Labor and the Internal Revenue Service about Moon's possible use of UM members as violating minimum wage laws, the condition of Moon's tax-exempt status, and his "importing" of foreign nationals to help in fund-raising, only to be cut short with the firm apology that such questions could be answered only after a formal list of allegations in writing had been submitted, reviewed, and investigated. An outside observer might have asked what remedial action of any importance had been achieved (or promised) by the end of the two hours, and the conclusion would have been that the hearing produced satisfaction among ACM proponents only for its cathartic effect and the *expectation* that it was the harbinger of future government action.

The 1976 "Dole hearing" did have several significant consequences, though not all of them were intended. For the first time, the anti-cult associations together enjoyed a well-publicized, credible forum to air their concerns before important national-level figures. This was testimony to their hard-won abilities to gain access to bureaucracies and articulate their case. Dole's evident sympathy for the associations' spokespersons' plights had a profound, reinforcing effect on their sense of legitimacy and feelings of urgency. In addition, the attention given by both media and national leaders reaffirmed anti-cult leaders' conviction that the time had propitiously arrived for instituting a single, umbrella organization which could more efficiently coordinate ACM activities and resources nationwide. Since the days of the ill-fated Volunteer Parents of America, anti-cult activists such as William Rambur and others had perceived that the ACM, fragmented into geographically disparate organizations of various sizes and emphases, could never hope to achieve the "clout" necessary to elicit an institutional (a *political*) response until these groups first achieved some degree of organizational coherence.

Yet, at the same time, the hearing raised hopes and created expectations that made the subsequent bureaucratic inaction a harsh fact to face; while they had become well versed in the procedures of getting a major bureaucracy to listen, ACM proponents were not appreciably closer to moving it to act than they had been five years earlier. This became apparent in October 1976 after the first national umbrella organization of anti-cult associations had been created (to be discussed shortly). Its president bitterly reported to members that not only was the government unwilling "to go after the cults" but that it was unwilling even to support the parents' efforts. CFF's application for tax-exempt status as an educational organization had been rejected because its principal function (said the IRS code) "was the mere presentation of unsupported opinion." He commented:

All the tragedies, illnesses, involuntary servitude, broken homes, inveiglement, hypnotizing, threats, murder and suicides—all of those things that have and are happening today because of the results of mind-manipulating activities of the leaders of destructive pseudo-religious cults—which our organizations report on have been determined to be "mere unsupported opinions" as determined by *YOUR* Treasury Department. . . . It seems that "Big Brother 1984" is almost here. *YOUR* Federal Government is going to tax *YOU* on each dollar you spend trying to expose the illegalities of cults and trying to help others who are (or will be) caught up in this personal tragedy, and you'll be taxed on your effort to see that all citizens have the constitutional right of self-determination [CEFM, 1976d].

Likewise, in 1976 CFF President William Rambur, expressing his frustration in dealing with officials, stated:

Their offsprings' lives are surely being destroyed and their families torn apart because far too few are willing to investigate and then take positive action. Many Congressmen say it is a local problem while local officials are saying write your Congressman [CFF, 1976c].

He vowed:

We no longer will accept, from those mandated by law to protect our rights, the stock answer that "nothing can be done at this time because of the protection of the Constitution." Only those individuals with no sense of justice could interpret the Constitution to grant protection at the expense of others [CFF, 1976b].

This frustration at the lack of official response had been clearly voiced a year earlier by Chalenor (1975) in answer to his own rhetorical question, "Why don't the authorities do something?" He replied:

Those authorities who have reluctantly agreed to investigate this situation . . . claim that the First Amendment makes it impossible for the courts or other authorities to act. In other words, if you *CLAIM* to be a religion, this gives you the legal right to commit crimes of violence and to disobey other local, state and federal laws. Parents have appealed to local police, to District Attorneys, the FBI, the Justice Department, to their U.S. Congressmen and Senators: The answers are always the same:
1. This matter is out of our jurisdiction.
2. We cannot abridge freedom of religion or speech.
3. You are just over protective parents, unwilling to let your children grow.
4. Your charges are too vague, bring us hard evidence.
5. Ten thousand signatures on a petition mean nothing, we get them every day here in Washington.
What it really boils down to is: An apparent attack on "religion" can bring political death.

Efforts to Sustain a National Movement

The 1976 "Dole hearing" provided the ACM with its first national exposure and one of the few occasions on which federal officials dealt with ACM grievances in a quasi-formal manner. Anti-cult association leaders at this juncture believed that they had laid the groundwork for further dialogue with officials who could and would act on their behalf. Bouyed by this optimistic view of the future of their movement, they then sought to erect a national organization which would sustain their hard-won victories. Such a national-level operation would, they thought, serve as clearinghouses of information on "cults" which would both raise national consciousness about the "cult problem" and provide the expertise and direction for anti-cult legislation. To this end two very different models of national organization were subsequently adopted; a centralized organization in which the national headquarters was preeminent and local/regional organizations were to assume the status of chapters (as with VPA, CEFM, and IFIF), and then later a federated structure in which autonomy remained with the separate, distinct, local anti-cult associations while the national headquarters served as a coordinating umbrella structure (as with CFF-IS). In both cases, anti-cult leaders realized that the development of a national movement was dependent upon three indispensable resources: (1) a larger, more stable flow of financial resources; (2) an expanded membership/supporter base; and (3) a clear-cut, ideologically consistent definition of those groups against which anti-cultists wished to mobilize political sanctions.

ORGANIZATIONAL CENTRALIZATION

The first attempt at a centralized national organization following the earlier Volunteer Parents of America was the National Ad Hoc Committee Engaged in Freeing Minds (CEFM). Shortly after the "Dole hearing," representatives of the major anti-cult groups met in Grand Prairie, Texas, at the home of George M. Slaughter III, a prominent independent business-man in the Dallas-Fort Worth Metroplex whose own daughter Cynthia had been a brief cause celebre in the media shortly after her deprogramming from the UM in 1975. In part because Slaughter's business permitted him considerable discretionary time and funds which he could devote to anti-cult efforts, the assembled representatives selected him to be the Interim Coordinator of CEFM. There was little doubt in the minds of either Slaughter or other anti-cult leaders that CEFM was not to be a duplication of other groups; rather, it would serve as the national ACM coordinating body. As Slaughter formally announced in his statement of CEFM's objectives (CEFM, 1976b): "We are forming a permanent national administrative office, professionally staffed, to coordinate the efforts of the various regional citizen organizations who wish to protect and preserve the individual's right to freedom of choice." CEFM encouraged other groups to pool information for its newsletter, to contribute money for its lobbying and communications costs, and to pledge its loyalty as the new central ACM organization. There is some evidence that this process of consolidation began to occur. For example, the Citizens Freedom Foundation ceased publishing (for a time at least) its monthly newsletter (CEFM, 1976f). In Columbus, Ohio, the first official *new* local CEFM chapter was formed in October 1976, and in the same month Slaughter claimed other CEFM chapters (presumably with various former identities) in Indianapolis, Milwaukee, San Antonio, Phoenix, Tempe, and Virginia Beach, as well as others in Connecticut and Vermont (CEFM, 1976d).

Elsewhere (Shupe et al., 1977a), we have described in greater detail the daily operation of CEFM based on participant observation in its "central office" (George Slaughter's private residence). Suffice it to say that the almost exclusively volunteer staff was regularly inundated with the large number of inquiries about "cults," missing offspring, and CEFM's service that arrived at all hours of the day and night through the mail and by telephone. Within a year, the uphill pace and ever-increasing strain on CEFM's fragile resources caused by the large volume of response to its mission began to be apparent. CEFM could not secure tax-exempt status as an educational organization,[4] and the daily round of trying to cope with frantic parents, the never-ending flood of correspondence, and other demands began to swamp the personal resources of the volunteers involved.

The next attempt at central organization was made in January 1977 when leaders of anti-cult associations throughout the country held another summit meeting on their common problems (personal interview, 1977). One month later, in late February, the leaders of six major anti-cult associations (the National Ad Hoc Committee Engaged in Freeing Minds, Citizens Organized for Public Awareness of Cults, Citizens Engaged in Reuniting Families, Free Minds, and the Individual Freedom Foundation Interim "Direct Action Program") met with several dozen other persons for a three-day conference at the University of New Hampshire's (Durham) New England Center for Continuing Education. Out of that conference emerged the decision to merge into the International Foundation for

Individual Freedom, located in Ardmore, Pennsylvania, which had obtained the long-sought status as an Internal Revenue Service tax-exempt 501 (6) (3) educational trust. On March 1 the assembled anti-cult leaders announced a new "united front in order to pursue our mission effectively" (IFF, 1977a). The Individual Freedom Foundation Education Trust (IFFET), the IFIF's new tax-exempt designation, offered hopes of greater solvency and the promise of a more stable centralized organization, as Slaughter announced to CEFM supports in April:

> Thirty delegates from all over the nation attended and found that we all had such a commonality of purpose that we could and should form one central national organization under which we could combine our individual efforts as well as our local groups to give us a strong national united voice [IFIF, 1977c].

As with CEFM a year earlier, ambitious plans were made by IFFET. National conferences and conventions that were to include seminars, training workshops, and goal-deliberation discussions in coordination with interested religious groups such as the American Jewish Committee were planned. IFFET began making arrangements with R. F. Dini and Associates, a professional consulting firm in Texas, for a Dallas office from which to coordinate a major fund-raising campaign. On April 24, 1977, IFFET's national steering committee held its first meeting in Philadelphia, electing Ben Roeshman (President of IFIF) as Executive Director and staffing the executive offices primarily with anti-cult "old guard." William Rambur, for example, chaired the finance committee, George Slaughter became Fund-Raising Chairman and Executive Coordinator, and other familiar anti-cult names (such as George Swope, Jack Eckhardt, and Henrietta Crampton from CERF, EFF, and other groups) appeared among appointees to the steering committee (IFIF, 1977c).

Yet, almost as soon as IFFET embarked on its national crusade, events began to go awry. The first national meeting of IFFET, to be held at Georgetown University and at which 1000 persons were expected to attend (IFIF, 1977d), was canceled after the university apparently had misgivings about the purpose of the group. IFIF members had poured a great deal of energy into making arrangements for the conference, and its cancellation dealt a blow to morale. More important, stubborn problems of organization and leadership were not resolved. The proposed fund-raising campaign never materialized, local and regional organizations were uncertain as to whether they were to retain their former identities or become local IFFET chapters, and IFFET executives could not reach agreement with the heads of other groups as to how flows of limited funds were to be coordinated. In this uncertainty the various regional anti-cult associations were understandably reluctant to surrender their autonomy, dissolve the separate structures and channels of fund-raising which they had established after prolonged effort, and cease much of their ongoing activities. Finally, an additional factor must be located in the forceful personalities of individual association leaders whose sheer perseverance had built the respective grass-roots organizations but who, in the absence of a clear, centralized authority in more than name, could not settle differences over the coordination of IFFET (personal interviews, 1977.) The result was confusion and disintegration of some local anti-cult groups. For example, after IFFET's formation in spring 1977 George Slaughter's national ad hoc committee of Citizens Engaged in Freeing Minds became the Dallas-Fort Worth Metroplex IFFET chapter, but by August of that year it had folded. Apathy, cited by a local journalist (Weatherly, 1977) in an obituary, was as much a product of inefficient management by IFFET as it was of public disinterest:

> Apathy was ruled as the cause of death. The Individual Freedom Foundation Educational Trust (IFFET), which offers advice, counseling and information to families who have a child in a cult, died a lingering death, said George Slaughter, life source of the organization. No support, no money, no office, and no interest in the Metroplex area killed efforts to establish an IFFET chapter here, he siad. "It (interest in a local chapter) has never been a thing that any group in Fort Worth or Dallas . . . has really taken off on," he said. "They are not really behind it in this area. . . . We're closing down operations," said Slaughter, "because there is apathy."

Following IFFET's failure to provide the long-sought centralized leadership role, another assessment of the possibility of nationally coordinating anti-cult associations occurred in late summer 1977. Leaders and activists from various groups met in Dallas to discuss their mutual interests and problems and to consider alternatives for viable reorganization. Given the failures of VPA, CEFM, and, most recently, IFFET, the option chosen this time (originally considered at the earlier February conference at the University of New Hampshire but tabled at that time) was a decentralized structural arrangement that seemed most compatible with the realities of the associations' resources and needs and one that continued through the subsequent two years. Those present at the Dallas meeting divided the continental United States into eight regions,[5] each supervised by a volunteer director who assembled mailing lists, maintained legal/media/"cult" activities in his or her region, and served as liason between the region and the still-continuing IFIF organization. Former groups such as Citizens for Public Awareness of Cults, Citizens Freedom Foundation, and Love Our Children were also to continue activities; in some cases their leaders would work closely with the new directors and in others they would take turns in that new role themselves.

Thus, despite plans for IFIF to perform its coordinating functions, the organization never successfully gained sufficient support from its regional allies to carry out its mandate. As a result, the anti-cult associations continued in a de facto state of decentralization for almost three years. However, the new decade of the 1980s witnessed yet another attempt to achieve national coordination. In November 1979, 65 delegates representing 31 ACM groups met in Chicago for a three-day summit conference. Out of their deliberations came a new umbrella organization: the Citizens Freedom Foundation—Information Services (CFF-IS), to be located in Los Angeles where it could rely on the superior organization and larger number of members of the CFF, undoubtedly still the most stable and largest ACM organization in America at that time. The delegates elected a board of directors, selected a national chairman (John Sweeney, President of CFF), and agreed on a preliminary budget. The national CFF-IS's goals were remarkably unchanged from the aims of the first attempts at national-level organization: to educate the public and legal and medical professionals as to the dangers of "mind control"; to disassociate the issue of religious freedom from legal and moral attempts to deal with "cults"; to promote legislation aimed at correcting the "cult problem," such as requiring honest identification of organizational origins during fund-raising; to provide public information and counseling instruction for clergy and other professionals dealing with "cult" victims; and to not only launch a public relations campaign designed to discredit "cults" and favorably present the ACM message, but also foster research into the mental health conditions conducive to prevention of youthful victimization by "cults."

Organizationally, CFF-IS was not intended to become a "super" anticult association into which all regional and local groups would merge (as VPA, CEFM, and IFFET were to have been) but rather as a coordinating body to monitor more effectively the decentralized activities of all anticult associations. In its founders's words: "The National organization was formed not to be an authority over the local groups, but to coordinate various jobs that local groups volunteered to do to provide important services for everyone" (IFF, 1980). Specific functions, such as monitoring

the media, establishing and maintaining an information library, publishing
a regular newsletter, training in counseling and deprogramming, and coordinating referrals, were identified and assigned to specific regional anti-cult
associations in an attempt to divide the labor of a national-level movement. A number of ambitious projects, including the production of eight
hour-length documentaries to be shown on public television (an edited
version to appear on an unspecified commercial network) at an estimated
cost of $2.5 million, and a series of major seminars across the United
States, were planned (CFF-IS, 1980). Thus, as the ACM entered its second
decade, a plethora of anti-cult associations possessing a bewildering set of
acronyms, widely disparate in terms of experience, size, and financial
resources yet committed to achieving a united anti-cult effort, covered the
continental United States.

MEMBERSHIP

It is important to note at the outset of any discussion of membership in
the anti-cult organizations that the number of individuals and families who
were directly affected by "cults," despite media reports of tens of thousands of youths in various new religions and ACM spokespersons' fantastic
claims of millions, always remained relatively small with high rates of
turnover.[6] As a consequence, there never was at any given time an
enormous pool of potential aggrieved parents who might join the ACM.
This situation was compounded by the fact that the local anti-cult associations never actively recruited new members. Rather, as in the case of
FREECOG, media publicity, word-of-mouth referral, and sheer chance
brought persons into contact with these groups. It is true that anti-cult
association membership lists grew rapidly after 1974; for example, CFF
claimed 1500 members in 1975 (CFF, 1975b), while CEFM's mailing list
contained almost 4000 addresses by 1976 (personal interviews, 1976).
However, most of those whom the anti-cult associations counted as members in reality were seeking rather than offering assistance. As we shall see
in the next section, this situation presented an enormous drain on organizational resources.

The relatively small proportion of parents and individuals who became
activists in these anti-cult associations did so somewhat reluctantly after
unsuccessful individual attempts to recover their children had impressed
upon them the importance of cooperative efforts in achieving their restorative goals. Moreover, once publicly identified as protagonists in the effort
to win back offspring, these individuals were inundated with requests for
help by other distraught parents and, out of feelings of both empathy and

civic responsibility, felt that they could not refuse to at least try to cope with the requests for aid. Interestingly enough, this small coterie of activists never attempted to recruit other community actors (that is, those who supported and sustained other local charitable causes), limiting their potential constituency to those persons who took the initiative to contact groups for information, solace, and support. However, because (until the late 1970s) anti-cult groups did not distinguish the larger number of requests for services from the considerably fewer offers of financial and/or volunteer assistance, membership rolls often lent an inflated picture of the actual membership base on which leaders could depend for everything from participation at rallies and demonstrations to donations. As a consequence, the nucleus of committed, working activists remained small; in fact, as requests continued to mount and the rolls gained protracted length, it became a perennially beleaguered, proportionately shrinking minority in the movement.

That anti-cult associations did not systematically recruit new members was compounded by the fact that even those who did join such groups had only one common, narrow base of interest—restoring their previous family relationships. Thus, usually as soon as parents managed to extricate their offspring from a "cult" or their offspring defected, their participation in anti-cult associations dropped off almost as rapidly as it had begun. This rapid turnover of membership and single common interest continued to plague anti-cult associations. As a result, they never achieved a sufficiently large, stable base of membership to launch the kind of anti-cult campaigns which their founders had envisioned.

These two membership problems were in turn exacerbated by the nature and size of the ideology that the ACM had constructed. Among the chief targets of the ACM, the Children of God and the UM were either organized into what were low-visibility, isolated communes or highly mobile fund-raising/witnessing teams. Therefore, it was difficult to arouse sustained interest in local communities, either because no group resided in or near them or because mobile teams appeared unpredictably and for only brief periods. Further, of course, since the "cults" were relatively small in size, relatively few parents in any locale had, in fact, "lost" their children to them. The elusive nature of "cults" simply meant that it was difficult to provide local communities with a sense of ongoing threat or meaningful targets for concerted action. Where the ACM was able to identify such targets, such as regular fund-raising in airports or attempts to witness on local university campuses, anti-cult association members were, in fact, relatively successful in at least impeding "cult" activities.

The ACM ideology also functioned as "blinders" in impeding the building and accurate assessment of a membership base in an ironic way. ACM leaders (at least publicly) were compelled by the brainwashing metaphor to contend that it was impossible for "cult" members to voluntarily leave such groups, hence that the actual high turnover rates that researchers such as ourselves (personal interviews with UM Officials, 1976) found did not exist. Therefore, they tended to assume that parents in contact with anti-cult associations were certain to be long-time ACM advocates and supporters. In fact, members of new religions were likely to join such groups for periods of time typically ranging from a few months to, at most, a few years during young adulthood. Within two or three years of joining, the attrition rates for given cohorts became substantial. (For example, according to one informant, the defection rate of the first graduating class of Reverend Moon's Unification Theological Seminary, composed of the "cream" of his millenarian movement, was 17 percent.) Because anti-cult association leaders chose—indeed, were *forced* on pain of abandoning the key metaphor underlying their entire enterprise—to ignore this fact, they never accurately appraised the real base of support from which they were operating and continually were disappointed with the turnouts they achieved for various ACM activities.

The anti-cult associations alternately experimented with both the centralized and federated models of organization at a national level. However, in each instance the factors just discussed plagued attempts to sustain a viable national-level organization. If, on the one hand, anti-cult associations chose a federated structure with only loose coordination at the national level, as they did after the disappointment with VPA, CEFM, and IFFET, what was then needed was a series of vital aggressive local organizations. Under such a system the national coordinating body would be reliant upon local groups with common interests and grievances to bring to it an agenda for action, provide sufficient surplus resources to allow it to conduct national campaigns and projects, and recruit sufficiently large memberships at a local level to convince federal officials that a problem of substantial proportions existed which justified or even required a commitment of their own limited time and resources. However, most of the anti-cult associations, aside from more experienced ones such as CFF and Love Our Children, Inc. (LOCI), never did generate surplus resources to forward on to the national level and never developed sufficient membership bases from which a national federated organization could mobilize an effective lobbying force. Moreover, not only did local groups funnel their local problems to the national organization as soon as it was established, but the national organization began directly receiving requests for information and services from all over the nation, straining part-time volunteer staffs and distracting them from coordinating functions originally mandated to them. It was not long, for example, before the de facto federated arrangement of anti-cult associations following the collapse of IFFET in 1977 bogged down in such problems. As a result, rather than serving to coordinate aggressive local initiatives, the national organization simply became a dumping ground for unresolved local problems, handed the responsibilities of a broad agency but expected to make do on the limited budget of a regional group. Herein lay the inescapable paradox for any attempts to coordinate anti-cult associations' activities. Local groups formed the national federation because they began to recognize that their problems and interests transcended local boundaries. However, the national organization they sought was premised on strong local-level organizations which were largely nonexistent. Thus, the federated structure seemed doomed from the outset, and indeed the ACM offers evidence of its unworkability.

On the other hand, the anti-cult associations repeatedly pursued a centralized national structure—as in VPA, CEFM, and IFFET—but this alternative, too, foundered amidst apparently irresolvable organizational problems. Under this second model, the national body needed to possess substantial autonomy in order to formulate policy and strategy and disburse funds to local units which would, in turn, assume the status of chapters. However, neither the more recent CEFM nor IFFET (and certainly not the distant VPA) ever achieved any significant degree of autonomy with respect to membership or financial resources and local organizations giving up their own organizational identities and limited resources. As in the case of federated structures, the centralized attempts found that local groups simply passed local problems, referrals, and requests for information (along with the costs) up to the national level organizations. An average day for CEFM workers, for example, saw anywhere from 50 to 100 pieces of ACM-related mail to be sorted, read, and answered as well as innumerable phone calls during which information was also requested and transmitted.[7]

FINANCIAL RESOURCES

A viable ACM national organization, whether centralized or federated, required a steady, sizable influx of money to meet the expenses of lobbying, information-gathering/disseminating, and day-to-day maintenance/operation. Meaningful action at the federal level implied at least a small, full-time, paid staff of workers who could pursue the myriad of officials in pertinent Washington bureaucracies. This no national-level anti-cult association ever achieved. As we pointed out, local anti-cult associations never accrued substantial surplus funds which could be funneled to a national organization (indeed, most barely sustained a precarious solvency of their own), and national organizations, for the most part, failed to develop independent sources of membership/financial support.

This is not to say that national anti-cult leaders were unaware of the need for "big money" a substantial initial donation that would permit the establishment of adequate staffing, supplies, and office. They did discuss at various junctures means of obtaining "seed money," projects that would raise large sums in a short period of time, and expanding the scope of financial supporters.[8] However, consideration of such options never lead to successful courses of action. Anti-cult leaders periodically called for a large initial input of funds to "get the national movement going." In October 1976, Slaughter complained to CEFM constituents:

> The formation of a national organization or central office is at a standstill for lack of adequate funding. No one has come up with a tax-exempt organization to allow us to go to "big money" for a donation. We need at least $50,000 pledged or in the bank to hire an executive director, obtain an office, and employ a small staff [CEFM, 1976d].

In a communication the following month, after contrasting the "tremendous wealth available" to "cult" leaders such as Sun Myung Moon, Slaughter reiterated this theme:

> Try to interest an individual, organization, foundation, or company in contributing to our cause—one who would be capable of supporting us with a gift *in the five digit area* [CEFM, 1976a].

The only cases of which we are aware in which anti-cult associations sought to raise substantial amounts of money in a short time involved, respectively, a lottery and a national advertising campaign following the tragedy at Jonestown. Harper (1979: 29) reported that Love Our Children, Inc., in Omaha successfully ran a lottery, selling prizes donated by members and sympathetic organizations and businesses, raising $1000—a mere pittance by the standards of LOCI's "cult" opponents (one UM fund-raiser of our acquaintance raised that sum in a single day of street soliciting). In the other case, a large advertisement appeared in the Sunday New York *Times* which featured the headline "Cult Activity Didn't Die at Jonestown" over a photograph of a corpse-strewn field in Jonestown, Guyana. The advertisement began: "Cult activity is still alive in this country. Maybe in your own neighborhood. They're stealing your children and possessing their minds." It ended with the bold-face letters over a form to send with a donation: "Prevent another Jonestown." With these two exceptions, however, the ACM's failure to seek financial resources in the wider community, relying primarily on supporters from their limited, only partially active, membership lists, severely restricted the potential and actual monies with which anti-cult associations had to work and resulted in the frequent harangues on the inadequacy of operating capital found throughout ACM memoranda and newsletters.

Because both the national and regional anti-cult associations depended upon a small membership base (many of whom fit the description of isolated constituents--see McCarthy and Zald, 1977) and made only a few, largely unsuccessful, appeals to anyone not already associated with the ACM, the persistent pattern was one of relatively large donations by a small number of individuals. For example, in reporting on progress toward a financial goal of raising $40,000, Slaughter reprovingly noted that in the entire United States only 78 persons had pledged funds, 34 of whom had averaged $366 per pledge (CEFM, 1976b). This meant that the few individuals already giving large amounts were constantly besieged with requests to be even more generous, and the anti-cult associations sought to extract every possible dollar from a narrow resource base rather than tapping the lucrative charitable giving pool which was at least potentially accessible to them. As a result, anti-cult association newsletters were filled with requests and even pleas for funds which never yielded large returns, and much of the directors' efforts were spent on simply trying to maintain near-solvency.[9] For example, in 1975, William Rambur bluntly wrote to CFF members:

> I'm going to lay it on the line! Thank you's and praise are most welcome but they do not provide facilities, equipment, educational materials, staff, etc. Nor do they pay the bills. To succeed *we* must be equal in strength to those forces we are combatting [CFF, 1975b].

In 1976, George Slaughter wrote to CEFM members:

> Dadgumit, every parent should pledge $10 to $20 per month to CEFM: if you are not doing it, you are not doing your share--where

is your pledge? A few parents are doing most of the work as well as giving financial support. Are you one of them [CEFM, 1976b]?

Several months later, he reiterated the same pleas for financial support that Rambur had been issuing from CFF for half a decade:

WE APPEAL TO YOU FOR FUNDS once again. This memo alone costs several hundred dollars. The office expense necessary to gather and file information for it costs money; telephone, photocopies, and printing materials and mailing costs require several hundred more each month. We need a professional secretary so more letters can be answered and written. PLEASE HELP IF YOU CAN [CEFM, 1976d].

Three years later, the shortage of funds was still an issue largely unresolved. When John Sweeney, Rambur's successor as president of CFF, became national director of the Citizens Freedom Foundation—Information Service (CFF-IS) in 1979, he again pleaded in a mail-out solicitation:

This letter was made possible by a contribution from another family who cared. If you toss this letter into the waste basket, both your contribution and theirs will be lost forever. . . . For if we do nothing, 914 poor, brainwashed souls in Guyana will have died in vain [CFF-IS, 1980].

IDEOLOGICAL CONSENSUS

In addition to the strictly organizational problems which the ACM was confronted, it was also faced with a basic inability to define its target groups ("cults") consistently and with any precision or to agree upon a strategy for opposing "cults." As we have already noted, the brainwashing ideology represented a means of transforming families' private troubles into public issues. For if they were to garner support at a national level and mobilize governmental agencies to impose sanctions, it was imperative that they convince the general public and officials that a concrete, identifiable threat to commonly shared values and interests now presented itself. The ACM, however, was not completely successful in this effort, in part because it could not reach agreement on the definition of a "cult" (though it never abandoned the confidence that such a definition was achievable) and in part because ACM members and organizations disagreed on the extent to which radical actions (such as kidnapping and deprogramming) were justified.

The definitions of precisely what constituted a "cult" or "pseudo-religion" ran the gamut of personal preference and idiosyncratic prejudice for and against religious orthodoxy and theology, style of worship, belief origin, and virtually every other dimension of religious experience. This was never more evident than when anti-cultists attempted to estimate the number of "cult" members in the United States. For instance, a "partial list of cults, not all necessarily classed as destructive" that made the ACM rounds in 1976 and 1977 entitled "Magnitude of the Cult Phenomenon" (CEFM, 1976), claimed 30,000-50,000 "cult" members (a modest estimate by later standards). It listed groups on which all anti-cultists were in agreement as to "cultic" characteristics—for example, the Hare Krishna, the UM, the Children of God, and Scientology—but it also included groups that either were only nominally religious or were patently secular (such as Transcendental Meditation and Erhardt Seminars Training, or EST) or ones that, while sectarian, were certainly not part of any recent "cult explosion" (Jehovah's Witnesses, Herbert and Garner Ted Armstrong's World Wide Church of God, and the Old Catholic Church, for example).[10] Some anti-cult activists in conversations with the authors lumped charismatic Catholics (and all charismatic Christians) together with most yoga groups into the "cult" category. Ex-Moonie Gary M. Scharff, during an interview in which he attempted to present evidence that UM members might recapitulate the 1978 Peoples Temple massacre in Guyana, stated:

> The seeds are definitely there for the same kind of thing happening. . . . *"Whenever you're dealing with religious categories like resurrection and rebirth, you begin to blur the categories between life and death."* [Carroll and Bauer, 1979: 68; italics added].

Ted Patrick put Scharff's sentiments even more bluntly: "The Bible will drive you crazy if you take it literally" (Siegelman and Conway, 1979: 68). One fundamentalist Christian tract condemned the usual assortment of gurus, meditators, and "Moonies" as well as popular martial arts such as kung fu, karate, and aikido as "cultic" and inherently un-Christian (Means, 1976: 121-123), *not* because of their potential for violence but rather for their alleged Buddhist/Taoist linkages. Ted Patrick, in a free-wheeling *Playboy* interview, even categorized evangelist Ruth Carter Stapleton, President Jimmy Carter's sister, as "one of the biggest cult leaders in the nation," albeit a "good cult leader" (Siegelman and Conway, 1979: 220). Patrick explained that Stapleton employed "hypnotic techniques in her faith healing" and charged that she used these techniques on government officials, including cabinet members: "I saw one Cabinet Member on TV talking about how he was born again through Ruth Carter Stapleton. He looked just like a Moonie, glazed eyes, the works."

Perhaps the classic example that demonstrates the ultimate relativity of determining what constituted a "cult" occurred when one of the authors attended a meeting of the Interreligious Affairs Committee on Cults of the American Jewish Committee's Dallas Chapter in 1978. Working with a Dallas citywide interfaith council composed of all major Judeo-Christian denominations, the AJC came to loggerheads over the issue of Jews for Jesus, a group which the AJC defined as "cultic" and subversive to the Jewish family but which conservative Dallas Christian groups regarded as a "legitimate" mission. Later at this meeting one member (a professional with a Ph.d.) took the Stoner-Parke monograph *All Gods Children* (1977) and played devil's advocate by critically examining the stereotype of a "cult" (such characteristics as deceptive fund-raising and recruitment practices, an exploitive leader who lived in a luxurious manner significantly different from his followers, and communal group lifestyles) in a group-by-group consideration of the UM, the Hare Krishna, the Divine Light Mission, and others. Very quickly the discussion broke down and the analysis was abandoned as the group failed to fit various groups into the "cult" stereotype and the inconsistencies became apparent.

An important consequence of this tendency of anti-cultists to operate by an "I'll accept that group as a cult if you'll accept this group as a cult" procedure for defining groups as "cultic" was that potential allies of the anti-cult movement were likely alienated. A number of religious bodies—in particular, sectarian/fundamentalist and charismatic groups which otherwise were stridently opposed to the UM and other new religions—could have been enlisted in the movement. The tendency of anti-cultists to suspect any group whose practices strayed from a rather narrow Apollonian ideal, however, lost them the support of a number of orthodox Christian and other sympathetic persons. Patrick's anti-biblical statement above and others like it hurt ACM's chances to build alliances with other seemingly "natural" allies. Indeed, the latter correctly perceived that by the end of the decade there was very little in the area of religious belief or practice that could not be classified as "cultic" by some anti-cult spokesperson.

Further, not all ACM proponents held such broad definitions of what phenomena constituted "cults." Many would admit in private conversation that not all UM members were brainwashed, for example. Harper (1979: 30) noted in his study of the Omaha anti-cult association Love Our

Children, Inc., that sensitivity to overreaction (what Harper termed "a degree of restraint") developed on the issue of expanding the number of potential "cults." In one excerpt cited by him, a LOCI leader stated:

> As persons who are personally affected by and interested in the cult phenomenon, we recognize a need to exercise caution and not denounce every group united around an uncommon or foreign religious belief or practice. Blind intolerance can be an attitude just as injurious and as "unfree" as we perceive the practices of some cults to be. There is a need for more careful thinking about religious groups and their activities.

These kinds of disagreements, of course, served to limit the effectiveness of ACM campaigns, particularly given the limited membership base.

Not only did a precise definition of "cults" prove elusive, but also the ACM, in an attempt to broaden its public appeal, kept expanding the category "cult" to include groups which hardly were perceived to constitute a public threat. This became a liability to the ACM. Definitions of Mormons as "cultic" in Waco, Texas, simply did not "wash" in Provo, Utah, and Christian evangelists' encroachments into the ranks of college-age Jews did not look nearly as threatening to Southern Baptists as it did to American Jewish leaders. In addition to the previous illustrations of groups which became included in the "widened net" of ACM definitions of "cults" (for example, Jews for Jesus, the Jehovah's Witnesses, and Christian Scientists), the ACM also became associated with the deprogramming of Catholics, Greek Orthodox persons, and even individuals who had not joined or left any religious or communal group at all (see the following chapter). At the end of the decade of the 1970s there were even indications that the ACM might take on television evangelists as well. In one newsletter (IFF, 1979f) a reprinted newspaper article (Sunday Gazette Mail, [Charleston, W.VA.], Sept. 8, 1979) "exposed" the annual collections of various "electronic pastors" (such as Pat Robertson, Garner Ted Armstrong, Oral Roberts, Rex Humbard, and Jimmy Swaggert). Given such a pattern, it is not surprising that federal officials and others called upon by the ACM to act against "cults" held grave reservations about initiating or promoting what easily could develop into a colossal witchhunt. In this sense the expanded definitions of "cult" which were intended to broaden the ACM's appeal not only actually reduced the number of potential allies among religious bodies but also left the impression that the

ACM would run amok over religious pluralism and individual rights if granted support by the political institution.

The second major issue dividing the ACM was the propriety and morality of various strategies for combating "cults." While virtually all anti-cult associations agreed that public education warning of the dangers to young adults of "cults" constituted responsible, necessary public service, there were some who even questioned the advisability of trying to legislate a definition of "pseudo-religion" due to the difficulty of accurately identifying "cults." More important, however, was the division between supporters and opponents of deprogramming. To those distraught and sometimes hysterical parents who really believed that their offspring had become slaves and zombies, such radical action was frequently justified on the basis of its efficacy irrespective of ambivalence about its morality. For other parents, however, the issue was not so clear-cut. While the latter despaired of their offsprings' choices of lifestyle, they simply were unable to bring themselves to abduct forcibly and put their adult offspring through the trauma and humiliation of the coercive deprogramming process. Such division, of course, provided another reason to separate the anti-cult associations and the deprogramming wings of the ACM. (In Chapter 5 we discuss the legal implications of this organizational separation.) The anti-cult associations were able to indirectly and informally offer support to deprogrammers but were not faced with taking formal actions which would have divided their membership. Yet, even this disagreement about strategy and tactics served to weaken the anti-cult associations' drive to establish national-level organization, since virtually every bit of the limited membership's energy would have been necessary in order to achieve any measureable impact.

STRATEGIC REASSESSMENT AND READJUSTMENT

In the approximately half-decade during which the anti-cult associations expanded from FREECOG into a loosely confederated coterie of organizations with similar structures and goals, much and yet at the same time very little had been accomplished. On one hand, the anti-cult associations had learned a great deal about the various groups they sought to combat, about the procedures and tactics involved in interest group politics, and about the rigidity and cumbersomeness of bureaucracies. On the other hand, they failed both to generate and sustain an effective national-level organization and to achieve the imposition of significant sanctions via federal agency action which they lobbied for so assiduously.

In the latter half of the 1970s the ACM as a whole shifted emphases in a number of ways as its members' hopes of strong federal action increasingly waned. Efforts to influence federal officials continued, but over time the anti-cult associations began to recognize that only symbolic victories (in the form of governmental "lip" support for their definition of the situation) and not imposition of behavioral sanctions were likely to be forthcoming. This is not to say that anti-cult groups did not seize the opportunity to marshal various federal agencies when the time seemed ripe; however, these few opportunities emanated not from the constituency or organization of the anti-cult associations themselves but rather from serendipitous events in the larger society which the groups sought to turn to their own purposes. The two foremost examples of such opportunities were "Koreagate" and "Jonestown." In the former case, when a scandal surfaced involving influence-peddling in Washington by agents of the South Korean government and questions were raised about the linkage between the UM and the government of South Korea, the anti-cult associations sought to "expose" Moon and the UM for what they "really were." The occurrence of the tragedy at Jonestown, of course, provided the quintessential event which confirmed ACM members' own worst fears and most nightmarish predictions. As we shall show in Chapter 8, they believed that the specter of Jonestown would at last convince officials and the public alike that the "cult menace" was indisputable and explosive in its potential consequences. When even this dramatic event did not bring formal governmental support for the cause which anti-cult groups advocated, their members began to recognize the futility of their long-hoped-for goal of federal support.

The other two developments which emerged during the decade were renewed interest and activity at the local level and increased direct action to fill the void of state and federal inaction. The anti-cult associations gained sufficient national organization and political sophistication to intervene more effectively at local and state levels where their limited strength actually lay. Thus, anti-cult associations frequently were able to enlist the aid of local law enforcement agencies in monitoring and reporting the movements of UM witnessing and fund-raising teams, among local political officials and businessmen in denying the opportunity to solicit funds, among local judges to escape potential legal penalties associated with attempting to "rescue" their offspring, among local Parent Teachers' Associations and church groups to take a public stand against "cults," and even among state legislators to hold hearings and introduce bills designed to deny the "cults" constitutional protections accorded to "legitimate" and "bona fide" religions. Indeed, as we shall discuss in detail in Chapter 7, these local and state campaigns were considerably more effective than their national counterparts.

Nevertheless, the anti-cult associations were not successful in gaining sufficient support from other institutions to legitimate a means for "recovering" their offspring from the "grasp of the cults." The more obvious it became to distraught parents that appeals to authorities to act on the basis of existing laws and efforts to redefine religion and/or mental competency in such a way as to gain leverage on the "cults" were not going to succeed fully, the more those parents who could justify doing so turned to direct, vigilante-style actions to achieve their goal. As a result, deprogramming as a tactic and later as an occupation began to emerge as a remedy in the face of what parents deemed the unresponsiveness of duly constituted authority. Individual families had, of course, turned to direct action from the onset of the new religions' growth because they simply did not know where to turn for help. What increasingly characterized the initiation of direct action as the decade wore on, however, was not ignorance of available avenues of appeal but conviction that such appeals were fruitless. Thus, parents typically were left either with the option of waiting out their offsprings' zealous crusades while seeking solace among similarly situated anti-cult association parents or defining their children as incapable of rational, autonomous action and undertaking desperate deprogrammings to "restore their children's individuality and free will." It is to the latter course of action, which became what we have termed the deprogramming component of the ACM, that we now turn in order to complete the analysis of ACM organization.

Summary

The anti-cult associations composed one of the ACM's two organizational components. Largely a grass-roots phenomena composed of "cult" members' families, the latters' overriding goal was always the "recovery" of young family members and their "restoration" to valued patterns of family interaction and career preparation. Our account of such associations' origins and growth did more than provide historical details on their expansion; it also revealed the emergent problems which this ACM component encountered as it moved from local to state and national levels of influence. The dynamics of attempting to mobilize officials and power-holders at each level forced anti-cultists to develop a more coherent explanation of their dilemma in order to justify official intervention. Such mobilization efforts also involved families of "cult" members in a gradual "drift" away from their immediate, direct, concrete goals of "recovering" younger members to more indirect lobbying and political influence strategies within bureaucratic contexts.

The first decade of their existence revealed a series of repeatedly unsuccessful attempts by anti-cult associations to forge a more viable social movement. This lack of success, in sociological terms, can be traced to four critical dimensions around which such groups failed to solve organizational needs: (1) moving beyond immediately affected families of "cult" members for membership, (2) tapping possible sources of financial resources beyond the same affected families, (3) reaching agreement on what sort of national-level organization (that is, decentralized confederation or centralized federation) was to be established, and (4) achieving an ideological consensus on delineating "cults" that might lead to a finite operational definition of just what constituted a "cult." That anti-cult association spokespersons, in the midst of ongoing reincarnations of the same inefficient organizational structures, were from time to time aware of these shortcomings did little to correct these group level deficiencies.

NOTES

1. A critical review of Patrick's narcissistic claims and quasi-autobiographical recounting of how he became involved in the ACM can be found in Shupe (1978). The Alliance for the Preservation of Religious Liberties (APRL), which, together with the American Civil Liberties Union, co-sponsored a conference in 1977 on the deprogramming issue, offered a purported organizational chart of the so-called "deprogramming movement." Patrick was placed at the top center of the page in the position analogous to a corporate president with all ACM organizations, regardless of separate origins or ideological variance, flowing directly from him.

2. That the state of California itself may be a bellwether or experimental cauldron, out of which the new religions of the late 1960s and 1970s emerged, has been suggested by Needleman (1972), among others. This idea does not seem to be arrived at ecologically or sociologically but rather almost mystically. Hence, Needleman's speculation (p. 5): "I wish I could state clearly what it is about California that makes so many of its people—and not just the young—so much more accessible to the cosmic dimension of human life."

3. Officials from those bureaus and departments whose legal jurisdictions could have conceivably been trespassed by "cults" were particularly encouraged to attend. These included high-ranking bureaucrats from the Internal Revenue Service, the Departments of Justice, Labor, and Health, Education and Welfare, the United States Postal Service, the National Institute of Mental Health, and the Federal Trade Commission. In addition, Dole stated that he had received inquiries about the hearing from 31 senators and 42 representatives (CEFM, 1976a: Vol. I, 3-7).

4. At one point Slaughter even tried to have the cost of his daughter's deprogramming deducted from his income tax as a medical expense but failed (personal interviews, 1976).

5. These regions were New England (Connecticut, Maine, Massachusetts, New Hampshire, Vermont, Rhode Island, New York); the Great Lakes (Michigan, Indiana, Ohio, Kentucky); the West Coast (California, Washington, Oregon, Nevada); the Midwest (Minnesota, Wisconsin, Iowa, Missouri, Illinois); the Southwest (Texas, Arizona, New Mexico, Louisisna, Oklahoma, Arkansas); the Rocky Mountains (Idaho, Kansas, Wyoming, Montana); the South (Mississippi, Alabama, Georgia, Florida, South and North Carolina, Tennessee); and the Mid-Atlantic (Virginia, Maryland, West Virginia, Washington, D.C., Delaware, New Jersey, Pennsylvania).

6. Exaggeration of membership size, whether deliberate or inadvertent, is a perennial feature of religious organizations (see Landis, 1967; Lambert, 1967), all the more so to be expected of fledgling or aspiring minority religious bodies acutely aware of their public relations' needs to appear to be growing rapidly and thus popular. Similarly, for a countermovement seeking to persuade the general public and officials of a pervasive, widespread, imminent threat to all persons, impressive statistics, however unsubstantiated, became important. At the 1979 "Dole hearing" in Washington, D.C. (see Chapter 8), for example, anti-cult spokespersons variously claimed two million "cult victims" and four million injured parents (AFF, 1979a: 79) and ten million "victims" (AFF, 1979a: 25), while elsewhere deprogrammer Ted Patrick freely estimated twenty million Americans involved in cults (Siegelman and Conway, 1979: 56).

7. Two of the authors' colleagues, while doing participant observation at CEFM headquarters as clerical assistants, found it next to impossible to determine the daily number of incoming and outgoing phone calls. Slaughter had two phone lines installed with a number of extensions in various rooms of his home. At one point in October 1976 he was considering adding a full-service WATS line but the $2750 cost was prohibitive. Slaughter's estimate of total long-distance phone time for that month was 120 hours, three to five hours *per day* (CEFM, 1976d).

8. As McCarthy and Zald (1973: 15) noted, American society in the twentieth century has witnessed "the growing institutionalization of dissent," a process characterized not only by a professionalization of social movement leadership but also by the growth in amount of foundation/governmental grants and private funds that go to support various social movements. Anti-cult leaders seemed at least intuitively aware of this trend, however frustrated were their attempts to obtain such funding.

9. McCarthy and Zald (1977), in formulating propositions based on resource mobilization theory, hypothesized just such a situation; in organizations with large numbers of isolated constituents (hence without solidary incentives), (1) not only will financial support arrive at sporadic, unreliable intervals in less than adequate amounts, but (2) also such groups will have to expend a great deal of ongoing effort to solicit donations from members.

10. One "old guard" informant repeatedly voiced reservations to Shupe about Bromley when she learned that the latter had been raised as a Christian Scientist.

Chapter 5

THE DEPROGRAMMERS

In this chapter we shall discuss the second major component of the ACM, the deprogrammers. Like the anti-cult associations, the deprogrammers were supported almost exclusively by distraught parents of UM members (and of those participating in other religious groups) whose primary goal was "recovery" of their "lost" offspring. In this sense the deprogrammers were agents to whom parents delegated authority in order to restore their sons and daughters to career paths more in line with the parents' own conceptions of normalcy.

Deprogramming as a "service" emerged in response to "client" demand; it manifested considerably different activities from those in which ACM interest groups engaged because it involved full-time efforts, the use of coercion on at least some occasions, and a questionable legal status. As we shall show, although the deprogrammers functioned in a fashion relatively autonomous from the anti-cult associations, at the same time they derived both clients and moral support from anti-cult association members. As the direct action component of the ACM, however, deprogrammers faced two kinds of organizational problems. First, they encountered the necessity of establishing themselves as a legitimate occupation, one which, despite their protestations to the contrary, sometimes had extremely remunerative rewards. This resulted in several simultaneously ongoing efforts: creating a financial base for operations, distinguishing their efforts from those of other occupational groups which might claim responsibility and/or expertise for the problems they sought to address, and erecting centers where clients and deprogramming practitioners could be brought together. Second, the deprogrammers searched for a legal basis of operations under which their emergent occupation could be practiced. This was certainly their most perplexing and irresolvable problem. Parents clearly were willing to delegate to deprogrammers the authority to "treat" their offspring; yet, when the latter were themselves adults, their parents lacked the legal grounds for issuing such a delegation of authority. The history of deprogramming as an activity thus became a search among various possible legal options, a stretching of existing legal procedures to fit ACM activities, and in some cases a furthering of activities which were without any legal foundation. For a time, at least, the use of temporary writs of conservatorship which promised to lend the coercive aspects of deprogramming the "color of law" appeared as if it might be one viable solution to this problem. As we shall show, however, this strategy was not the permanent answer to questions of deprogramming's legality, and because no other answers were forthcoming, deprogramming remains in the 1980s what it had always been—a risky, tenuous operation.

Defining Deprogramming
and Locating Its Origins

It is important to emphasize at the outset of any discussion of deprogramming that for its proponents, and indeed for the heterogeneous membership of the larger ACM, the term referred to a wide array of behaviors, some of which deserved the notoriety accorded them and others which were relatively innocuous and infringed on no one's civil liberties or moral sensibilities. The best-known form of deprogramming was the coercive type as espoused by Ted Patrick, the man who coined the term deprogramming and who relentlessly promoted both its logic and practice despite law suits, court orders, and even imprisonment. Coercive deprogramming was marked by abducting and detaining members of "cults" against their will, haranguing them for extended periods of time under emotionally charged conditions, and then achieving in such individuals rapid redefinitions of their former religious experiences and beliefs that culminated in their apostasy. (This is, of course, not the interpretation given to this sequence by anti-cultists.) Less publicized but also included under the deprogramming rubric by anti-cultists, however, was the opposite noncoercive extreme, as when a parent or clergyman, whether by telephone, mail, or face to face, created doubts or second thoughts in the mind of a young "cult" member who, in the absence of any coercion, decided to leave the new faith. Rabbi Maurice Davis, founder of Citizens Engaged in Reuniting Families, termed this noncoercive alternative *re-evaluation.* We shall restrict our use of the term deprogramming to refer only to the more coercive type.

Generally speaking, neither the public nor the media were aware of the ACM's often imprecise use of the term. Certainly, the American Civil Liberties Union (ACLU) and the Alliance for the Preservation of Religious Liberties (APRL), two outspoken opponents of the ACM, assumed all advocates of deprogramming were ipso facto proponents of the coercive type. Their references to the ACM as "the deprogramming movement" did not reflect a perception of the broader meaning of the term deprogramming but, rather, just the opposite.

Furthermore, while we have delineated the anti-cult associations and the deprogrammers as two organizational components of the ACM, we also qualify this distinction. Unlike anti-cult associations, the deprogramming component manifested considerably less formal organization and coordinated leadership or hierarchy. There were never, for example, national or even regional conferences of deprogrammers, and any narrative of the origins and development of deprogramming trends needs to rely more on the actions of specific individuals than it does on organizational history. Nevertheless, the deprogramming component made some initial, if frustrating, attempts to institutionalize both internally and externally, by achieving a working relationship with anti-cult associations and seeking acceptance as a legitimate profession by the larger society; for those reasons it can be regarded as a viable, if precarious, organizational component.

Deprogramming began in 1971 as the ad hoc vigilante response of one man, Theodore Roosevelt "Ted" Patrick, Jr., to proselytization activities of the Children of God sect at about the same time that concerned parents began meeting to discuss their common grievances against that group. Patrick's personal background as a civil rights activist and Special Representative for Community Relations under California Governor Ronald Reagan as well as his own family's initial encounter with the Children of God are discussed at length in his apologetic, quasi-autobiographical account of his deprogramming activities (see Patrick and Dulack, 1976).[1] Deprogramming as a systematic activity grew out of Patrick's own personal contact as a parent with Children of God recruiters. Patrick's version of his creation and development of the deprogramming process can be summarized as follows:

In early July 1971, Patrick's teenage son and nephew met several street missionaries from the Children of God sect who allegedly left the two boys noticeably but "mysteriously" disoriented. One week later a woman who had unsuccessfully appealed to various other officials appeared in Patrick's San Diego office to file a complaint against the Children of God for abducting and exploiting her offspring. In two day's time Patrick claimed to have received reports of parallel experiences from 26 families; by the end of the week a total of 52 families had contacted him with similar complaints. (Whether Patrick simply exaggerated the number of complaints or whether there already existed an informal network of concerned parents—not an impossibility—is not clear.) Patrick reacted to this unexplained epidemic of parental concern in his official capacity as state "ombudsman" by instituting a one-man investigation, approaching Children of God street missionaries and allowing himself to be taken to a weekend COG "training session." After little sleep, inadequate nourishment, and the constant "bombardment" of biblical passages and religious lectures that allegedly began to "erode" his rational thinking process, Patrick claimed he was becoming programmed by COG's propaganda. After managing to "resist and escape," Patrick began following up other complaints against the sect and soon was "rescuing" young adults from COG. From the outset, this process involved forcible abduction, detainment, and argumentation, a sequence he later termed "deprogramming" or the reversal of the seductive, manipulative indoctrination process (programming) which he believed he had experienced. Doubtless, there occurred an evolution in the procedures of deprogramming; however, details of this development were not provided by Patrick. Nevertheless, the core of the deprogramming process appears to have remained constant since its inception: Constant verbal assault on the integrity, values, and activities of the various new religions and their leaders, frequently combined with biblically based refutations of their doctrinal heresies (see West, 1975).

By fall 1971 Patrick resigned from his state position to devote his full-time energies to deprogramming. Indeed, by early 1972 he was actively pursuing deprogrammings on a nationwide basis and building not only a clientele that provided him with a constant number of referrals but also a small coterie of assistants and apprentices who helped handle the expanding demand among desperate families of "cult" members. Foremost among those who trained under Patrick was his protege and later competitor Joseph Alexander, Sr. (later joined by his son Joseph Alexander, Jr.), who began as Patrick's assistant in 1973 and who later managed the Freedom of Thought Foundation "rehabilitation" ranch for deprogrammees in Tucson, Arizona (to be discussed shortly). Boasting that "cults" had grudgingly given him the nickname "Black Lightning," Patrick proceeded to carry out coercive deprogrammings on a prolific basis throughout the rest of the decade, though his own estimate of 1600 total personally deprogrammed persons was undoubtedly an exaggeration (see Siegelman and Conway, 1979: 77).[2]

As we noted in the previous chapter, after an initial period during which the ACM focused solely on the Children of God, the former movement broadened its concerns to a wider range of religious groups. This naturally expanded Patrick's clientele and made it possible for a number of other individuals to become full-time or part-time deprogrammers. Thus, what began to emerge in the early to mid-1970s were the first signs of a possible new occupation. Deprogrammers, as we already discussed, offered a number of advantages (from families' perspectives) over psychiatrists and psychologists; and there was—at least for a short time—an increasingly larger pool of distressed parents eager for their services as the new religions grew in size during the early 1970s. In order to reduce the substantial risks involved in deprogramming, these individuals deliberately began to develop a set of skills and practices that distinguished them from other "helping professions" and at the same time cultivated an image of legitimacy for their activities.

The Role of Deprogrammers in the ACM

THE DEPROGRAMMING OPTION

The ACM's gradually emergent ideology was intended to confer a specific deviant status on those individuals who joined new religions and thereby legitimated the exercise of specific forms of social control over them. Because members were defined as "brainwashed" and therefore considered completely unable to manage their own lives and decisions, a correspondingly extreme form of social control termed deprogramming that treated individuals as dehumanized automatons whose apparent volitions and actions were not really their own emerged to aid in restoring earlier-valued social relationships. However, the anti-cult associations, as we have shown, were largely incapable of undertaking individual recovery attempts. These associations were essentially interest groups; hence, their members' participation in terms of time, energy, and resources was limited. Indeed, the structures of anti-cult associations rarely provided role definitions or opportunities for more intense involvement by constituents. Thus, despite the fact that the major objective of the ACM was always the "recovery" of individual family members who had become involved in "cults," the members of these ACM groups were frequently in a poor position to carry out coercive deprogrammings.

Such direct action became by and large reserved for the ACM's deprogramming component, a group at its small nucleus composed of full-time ACM proponents who were to struggle throughout the 1970s with mixed fortunes to gain public and legal acceptance for their assumptions and techniques and to have deprogramming recognized as a new, alternative profession. As we shall show, deprogrammers performed several vital functions for the entire ACM. The "cult" members whom they abducted and persuaded to recant their faiths seemingly reinforced the validity of the brainwashing ideology and reaffirmed the "cults'" presumed perniciousness. Perhaps just as important for frustrated, distraught parents, the deprogrammers provided dramatic evidence of hope, should the right circumstances arise, that something severe but effective could be done to "recover" offspring. They even began to assume a somewhat heroic, even romantic image within the ACM (see Testa's [1978] analysis of the deprogrammer role in a series of Canadian newspaper articles). Just as important, however, the deprogramming component of the ACM was highly dependent on the anti-cult associations for their clientele (not to mention monetary compensation) as well as for whatever legitimacy the ACM as a whole possessed, and in this sense the two components existed in strongly complementary fashion.

There were numerous options available to parents who were unable to accept their offsprings' participation in deviant religions. Undoubtedly, achieving a formal definition of them as mentally ill, for example, which some parents tried (see APRL, 1977: 65, 118, 15), would have yielded the same degree of social control over rebellious offspring as believing them brainwashed and then having them deprogrammed. However, deprogramming offered a number of advantages. One obvious advantage was expedience: Deprogrammers often were willing to "cut corners" and violate the law by outright kidnapping and forcibly detaining young adults. Psychiatrists, conversely, would have had to rely on either voluntary compliance which would not compromise their professional ethics or lengthy mental competency hearings at which the "cult" members could have right of counsel. (This is assuming that a psychiatrist or clinical psychologist was willing to interpret specific behaviors of "cult" members as fitting within existing diagnostic categories and therefore legitimate the brainwashing ideology.) Deprogrammers thus extended to parents unilateral action unavailable through legal/psychiatric procedures.

A second major advantage was the relative lack of stigma which accrued to the deprogrammee. Once applied, a label of mental illness could prove exceedingly difficult to remove and would likely confront both the young adults and the parents with a semipermanent stigma that could prove detrimental to a number of later careers. By contrast, once deprogrammed, an individual could be returned relatively quickly to conventional social activity (although there was alleged to be some period of lingering vulnerability called "floating") with little stigma. The brainwashing ideology provided an honorable basis for accounting for the individual's past bizarre behavior, one which did not imply inherent personal weakness or family problems and which, when properly implemented, posed no danger of future reoccurrence. Brainwashing/deprogramming as a package explanation placed blame for the individual's problems or mistakes squarely on the "cult." Thus, deprogramming's "diagnosis and treatment" absolved both individuals and their families of any fault for the "misfortune," returned the "cult" member to "normal" social functioning, and condemned the "cult" for its destructive practices. Of course, if all else failed, the difficulties of trying to obtain psychiatric treatment could be undertaken, and there were some in the mental health profession who endorsed clinical therapy for ex-"cult" members or for members undergoing deprogramming (Aversa, 1976: Clark, 1976; see also the description of the Freedom of Thought Foundation ranch later in this chapter.)

DEPROGRAMMING AS A DISTINCT ACM COMPONENT

The necessity of having a separate wing of the ACM devoted to programming is reflected in the ambivalence shown toward deprogrammers by the anti-cult associations. They alternately praised deprogrammers and yet strove to maintain a certain distance between the two units. For example, in 1975, the *Citizen Freedom Foundation "News"* (1975b) published an "Open Letter To Ted Patrick" that stated: "We are much impressed with, and applaud your wonderful work in freeing individuals who have been brainwashed by cults." William Rambur, CFF founder and President, wrote in two separate editorials:

> The severe threat imposed by these cults justifies the action taken by the parents to save their children, however labeled, but more important is why such drastic action is necessary [CFF, 1975a].

Each attempt at rescue, *whether successful or not,* further reveals
the need for such action. Since there are so few people who have had
the experience in rescue techniques, you cannot wait until someone
becomes available to you. You must use their knowledge and effect
a rescue yourself [CFF, 1975c].

Yet, at the same time Rambur simultaneously engaged in an ongoing effort
to separate his organization from Patrick and the deprogramming component, he lauded the latter. In November 1974, Rambur stressed CFF's
educational functions when he stated:

Although we subscribe to the need for Mr. Patrick's activities, none
of the parents' organizations have programmed funding in support of
his activities. Mr. Patrick's financial arrangements are totally exclusive of parent group control and accounting. As an organization,
CFF is not involved in any phase of deprogramming.... Undoubtedly there is a need for deprogramming, but there is an even
greater need and that is to prevent use of detremental [sic] mind
control methods whether being practiced deliberately or otherwise.
This is the function of CFF [CFF, 1974a].

One year later (CFF, 1975c), in an eassay entitled "Issues That Are
Plaguing CFF at the Present Time," Rambur wrote:

One such issue is the functional and financial connection between
CFF and Mr. Ted Patrick. THERE IS NONE! Mr. Patrick concentrates on rescuing victims from pseudo-religious cults on an individual basis, while CFF concentrates on removing the source of
victimization in addition to assisting victims, utilizing every established agency available in our society.... CFF operates solely on
contributions and is open to proper audit whereas Mr. Patrick's fees
and contributions are his own personal business open to no one.

There were four fundamental organizational reasons for the emergence
of deprogramming as a seperate component of the ACM and which explain
the persistent ambivalence of anti-cult associations toward the deprogrammers. First, anti-cult associations were not structured in such a way as
to allow members to engage in full-time activities. These associations were
limited interest groups devoted to maintaining solidarity among families
whose members had joined "cults," monitoring the whereabouts and
activities of various "cults" and their members, and lobbying to influence
public opinion and to secure passage of anti-"cult" legislation. Depro-

grammers, by contrast, in some cases gave up former occupations and thus job and income security, were always "on call" (consequently unable to live conventional lifestyles), and were frequently running afoul of the law and hence were subject to legal prosecution.

Second, the anti-cult associations sought to build broadly based public and official support for their cause. This implied working with and gaining the support (financial and legal) of individuals and groups with a variety of differing perspectives and interests with respect to the "cult problem" and religious minorities in general. Thus, many members and supporters of the associations' proposed anti-cult legislation (for example, curtailment of solicitation and recruitment activities and government investigations) did not approve of coercive deprogramming. For the anti-cult associations to have directly undertaken deprogramming, an activity which was never able to shed its legally ambiguous and unsavory reputation, would have alienated at least part of their base of support.

Third, for several years ACM organizations had been engaged in an ongoing attempt to gain tax exempt status from the Internal Revenue Service as educational foundations. One major reason why this status had been withheld was the perception of officials that these groups were involved in deprogramming and other partisan activitis. So, for example, CEFM, the first national coordinating ACM organization, was more aggressively supportive of deprogramming than some other groups such as CFF (perhaps because CEFM Director George Slaughter successfully "rescued" his daughter from the UM with the assistance of Ted Patrick). In fact, in one CEFM newsletter (1976f) Slaughter urged readers to go to court to obtain legal temporary conservatorships and to publicize successful deprogrammings:

> CEFM has a legal packet which contains advice on the procedure and techniques of legal deprogramming. It is for the family attorney's use only. Write us giving his name, and ask him to request it—we will mail the information directly to your attorney.

It is significant that CEFM was never able to obtain tax-exempt status while other anti-cult associations less strident in their support of deprogramming (such as CFF) ultimately did.

Finally, anti-cult associations maintained their separation as a means of avoiding legal liability from the lawsuits attending unsuccessful deprogrammings. Had the UM, for example, been able to sue the deprogrammer, a "cult" member's parents, *and* anti-cult association officials and organizations, the latter would have been financially decimated. As it was, anti-cult associations were able to attempt to raise money and channel it to support deprogrammers' legal expenses, but they did not thereby become liable for the deprogrammers' actions.

The Search for a Legal Basis
for Deprogramming

Perhaps the most important single activity deprogrammers undertook was an attempt to define the legality of their activities. The forcible abduction of adult individuals who at least ostensibly had voluntarily joined the new religions, after all, legally constituted kidnapping. This was a problem the deprogrammers never were able to resolve satisfactorily and indeed was the single most important reason that deprogrammers were not able to establish themselves as a legitimate occupation. When Patrick and others first began their deprogramming activities, they appear to have been relatively successful at escaping prosecution, legal suits, and incarceration. It is true, however, that from the outset Patrick was arrested and jailed repeatedly, if temporarily, when leaders of religious groups from which members had been abducted made formal complaints to police agencies. However, as time went on, the religious movements began to discover that they enjoyed formal protection under law and that such protection was extended in most (although certainly not all) instances.

The reason that the legal status of deprogramming did not immediately, and to some extent has not yet, become clear hinged on a variety of factors related to the strategies of the new religions and the deprogrammers, as well as to the attitudes of the police and public officials and vagaries of the law itself. Within several years after the inception of deprogrammings and after Patrick and others had coercively deprogrammed a number of members of the new religions, the latter began to seek legal redress. Thereupon each side engaged in a series of moves and countermoves resembling a chess game, designed to solidify the legal position of each and erode that of its opponent. The UM's response to what it regarded as repeated harassment of its members by deprogrammers illustrates this conflict process.

At first the UM attempted to sue the deprogrammers for libel, violation of civil rights, and false imprisonment. However, the deprogrammers saw in such litigation the opportunity to subpoena UM officials and records in order to substantiate more general allegations about the UM's political and financial irregularities. Correctly perceiving a Pandora'a box of potential public embarrassment or worse in that route, the UM adopted subsequently a policy of having individual members sue deprogrammers with the UM simply paying the legal expenses. The deprogrammers in turn responded by always arranging to have parents present at the time of abduction and detainment so that the latter would be legally liable in criminal or civil proceedings, a tactic on which Patrick (1976: 59) was quite explicit. This latter move had the effect of reducing the number of legal actions, since UM members often were less willing to prosecute their own parents, however angered they were by the abduction/deprogramming sequence.

Another issue related to the legal grounds on which abduction/deprogramming could be justified or prosecuted. Initially distraught parents, unable to make contact with their children, served the UM with habeus corpus writs (a tactic never completely abandoned.) However, the UM was able to deny either knowledge of the individual's whereabouts or alternatively that it had any control over the individual and therefore that it was unable to force him or her to appear in court. The case of Barbara Larsen, a 25-year-old "Moonie," illustrates this exchange of manuevers. In mid-December 1978, New York State Supreme Court Justice Alvin Klein ordered the UM on a writ of habeus corpus to produce member Barbara Larsen to answer her father Louis' charges that she was being held by the UM against her will and simultaneously being deprived of proper nourishment and sleep for extended periods of time. A UM member for six years, she had been abducted in October 1978 by seven persons, including her father and brother, in St. Louis, Missouri. Held until a hearing when they obtained custody, the group then flew Barbara from St. Louis to Washington, D.C. and then on to a small town outside Wilkes-Barre, Pennsylvania, where she was placed in the Freedom of Mind Rehabilitation Center run by attorney/deprogrammer Gifford Cappelini (to be discussed later in this chapter). On December 10, after six weeks, she escaped with the help of an undercover newspaper reporter employed by the UM's New York daily newspaper *The News World* and made her way to the sanctuary of the New Yorker Hotel, a recent mid-Manhattan purchase of the UM. From there she declined to appear in court for fear (she stated in messages delivered to the court and media via her lawyer, ACLU president Jeremiah Gutman) of another abduction. Before the angry judge who ordered the habeus corpus, the UM contended it had no jurisdiction or control over her actions, and UM lawyers representing her at one point claimed they had no knowledge of her exact whereabouts. Finally a compromise was arranged wherein her physical safety was guaranteed by the court and she

appeared to argue (ultimately with success through further legal manuevers) her competence (see The New York Post, Jan. 20, 1978; The News
World, Dec. 23, 1978; The Washington Post, Feb. 15, 1979).

The legal objective of the use of habeus corpus writs by deprogrammers
was, of course, always to demonstrate the "cult" member's mental incapacity in open court. When such a tactic generally proved unsuccessful,
deprogrammers seized upon existing temporary conservatorship laws
which were originally established by states to place legal guardianship of
one adult in the hands of another (often a family member) on short notice
without a formal legal hearing at which the adult in question was present
or represented. Such provisions were intended to allow emergency action
in the event that a senile or unstable person was imminently to commit an
irrevocably injurious act, such as an elderly relative about to squander
savings. Serving temporary conservatorships (obtained often from local
judges on a 30- or 60-day basis based on the testimony of a physician or
psychiatrist who had not even examined the person in question) provided
deprogrammers' activities "with the color of the law" that assuaged
parental fears of law suits from "cults" and/or their own offspring should
the deprogramming fail. For a time, at least, such proceedings, tantamount
to declaring one's adult child mentally irresponsible or at least incom-
petent to handle his or her affairs, promised to undergird an expansion of
deprogrammings.

However, by the late 1970s conservatorships began to be more difficult
to obtain as local judges became more informed about the deprogramming
controversy and recognized that evidence for and against brainwashing
charges was by no means clear-cut. Judges also became aware that such
conservatorships had been misapplied and exploited in ways that law-
makers had never intended. The demise of the conservatorships strategy as
a major weapon in the deprogramming arsenal stemmed from, first, the
fact that conservatorships obtained in one state were frequently served in
another state where they had no legal status, and, second, that these
conservatorships were served on members of "legally recognized" religious
groups who demonstrated no signs of mental incompetency. The most
sensational national deprogramming trial, that of the "Faithful Five" in
San Francisco during 1977 and 1978, had landmark implications for the
use of conservatorships and became a benchmark by which this strategy's
decline can be dated. In that trial five members of the Unification Church,
represented by UM attorneys, had gone to court to prevent their parents
from obtaining temporary 30-day conservatorships and sending them to

the Freedom of Thought Foundation deprogramming ranch (discussed in a subsequent section). On October 7, 1977, after a complex and sensational trial,[3] Judge Lee Vavuris gave custody of the five "Moonies" to their parents on the grounds that parental responsibilities did not end regardless of the offsprings' ages and that the parents in this case were acting out of the noblest motives and in their children's best interests. Judge Vavuris' stated logic, closely in line with ACM opinions regarding parental authority and responsibility, was widely quoted: "The child is the child even though a parent may be 90 and the child 60. We are talking about the essence of civilization—mother, father and children" (see The Boston Globe, April 13, 1977). Aware of the complexities of the case, however, Judge Vavuris invited higher court review of his decision, and on March 28, 1978 an appellate court agreed to hear an appeal. Little more than two weeks later the appellate court stayed Judge Vavuris' ruling, rejecting both his reasoning on the limits of parental authority and the use of temporary conservatorships to remove legal adults from unpopular or unconventional religious groups. (Interestingly enough, four of the five young Unification Church members soon after announced their "deconversions" and voluntarily left the Church without going through deprogramming, a somewhat telling reflection on the validity of the "mind control" argument. One ACM informant told the authors that the court testimony against the UM had actually acted to deprogram the four apostates during the trial without their awareness.)

For a time it appeared that with the loss of conservatorships as a primary, fail-safe strategy, at least in any legal fashion, deprogramming had been halted. However, Patrick did not slacken his deprogramming activities, ran into further troubles, and came to rely more heavily on a defense originally used unsuccessfully in an earlier trial in which he was incarcerated in California in 1975 (Patrick, 1976: 266). According to Patrick,

> most states have a law of justification that permits a person to do something that would ordinarily be considered illegal if he was committing that act to prevent a greater harm, the greater harm being what is happening to the mental and physical health of the person in the cult. . . . It's called the lesser of two evils [1976: 56].

At the end of the decade, this defense was a surprisingly resilient and effective one for Patrick. In both upper- and lower-court cases in 1978 he used this defense. In 1979 in Colorado Springs, Colorado, he was acquitted by a jury after holding a 24-year-old member of The Way International against her will for four days (see Boston Sunday Globe, "Cult Fighter Cleared of Kidnapping, Assault," Feb. 25, 1979). An even more recent, incredible acquittal was handed Patrick and a 52-year-old widow named Marti Schumacher in a trial on the west coast. In July 1979 Schumacher hired Patrick to deprogram her daughter Janet, age 31, *not* because the latter had joined any sectarian religious group but rather because the mother claimed that the daughter's fiancee, Charles Connefax, exerted apparent undue psychological influence over her daughter. The daughter was unsuccessfully deprogrammed, married Connefax anyway, and subsequently charged both her mother and Patrick with second-degree kidnapping. Under the "choice of evils doctrine" in Oregon state law, upon which Patrick's attorneys based their case, the actions of Marti Schumacher (and her agents) were justified if she believed they were necessary as an emergency measure to avoid an imminent greater public or private injury. According to the judge's charge to the jury, in order to acquit Schumacher and Patrick they had to find that Mrs. Schumacher sincerely believed at the time that the "threatened injury is of such gravity that, according to ordinary standards of intelligence and morality, the desirability and urgency of avoiding the injury clearly outweigh the desirability of avoiding the injury sought to be prevented." The jury acquitted both Schumacher and Patrick on this basis, and deprogrammers continued to have hope (see The Oregonian, "Mother, Cult Deprogrammer Acquitted, May 19, 1979).

The final factor contributing to the ambiguous legal status of deprogramming was the ambivalent opinions and actions of individual citizens, police officers, and members of the judiciary. Numerous instances have been recorded (see Bromley et al., 1979) in which police officers were present at the time of forcible abductions and allowed parents and deprogrammers to forcibly remove UM members from the scene. Patrick (1976: 93-94) also recounted such instances. Further, judges varied widely in the receptivity to parental requests for conservatorships. At least for a time, deprogrammers were able to locate sympathetic judges, but this became much more difficult after the legal precedent set in the "Faithful Five" case. Finally, deprogrammers being prosecuted for false imprisonment were able to request jury trials and rely on the emotional impact of parental testimony and even testimony from psychiatrists sympathetic with the ACM to sway enough jurors to prevent conviction.

Deprogramming as an Occupation

FINANCIAL UNDERPINNING

When Patrick began his deprogramming career, it would appear that it was not with the conscious plan of converting it into a full-time vocation (1976: 28). He must have been uncertain about how successful his endeavors would be, the number of requests for his services and for how long they would continue, and his own personal financial responsibilities (to his family and so forth). In the beginning Patrick only accepted enough remuneration to cover his expenses. Later, however, as demands for his services increased, and after he had resigned his job with the state of California, deprogramming evolved into a livelihood as well as a personal crusade.

Patrick continued to contend that his involvement in deprogramming was altruistically rather than economically inspired; however, available financial evidence belies this claim. Much like his seventeenth-century English counterpart, Puritan Matthew Hopkins the "witch-finder" who built a brief but lucrative practice by "uncovering" witches through "witch-pricking" and other ad hoc innovative practices (Simons, 1974; Seth, 1969), the sudden uncertainty and fears of families for their offspring who had joined "cults" provided Patrick with an opportunity to begin an ersatz but considerably remunerative occupation. Though in his book (1976: 159) Patrick claimed he averaged a fee of only $1500 per deprogramming to meet expenses, his later statements on finances indicated a substantial income from deprogrammings even allowing for inflation. For instance, in a 1978 lawsuit connected with his book *Let Our Children Go!* Patrick testified in a deposition (Fitzpatrick, 1978: 8) that his average charge to families was between $2000 and $5000 per deprogramming, with $10,000 the maximum amount he ever demanded, in a *Playboy* magazine interview (Siegelman and Conway, 1979: 86) he reiterated the $10,000 figure. While over the years Patrick had held a variety of unskilled and manual jobs (among these numbers runner, chef, chauffeur, masseur, undertaker's assistant, barber, and truck driver), he was totally unemployed from 1965 to 1968, and during his employment as a community representative for the state of California he earned between $12,000 and $13,000 per year, Patrick could nevertheless report $71,950 on his 1975 tax return. By 1977 his checking acount alone revealed deposits totaling $97,000—and for four months out of that year he had been unable to work while in jail on account of his deprogramming activities (Fitzpatrick, 1978: 7). (Patrick [in Siegelman and Conway, 1979: 86] claimed his "competitors" charged around $15,000, a figure also quoted to us by ACM informants. Other newspaper accounts from parents whose offspring had been deprogrammed as well as from deprogrammers themselves suggested that fees as large as $25,000 were sometimes charged.) In addition, Patrick apparently had other sources of income. Royalties from the sale of just the hardcover edition of his book totaled $13,000 by 1978 (the proceeds from the softcover edition, which certainly substantially outsold the hardcover edition, were not revealed), and an additional unknown sum above $3000 was received by Patrick for movie rights to the book. Patrick also acknowledged receiving considerable sums in the form of "gifts" and "loans," which may or may not have been repayable, for his legal defense (Fitzpatrick, 1978: 8).

There seems to be little doubt that deprogramming provided Patrick and some other deprogrammers (see the later section in this chapter describing the Freedom of Thought Foundation ranch in Tucson, Arizona) with larger revenues than their previous occupations. In fact, what knowledge we have of those other individuals who engaged in full-time deprogramming suggests that they, like Patrick, had been employed in marginal occupations (for example, Galen Kelly, whose one-man private detective agency branched into deprogramming work, or Joe Alexander, Sr., who had previously been employed as a used car salesman) or low-ranking bureaucratic jobs in what otherwise would have seemed to be prestigious professions (for instance, Michael Trauscht worked as a special attorney in Pima County, Arizona'a finance department). However, the potentially lucrative returns from deprogramming were reduced or endangered by the high costs of legal defense, fines, and civil suit settlements. There is, of course, no available record of the costs which deprogrammers incurred or of their overall profit figures; however, it seems abundantly clear both that the lucrative fees lured deprogrammers into continuing to accept clients after they had already become embroiled in legal disputes over deprogrammings *and* that legal prosecutions nevertheless significantly hindered deprogramming's emergence as a viable way of making a living.

BUILDING AN OCCUPATIONAL IDENTITY

As we have already pointed out, the deprogrammers utilized the brainwashing model described in Chapter 3. It was this ideology, defended by them in its most extreme form, which dictated that members of all so-called "cults" required deprogramming before their free will could be fully restored. They insisted that voluntary withdrawal was virtually impossible. To admit otherwise was to perceive cracks in the validity of the brainwashing argument. Thus, Ford Greene, an ex-"Moonie" who went on to become a well-traveled deprogrammer, voluntarily left the UM after eight months without being abducted and forcibly deprogrammed; however, to preserve the ideology, the story was told that Green reputedly *deprogrammed himself* (presumably through his superior will—see Testa, 1978: 66-67). In those rare instances when an individual might physically leave or "escape" on his own without being deprogrammed, that individual would never truly be free of a "cult's mind control" and would therefore suffer its effects indefinitely. For example, Conway and Siegelman (1978: 84) cited the instance of an ex-"Moonie" who managed to leave on his own. However, he never underwent deprogramming and "never snapped out of his cult state" despite later visits to psychiatrists. The combination of defending the most extreme form of the brainwashing model and insisting that all "cult" members required deprogramming was, of course, intended to buttress deprogrammers' claims that deprogramming was a unique and necessary occupation.

The deprogrammers accordingly made considerable efforts to distinguish themselves and their skills from existing occupations, particularly psychologists and psychiatrists. For example, Patrick (1976: 82) sternly informed a nervous parent contemplating deprogramming that no psychiatrist (much less anyone else) really understood brainwashing and the phenomenon of mind control better than he. Similarly, Conway and Siegelman (1978: 86-87) contended that America's mental health "establishment" had only outdated, ineffective concepts to explain a totally new, inexplicable outbreak of "snapping" personalities occurring in religious cults. In testimony at the 1979 "Dole hearings" ("The Cult Phenomenon in the United States," AFF, 1979a: 50; see Chapter 8) these authors went on to argue:

> The only remedy currently available for treating the states of mind produced by this cult experience is the controversial method of deprogramming; and we believe that deprogramming should be recognized as a new and valuable form of mental health therapy.

Yet, at the same time, deprogrammers carried out an ambivalent relationship with the established mental health profession. Because the former occupation's status was so vulnerable, it always enthusiastically accepted apologetic statements from John Clark, Margaret Singer, Kevin Gilmartin, Marvin Galper and other clinically oriented psychologists as well as research findings or corroborative testimonies which lent deprogramming credibility. On one hand, it was willing to castigate conventional mental health professionals as stodgy and conservative; on the other, when they rallied to its cause, deprogrammers unhesitatingly sought the acceptance and confirmation of the latter.

Although deprogramming was never specified in its procedural details with the standardized clarity of exorcism, for example, an attempt was made to describe and formalize its basic outlines, as we indicated in Chapter 3. However, the qualifications and training for deprogramming remained nebulous. Deprogrammers tended to have acquired their qualifications either by having served an apprenticeship to another deprogrammer (as Joe Alexander, Jr., did with his father) which gave them firsthand experience with "cults" or by themselves having been "cult" members who were deprogrammed (presumably these individuals had a special knowledge or an insight into "cult" mind control techniques and could effectively empathize with deprogrammees). Since the procedures, training, and qualifications were not clearly specified, deprogrammers tended to justify the validity of their credentials by reference to their success rate. This fact undoubtedly accounts for their frequently exaggerated figures of past deprogrammings. Patrick (Conway and Siegelman, 1979: 76), for example, in answer to an interviewer's query as to his qualifications, retorted:

> I think my experience and the proof I have presented speaks for itself. I've deprogrammed almost 1600 people. I have success record. Each and every person I've dealt with qualified me to do what I'm doing.

Likewise, Joe Alexander, Sr., variously claimed to have deprogrammed over 1000 persons (Gazette Times [Ferndale, Mich.], Dec. 23, 1976) and 600 persons (Los Angeles Times, Jan. 3, 1977) in boasting of his experience and credentials.

ESTABLISHING DEPROGRAMMING CENTERS

Because the brainwashing metaphor implied that the individual had been severely incapacitated by "cult" membership and also was incapable of breaking free of "mind control" on his or her own, deprogramming could not always be carried out quickly. While some deprogrammings required only a few hours, others took days or even weeks. In order to avoid the obvious problems associated with establishing a new base of operation in a motel or private residence for each such deprogramming, sometimes for extended periods, and to allow the employment of a full-time support staff, deprogrammers came to recognize the importance of having permanent physical facilities. During the 1970s several deprogramming centers were established throughout the continental United States. None of these, however, demonstrated much longevity as the necessary legal support failed to materialize.

The most successful deprogramming facility, and for our purposes the most illustrative, was the Freedom of Thought Foundation ranch located in Tucson, Arizona. The Freedom of Thought Foundation had its origins during the summer of 1976 when Michael Trauscht, special attorney for Pima County's finance department, heard complaints from several concerned parents that their adult sons had joined a nomadic communal religious group called The Body (alternately known as the Garbage-Eaters, after their practice of scavanging for scraps and unwanted leftovers in the waste bins of restaurants and supermarkets in strict observance of an obscure biblical interpretation). Posing as a pair of backpacking hikers, Trauscht and a police officer located the group in the nearby Tucson Mountains where Trauscht was reportedly "appalled" by conditions he observed at The Body's encampment. Shortly before this excursion Trauscht had been reading Vincent Bugliosi's *Helter Skelter*, an account of the Charles Manson cult, and noticed similarities between the regimented lifestyle of The Body and Manson's "Family." Trauscht eventually had the pair of young men arrested and obtained a habeus corpus writ to hold them on the grounds they were under the influence of "mind control." Joe Alexander, Sr., who had apprenticed under Ted Patrick three years earlier and then broken away on his own to deprogram full-time, was flown in to Tucson for a weekend and deprogrammed the young men.

Soon after, Alexander and Trauscht decided to form a partnership that would employ Trauscht's legal knowledge of ways to remove adults from "cults" utilizing temporary conservatorships and Alexander's experience at deprogramming. The catalyst for their establishing the Freedom of Thought Foundation came from a gift of $105,000 to Alexander from a grateful Detroit industrialist whose son Alexander had deprogrammed from the Hare Krishna sect. Together Trauscht and Alexander envisioned an "anti-cult capitol" of the United States that would eventually serve as a model to extend legal deprogrammings not only to all corners of this country but also throughout the world. With the money they purchased a trilevel, seven-bedroom house on five acres of land adjacent to Tucson and set up a permanent staff composed of Trauscht as director and legal consultant, Phoenix attorney Wayne Howard as the foundation's lawyer assigned to represent parents, Dr. Kevin Gilmartin (a Tucson psychologist) as psychiatric consultant, Joe Alexander, Sr., as chief deprogrammer, and (initially) five ex-"cult" members to serve as Alexander's assistants (Arizona Daily Star [Tucson], Sept. 11, 1976). Ex-members also participated in "rescue teams" which Trauscht employed in locating and abducting deprogrammees as well as serving as "security guards" to prevent the "guests" from escaping during their "rehabilitation" period of 30 days in the event that any "floated" (regressed to "cultic" inclinations).

Life for "cult" members during their stay at the foundation ranch was in certain respects unregimented and in other ways closely scrutinized. For example, Joe Alexander's wife Esther adopted a maternal role and "indulged" her "children" during their "rehabilitation." She allowed them to eat and sleep as much as they desired, to play games or engage in crafts, and to participate in low-key discussions with deprogrammers and with each other. She would, on occasion, take female "guests" into Tucson with her to shop. At the same time, however, "cult" members were given household tasks to perform, discouraged from smoking or imbibing alcohol (except wine at meals), forbidden sexual/romantic relations, limited in their contacts with their families (parents were permitted a four- to five-day visiting period during the month-long "rehabilitation"), and discouraged from reading the Bible ("because of the way it had been twisted and programmed in the converts' minds," Alexander told a newspaper reporter [Los Angeles Times, Jan. 3, 1977].[4]

It is difficult to construct more than rough estimates of the foundation's financial success and the number of young persons processed through it during its year of existence. Various figures offered to the press were at times contradictory and undoubtedly inflated. Regarding the size of clientele, for example, it is known that the ranch had facilities to accommodate 12-15 "guests" at a time (plus the Alexanders and their assistants). In one interview Alexander and Trauscht claimed that they had handled 70 cases "since going legal" (Los Angeles Times, Jan. 5, 1977), yet the foundation claimed about 100 deprogrammings that same month in a separate interview (Oakland Press [Oakland, Calif.], Jan. 5, 1977). In September 1976 (when the foundation was first established) Trauscht claimed he had removed 58 persons from "cults"; by February 1977 he claimed 85, implying the foundation only processed 37 individuals in its first five months. This figured squared with Dr. Kevin Gilmartin's estimate that he had only seen 25-30 cases as foundation consultant (Gilmartin was interviewed the month *before* Trauscht's estimate 37 persons appeared in the press—see Los Angeles Times, Jan. 3, 1977), yet that same month The Detroit *Free Press* (Jan. 17, 1977) reported another foundation estimate that it handled 80 cases during 1976. Suffice it to say that the figures are confusing and less than reliable. However, it is likely that the foundation did receive a minimum of several dozen "guests" during its operation and quite possibly more.

Finances are equally cloudy but possibly to estimate. Alexander was interviewed in early 1977 and "said he does not make any more money as a deprogrammer than he did as a car dealer, but he and Trauscht would not reveal their income from the group" (Detroit Free Press, Jan. 17, 1977). Some evidence, however, suggests that the foundation, even with a modest-sized clientele, did quite well—certainly beyond expenses. The Los Angeles *Times* (Jan. 3, 1977) reported estimates of deprogramming costs wherein legal fees alone ranged from $3000 to $5000 as well as involving expenses such as plane tickets for deprogrammers and assistants, motel rooms, long-distance phone calls that could easily add up to $25,000. The Detroit Free Press (Jan. 17, 1977) cited the foundation's figure of the cost of an average deprogramming as $9700, a figure corresponding to Trauscht's own frequently reported estimated of $10,000 (Framington Observer, [Linovia, Mich.], Jan. 20, 1977). The foundation's first year involved a reported budget of $150,000 (Tampa Tribune, May 5, 1977). If we subtract the $105,000 "gift" and assume that the foundation deprogrammed only a conservative maximum of two dozen persons at $10,000 each, hypothetically the foundation could have cleared $195,000 in its first and basically only year of operation.

What permitted the ranch to flourish for a brief period was the ability of Trauscht and Howard to obtain conservatorships; this provided a steady flow of clients without the problems of police and court intervention and long, costly legal custody proceedings. Even during this period, however, all conservatorships were not legally served, as they were often obtained in one state and served in other states. As we previously noted, once the case of the "faithful Five" had been adjudicated, conservatorships were no longer readily forthcoming. When the Freedom of Thought Foundation finally officially closed in December 1978, it had been functionally out of business for almost a year, collapsing under the weight of legal actions and injunctions designed to prohibit its anti-cult activities. Trauscht et al. had been for some time, and in a number of states such as California were (see News World, March 29, 1977), under suit for exploiting conservatorship statutes. At one point Trauscht, who resigned as director of the Freedom of Thought Foundation in March 1977 for reasons of "overwork" and became a "consultant/lecturer," cited the figure of $40 million in such suits against him and the foundation (Tucson Daily Citizen, March 25, 1978).

Thus, what finally undermined the establishment of physical facilities that would have given deprogrammers a large measure of stability and credibility was the lack of a legal basis for operations and not financial costs or shortage of clients. An attempt was made to continue the notion of a permanent deprogramming center in Sweet Valley, Pennsylvania, by Gifford Cappellini, Jr., and Joe Alexander, Jr., who together founded in late fall 1978 Freedom of Mind, Inc. Charging between $5000 and $15,000 per deprogramming, they, too, ran afoul of the law in attempting to employ writs of conservatorship improperly. For example, in the case of Mitch Dixon, an UM member who was "snatched" by the team of Cappellini-Alexander in front of the Empire State Building and who later escaped from them, Cappellini obtained a temporary conservatorship on Dixon in Arkansas and then illegally served it in New York State. When Cappellini tried to serve a similar writ on "Moonie" Barbara Larson (in the legal battle already mentioned) at a trial in new York City, he was arrested by police for kidnapping. In December 1978, a deposition was served to Joe Alexander, Jr., and despite a countersuit for $44 million filed against the UM and Sun Myung Moon by Alexander's parents, the Sweet Valley deprogramming operation closed down. Meanwhile, anti-cult associations tried to rally to the support of deprogrammers, but their efforts were largely symbolic. By mid-1979 a special anti-cult organization, the Recovery of Free Thought Charitable Trust, was formed to handle a "defense fund" for parents of young adults in such groups as the Hare Krishna, the UM, and The Way International who were being sued for literally millions of dollars and whose legal defense costs had run into the thousands—in some cases the tens of thousands—of dollars per family (RFTCT, 1979). The precarious financial situation of most anti-cult groups, however, precluded any major influx of money for such defense.

Summary

In this chapter we have analyzed the direct action component of the ACM, best known for its sensational practice called deprogramming. As we have shown, the term deprogramming actually referred to an array of activities, of which we have focused attention on only the most extreme form (coercive), since this provided for the emergence of a full-time occupation and a distinct wing of the ACM. This deprogramming wing relied almost exclusively on families, rather than the religious institution, for its clientele and financial support. These families delegated to the deprogrammers, albeit without legal foundation, the authority to abduct, detain, and "treat" their errant but in many cases adult offspring who had enlisted in various religious movements. Because deprogrammers engaged in controversial and frequently illegal behavior, the anti-cult associations, while composed of many families sympathetic with deprogramming, nevertheless maintained organizational distance from that arm of the movement.

Faced with the inability to dissuade their offspring from new religious leaders and beliefs, families turned to those individuals who were willing to take the risks inherent in coercive deprogramming. Deprogrammers offered families the advantages of gaining immediate behavior control over their offspring, avoiding the debilitating stigma associated with mental illness, and initiating action without entanglement in due legal process. In attempting to meet the demand for their services, deprogrammers encountered two major difficulties: defining and distinguishing themselves as an unique occupation, and securing a firm legal basis on which they could pursue their activities. For a brief time, conservatorships seemed to offer the promise of serving as a means to ensure legitimacy and stability in their endeavors. Their failure to do so, however, and the lack of other viabile alternatives rendered the ultimate status of deprogramming both vulnerable and marginal.

NOTES

1. *Let Our Children Go!* (Patrick and Dulack, 1976), written with the assistance of a college English professor (Patrick himself was a high-school dropout), is a "pot-boiler" mixture of anecdotes from Patrick's most sensational deprogrammings, personal reminiscences of his childhood in the gamy sections of Chattanooga, and assorted topics thrown together with minimal integration. It is lacking in all but the most general historical details concerning the development of deprogramming and abounds with justifications for it. It does provide, however, cogent statements of the "brainwashing" ideology (albeit in its most unsophistocated form) as well as an intellectual portrait of Patrick himself. In this chapter we simply note the 1976 publication date when referring to the Patrick-Dulack book rather than mention their names each time.

2. One ACM informant commented on this unlikely number of reasoning that if one considered *all* deprogrammings as having been inspired and hence indirectly originated by Patrick, then such a large quantity was possible. Even so, 1600 deprogrammings seems a gross exaggeration.

3. Attorneys for the parents were, of course, determined to provide evidence to show that their young adult offspring were under the influence of "mind control" and hence eligible for conservatorships, while the Unification Church members went

to great lengths, including performing original musical compositions and reading poetry to refute these claims.

4. The foundation was clearly ambivalent regarding its mission as to whether it should deprogram or reprogram (whether merely to "free" minds or to implant new ideas in them as well). In the Los Angeles Times article cited in the text, Alexander told a reporter: "No effort is made to introduce any specific religion to those being rehabilitated." Likewise, Trauscht said, "I'm not concerned about a person's religious beliefs. . . . We are concerned about the techniques used to achieve these beliefs." Yet, in the same interview, Alexander also stated: "We suggest they can see the Bible during their last week here with us. We make sure they can handle the Bible (understand it correctly) before they walk out of here."

Chapter 6

THE IMPACT OF DEPROGRAMMING

In this chapter we shall examine the impact of the deprogramming wing of the ACM on the new religions. As we pointed out in Chapter 5, deprogramming encompassed a wide range of activities, from the spectacular public kidnappings, forcible detentions, and exorcism-like rituals believed by deprogrammers to break "cult"-imposed mind control to quiet re-evaluation by a convert (together with, perhaps, family, clergy, or friends) of the full implications of his or her chosen conversion course. However, it was the former conception that dominated public discussion of deprogramming. This narrow and unrealistic portrayal prevailed for several reasons. First, as we have already noted, deprogrammers insisted that the formal deprogramming procedure was necessary both because it served their efforts to secure recognition of their undertakings as a legitimate occupational category and because it lent credibility to the brainwashing ideology. If members of the new religions could simply walk away from these groups of their own volition or be talked out of their faith by family or friends, then both the brainwashing ideology and deprogramming as an occupation were placed in obvious jeopardy. Second, disconfirming cases (that is, the underprogrammed majority of ex-cultists) remained largely outside the public view. Although a plethora of converts to the new

religions simply walked away from these movements on their own initiative at some point, they usually were uninterested in, or even eschewed,
public attention. What information we possess on this "invisible" majority
(see Beckford, 1978a, 1978b) suggests a mixture of feelings (among
others) of embarrassment and continued ambivalence toward their past
religious "questing." These cases, therefore, were not publicly recognized
as representing an alternative pattern of exit. Nor were new religious
movements eager to publicize such cases, since the high defection rates
undermined their claims to represent viable and/or inevitable alternative
lifestyles. Third, and most ironically, liberal opponents of the brainwashing ideology (at least indirectly) offered support to the coercive
conception of deprogramming. There was a tendency for liberal opponents
of the ACM to insist that members of the new religions were committed
zealots in reaction to ACM claims that such individuals were brainwashed
zombies. One effect of this polarization was that liberal critics of deprogramming sought to discredit the deprogramming procedure by highlight-
ing the most coercive, abusive practices. While this effort was at least
partially successful, it also helped sustain this unrepresentative depiction
of the dynamics of the deprogramming process and obscured the full range
of exit patterns by new religions' converts.

It is important that we give consideration to the real diversity and
complexity of the deprogramming phenomenon in order to place in
perspective the role that deprogramming and deprogrammed individuals
played in attacking and discrediting the new religious movements. The
most basic observation with which to begin is that deprogramming constituted an exertion of power. At one extreme, reevaluation involved verbal
suasion (in which there was only a moderate imbalance of power between
the two sides and therefore some meaningful exchange was possible). At
the other extreme was the exorcism-like, ritualistic handling of the members of a new religion (in which there was a drastic imbalance of
power, and converts' attempts to influence were treated as defenses
symptomatic of their "programming"). In the discussion which follows we
shall consider re-evaluation and coercive deprogramming as two polar
types of deprogramming.

It is our contention that the outcome of the deprogramming process
hinged on at least three major factors. First, both parents/deprogrammers
and the target "cult" offspring brought a range of preexisting personal
motivations and interests to the situation which influenced the latters'
responses to it (rather than such responses being explained by the stereotypical brainwashed personality configuration asserted by the depro-

grammers). In this sense individuals were differentially receptive to deprogramming. Second, the deprogramming scenarios varied enormously (and any one of a number of factors present in the situation might potentially influence the target individual), and parents brought to the situations varying types and levels of concern. Third, once the individual had been put through the deprogramming process, a number of outcomes were possible; these ranged from return to the movement to simple exit to assuming the role of active apostate. Which of these options was exercised was the product of the balance of power and interests of the two sides, as well as the availability of various roles into whch individuals might move if their roles in the religious movement were disavowed.

Individuals entered the deprogramming situation with different degrees and kinds of involvement in and commitment to their roles as members of new religions. For example, as we discussed in detail elsewhere (see Bromley and Shupe, 1979a), UM members were variously attracted to the movement by the relationships and lifestyles inherent in its communal organization, the integrated explanation of a broad range of phenomena offered by the theology, other members of the movement, and the sense of idealism and purpose which they perceived in the group. For some individuals, the bases of involvement broadened rather quickly; for others, they broadened slowly or remained narrow. Of course, individuals with a narrower basis of involvement were obviously more vulnerable to disaffection from the group. Since the group deliberately sought to expand any individual's basis of involvement soon after his or her joining, this is another way of saying that deprogrammings were most likely to be successful with newer "cult" converts.

Further, feelings of involvement and commitment varied over time. Many persons joining a communal organization such as the UM experienced feelings of liberation and fulfillment as a result of reduced interpersonal competitiveness, a sense of personal integration and purpose, elimination of a need to achieve or compete for wealth and possessions, and constant support from and interdependence with other group members. Frequently, such feelings presisted for some time and produced intense feelings of commitment. However, for many members, there came a time when they had to confront the fact that their chosen course involved continuous self-sacrifice for the good of the group and submission to group leaders, suppression of ego and foreswearing of conventional careers, and more encumbering social commitments (such as marriage and child-rearing within the group) which made any future change increasingly problematic. The realization that self-abnegation was a lonely and virtually unending struggle, which in many respects became more difficult as one sought to root out the last vestiges of egoism, gave some individuals pause. In addition, members began to perceive that despite proclaimed ideals of equality and a sacrificial life, structured inequality (in the form of privileges, prestige, and power), invidiousness, and competitiveness persisted, albeit in a muted, less visible form. This, of course, raised the question of whether the group's ideals were actually attainable on any level.

For their part, parents brought to the deprogramming situation a number of different concerns with respect to their offspring's decision to join and live in a new religious movement. In cases of milder concern parents/deprogrammers were likely to express disappointment or even personal anguish, arguing that the stigma of participation in this type of social movement would be difficult to live down if it went on for an extended period, that idealistic motives could be expressed in other ways, that the potential social and personal benefits should be balanced against costs and drawbacks, and that present idealism and happiness might end in despair and bitterness because the movement's goals were impossible to achieve. More embittered parents expressed fear and anger that lifelong sacrifices and investments for conventional careers were being thrown away, feelings of rejection, social embarrassment at their offspring's desertion of middle-class lifestyles, and real apprehension about their offspring's health and well-being.

Whatever predispositions parents/deprogrammers brought to the deprogramming situation, the relative power of the two sides determined the format of the exchange rather than the content of concerns which were relatively similar. If the deprogramming was deemed a re-evaluation by both parties, the deprogrammee possessed a greater degree of influence in the ensuing exchange. The mere fact that he or she was free to leave meant that the exchange of views would proceed on a relatively equal basis, though acceding to parentally orchestrated re-evaluation sessions did tacitly acknowledge parental authority. If the deprogramming was coercive in nature, the deprogrammee possessed virtually no influence in the ensuing exchange. The process therefore became a one-sided attempt to "educate" the deprogrammee, with any defense of his or her faith being interpreted and disparaged as evidence of the persistence of thought control.

In either re-evaluation or coercive deprogramming the deprogramee was likely to be confronted by new "information." Because individuals joining communally organized new religious groups such as the UM immediately assumed a full-time, consuming role requiring few substantive skills or detailed ideological knowledge, they were able to perform these roles without understanding of the groups' theologies or organizations. Nor were they likely to have been well-versed in critical media allegations about the UM before joining. In our own interviews with UM members in witnessing/fund-raising teams we found that on many occasions we possessed a greater knowledge of the *Divine Principle,* and certainly of UM organization on a national level, than a number of individuals who had been UM members for many months. These individuals could, therefore, be confronted with new "information" about Moon himself, political and financial aspects of the movement about which they knew little (and had obviously been discouraged by the movement from discussing or inquiring about), and even insider portions of the ideology to which they had not yet been privileged, any of which a member might find disconcerting. Indeed, deprogrammers usually relied upon a barrage of such "facts" about the religious group to shake the individual's faith.

Deprogrammees also were frequently confronted with an intense, emotionally charged situation. Whether the deprogramming was coercive or a re-evaluation, parental emotions might run the gamut from deep concern and visible apprehension to uninhibited outpourings of fear and grief. The fact that several family members might have suspended their own familial and occupational activities, had traveled long distances, were emotionally distraught, and tearfully pleaded with the deprogrammee to consider what he or she was doing to the family doubtless were powerfully persuasive. If parents had permitted forcible abduction, the deprogramee, despite any anger felt, might well be shocked that his or her parents felt compelled to take such drastic action.

Finally, the deprogrammee was faced with explaining a variety of inconsistencies which were more easily repressed within the context of the powerfully confirmatory communal group relations. Issues such as the use of deceptive practices in fund-raising and witnessing as compared with the group's lofty ideals, disconfirmation of theological predictions, and Moon's opulent lifestyle compared with that of his average follower were certain to be brought up by parents and deprogrammers as a way of discrediting the UM. Such charges frequently were difficult to refute, either because some were true (deceptive fund-raising) and deprogrammees had seen them occur or even engaged in them or because they did not possess sufficient organizational and theological knowledge to argue otherwise. When parents/deprogrammers presented confirming evidence of such accusations from published media reports or former group members, at least some deprogrammees were shaken either by the "new" information or by their own inability to challenge successfully the arguments.

The predispositions both sides brought to the deprogramming interacted with the dynamics of the process, yielding numerous possible and not easily predictable outcomes. Once the deprogramming was completed, the deprogrammees might (1) return to the movement either against parental wishes or with their reluctant consent, (2) agree to a trial separation from the movement, (3) leave the movement and resume former activities, (4) reject both family and the movement, or (5) reject the movement and join the ACM. For example, if parental concern was mild and the convert's commitment strong, the latter could successfully weather a re-evaluation session's emotional and/or intellectual onslaught and insist on returning to the group with reluctant parental blessings. If more serious doubts or ambivalent emotions were added to preexisting uneasiness, the deprogrammee might decide on a trial separation or severing of his affiliation entirely. By contrast, stronger parental concern and coercive measures might end up strengthening the deprogramee's resolve, convincing him or her that membership in the communal group was not worth the pain it was obviously causing the family, or creating the conviction that something must be terribly wrong for his or her parents to have taken such drastic action. In short, whether deprogramming was "successful" in any individual case was not (as the deprogrammers maintained in their crusade to establish themselves as a legitimate occupation) a function of applying certain standard therapeutic procedures, such as confronting converts with litanies of allegations about "cults"; nor was it (as the liberals charged) largely the result of the situation's coerciveness. Rather, the "success" or "failure" of a deprogramming was an interactive product of the factors listed above. In those instances of "success" deprogrammers were simply able, through intuition and from experience, to utilize a crude sense of group dynamics to pick up on and exploit the predispositions of the situation as located in both parents and converts as well as in the parameters (coercive or noncoercive) of the confrontation situation.

Apostasy

Our argument to this point has been directed at demonstrating that deprogramming was not a homogeneous process but rather involved a myriad of interacting factors which yielded numerous possible outcomes. Here we are concerned with explaining one specific pattern of exit, that which we have termed apostasy (leaving a new religious movement and joining the ACM). Apostasy is critical for understanding the impact of the deprogramming wing of the ACM because apostates played such a key role in discrediting the new religions through the recounting of what we have termed atrocity stories.

The emergence of apostasy as a solution to the problem of exit can most readily be understood by constrasting two polar scenarios. On one hand, if parents were only mildly opposed to their offspring's membership in a new religion and the latter decided, either on the basis of doubts raised (or confirmed) during the deprogramming or parental pressure, to disavow his or her membership, exit was rather easily negotiated. Parents' interests were served if the young person agreed to leave the group, and the exchange was sufficiently equitable that he or she did not have to define the situation as one of forced choice. The deprogrammee's decision to leave or recant the new religious faith could therefore be defined as a "mistake," "misplaced idealism," or "bad judgment"; and it was even possible for parents to acknowledge that there were some positive aspects about the movement to which a well-meaning person might have easily been attracted.

Apostasy, on the other hand, was more likely to occur when parental opposition to an offspring's membership in a new religion was strong and the deprogramming was coercive. In this scenario parents/deprogrammers were insistent that the deprogrammee renounce his or her conversion and leave the group; in these cases there was little room for meaningful negotiation.[1] Because force had been employed and a major confrontation created, the situation approached a zero-sum game. There was little likelihood that middle ground would be acceptable to either side. Thus, the deprogrammee either had to capitulate to the parents'/deprogrammers' world view or resist until an opportunity to return to the religious group presented itself. (Deprogrammees who successfully resisted the process used a variety of escape techniques ranging from literally breaking away and fleeing to feigning illness or even injurying themselves in order to be taken to a hospital, to playing along with deprogrammers to lower their surveillance. Once back in the group, having "survived" a deprogramming became a "red badge of courage," and atrocity stories comparable to those recounted by apostates were told by members to build solidarity within the movement; personal interviews, 1978; see also Barker, 1980, for a discussion of such functions.) Here, of course, we are more interested in those individuals who chose to capitulate to parents'/deprogrammers' perspectives.

For those individuals who were already experiencing ambivalence about their participation in the religious movement when they initially entered the deprogramming situation, who had doubts raised or confirmed during their deprogrammings, and/or who experienced the full brunt of parental fears, hurt, and grief, severing ties with the group constituted a reasonable decision. However, as we pointed out in Chapter 2, usually there had been an ongoing dialogue between family and offspring before the abduction/ deprogramming took place (if only to monitor the latter's whereabouts) in which the offspring usually vigorously defended the rightness of staying with the group. How, then, was the deprogrammee able to change sides so suddenly and dramatically, as if merely substituting hats or personae? Simply to admit a mistake and declare no further interest in the movement was not enough in this case. Parents, after all, had experienced humiliation in the form of their offspring's hostility and rejection during the period preceding the deprogramming and during at least part of the deprogramming process itself; they had felt forced to reduce their offspring to childlike status; they paid a substantial fee for deprogramming; and they had risked civil or criminal prosecution in abducting their own children. The price of reentry was now higher, and public admission of having been brainwashed and support of other ACM allegations comprised an explanation which would serve the interests of deprogrammers and parents alike. Public contrition for having abandoned parental values, in other words, was the cost of readmission into the community of respectability.

For the deprogrammers, of course, the success of deprogrammings buttressed both the brainwashing ideology and the rationale for extending to them legitimate occupational status. For their part, parents now possessed an assuaging explanation for their offspring's hostility and rejection ("he quite literally was 'not himself' "), a nonstigmatizing explanation for their offspring's participation in the new religious movement ("he had been subjected to a coercive force directed by malevolent individuals"), and a label which did not require an extended period of incapacity to remove (deprogramming by eliminating programming restored the individual to normalcy).

In one sense such a solution to the problem of exit sounds contrived, particularly with respect to the deprogrammee who manifested such a sudden reversal of positions. However, because doubts and ambivalence were in fact much more prevalent than the surface solidarity of communal organization suggests (or advocates of deprogramming would care to have admitted), the seeds of transformation frequently were already present. In fact, the distinctions between idealistic crusade and quixotic quest, subsistence, and deprivation; integrative world view and simplistic authoritarian cant; committed disciple and unwitting dupe; a secure, supportive family and dependency-inducing group; and selflessness and personality dissolution were largely a function of the *interpretation* rather than the *content* of behaviors. Therefore, once a process of retrospective interpretation began, with supports for the communal organization removed and with obvious rewards attending the adoption of the anti-cult perspective present, it was not surprising that migration to an opposite position took place rapidly. Of course, the fact that a deprogramee's shift in public statements doubtlessly masked the same doubts and uncertainties about the ACM's monolithic ideology and radical practices which the deprogrammee had previously possessed about his or her new religious movement remained unspoken and unspeakable from the apostate's standpoint. Such private doubts simply could no longer be expressed publicly in his or her new role.

Naturally, not all of the individuals who capitulated to the parents'/deprogrammers' perspectives became apostates. Assumption of the apostate role required recruitment by some combination of the anti-cult associations, deprogrammers, media, or investigatory agencies. However, there were a limited number of such roles and forums for their messages, and so many deprogrammers after a brief period in the limelight during which they were the objects of media reports and/or speeches to local groups resumed their former lives, for all practical purposes fading into obscurity. At the other extreme, some went on to become deprogrammers themselves or outspoken leaders of anti-cult associations. For a few deprogrammees, the experience of apostasy apparently became the basis for the direction of their future lives. Barbara Underwood, for example, co-authored with her mother a book on her UM experience, entitled *Hostage to Heaven* (1979), and married apostate Gary Scharff, a major figure in the deprogramming wing of the ACM during the late 1970s. Alan Tate Wood also co-authored an apostate's account of his UM experiences, *Moonstruck* (Wood and Vitek 1979), made frequent speaking appearances, and enrolled in a counseling psychology program at a southwestern university with the self-proclaimed goal of treating "cult victims." In any event, there is no question that the most injurious consequence of deprogramming for the new religions was the creation of apostates and the dissemination of the anecdotal atrocity stories which they told, and it is to these stories we now turn.

Apostates and Atrocity Stories

Apostates provided much of the drama which captured public attention and helped the ACM receive a degree of public credibility which might well have been unattainable without apostate testimony. One persistent problem the ACM faced was an inability to penetrate the new religious movements and gather firsthand evidence to support their allegation (although some young journalists did make brief forays into workshops, seminars, and meetings for this purpose). Yet, because the ACM's charges of brainwashing and proposed solution of deprogramming were so extreme, convincing evidence was vital to their case. While ACM proponents could allege that brainwashing occurred and describe the brainwashing process as they contended it happened to others, none of them had actually been brainwashed or seen brainwashing taking place. It was the apostate who could literally offer this "smoking gun" quality of evidence. Apostates could authoritatively state that they had been brainwashed, describe the process in detail, recount the irresistible nature of the process, and even elaborate on how they themselves had brainwashed others. Further, they described their personal exploitive fund-raising practices and uncontestably political activities as well as the authoritarian, regimented lifestyle which was intended to separate children from their parents. The effect of such testimony was to discredit new religious movements' claims that they were religious at all and that their members were in fact voluntary, committed converts.

It is this testimony that constitutes what we shall refer to here as atrocity stories. By an atrocity story we refer to the symbolic presentation of actions or events (real or imaginary) in such a context that they are made to flagrantly violate the (presumably) shared premises upon which a given set of social relationships should proceed. The recounting of such tales is intended as a means of reaffirming normative boundaries; by sharing the reporter's disapproval or horror, an audience reasserts normative prescription and clearly locates the violator beyond the limits of public morality. In the case at hand atrocity stories were constructed so as (1) to portray affiliation in new religious movements as the product of coercive, manipulative practices rather than voluntary conversion and (2) to portray new religions themselves as vehicles for personal, political, and economic aggrandizement at the expense of the well-being of members, their families, and the public at large.

ANECDOTAL ACCOUNTS OF BRAINWASHING

Apostates' atrocity stories uniformly conveyed a standard, even statistically predictable set of anecdotes (see Bromley et al., 1980) that portrayed their joining a given new religion as preceded by an overwhelming onslaught on their senses that swiftly eroded their (normally) critical

reasoning faculties and left them highly compliant to pressures for con-
formity. These accounts were characteristically replete with references to
zombie imagery, such as self-depictions as "robots," "automatons," and
"mental three-year-olds" as well as with other colorful metaphors, such as
UM apostate Kathy Knight's statement that she believed her mind (while
an UM member) had "been in a strong box for the past three years" (The
News Sentinel [Fort Wayne, Ind.], Nov. 20, 1976). All implied, if not
directly suggested, a malevolent, manipulative force that deliberately
orchestrated the destruction of their free will. To the extent that such
accounts were accepted, of course, they undermined any depiction of new
religions' membership as conversion in the conventional sense.

UM apostate Richard Greenwald, for example, recounted a classic tale
of having experienced a series of befuddling processes, incorporating
themes of hypnosis, sexual seduction, drugging, and thought reform:

> I think I was hypnotized at first. Basically by the girl that met me
> because she kept staring into my eyes and I kept being attracted to
> her eyes. Then, during the meal, its very possible for some sort of
> drug to make me more susceptible to the lecture. Then after that it
> was brainwashing because I was hooked. I wanted to stay there. I
> wanted to learn what they had to say. There was repetition all the
> time. Very appealing. The more I heard the more I rejected my
> family, the outside world [The Sun Messenger, (Cleveland Heights,
> Oh.), Oct. 16, 1975].

Another UM apostate, Dennis Carper, recalled how the group allegedly
combined sensitivity-training techniques and group dynamic strategies
with the vaguely occult method of "spot hypnosis":

> I became involved by going to a dinner and a few of their lectures,
> but, by attracting you and using spot hypnosis, placing suggestions
> in your mind on a person-to-person basis, using their hands a lot and
> telling you anything you are wanting to hear, they draw you deeper
> and deeper into the church and into the cult [The Pioneer, (Smith
> Center, Kan.), Dec. 4, 1975].

Other stories emphasized the mechanisms of inculcating guilt and fear
and reducing recruits to subservience and childlike dependence during
indoctrination. Many UM apostates in particular recounted details of
regimented daily routines characteristic of that movement's seminar training and operation of its field units, deploring the inability to act and think

autonomously within the context of the communal group. UM apostate Larry Gumbiner, for example, recalled of his workshop orientation:

> There were 14 hours of lectures interspersed with singing and games. The whole time I was never left alone. I went off to the bathroom and was reprimanded for being inconsiderate and breaking group unity [The Arizona Daily Star (Tucson), July 1, 1976].

Others emphasized the UM's penchant for rote memorization and "one-way" discussions with novitiates. Said UM apostate David Geisler, "We had to answer word for word from the lecture. . . . There was no freedom of thinking, dialogue, or originality allowed" (Columbus Evening Dispatch, Aug. 20, 1976). Such indoctrination techniques allegedly impaired one's ability to think either critically or independently. While it was not actual physical imprisonment that kept members within the group, they nevertheless maintained that they did not feel free to leave (thus preserving the coercion element necessary to make their stories analogous to prisoner-of-war brainwashing studies). Apostate Terry Sherven, for example, recalled what he termed a "psychological force" holding him in the Tony and Susan Alamo Foundation, a sectarian offshoot of the Jesus Movement:

> The brothers would form a ring around you and through the Scripture they would badger you, ask you how you believe, where you could find it in the Scripture that told you now that you were saved and in the house of the Lord [The Spotlight (Washington, D.C.), Oct. 18, 1976].

Much of this "psychological force," apostates were quick to affirm, resulted from the guilt and fear engendered by a movement's doctrines; for example, concerning the satanic/demonic world outside of the "cult" group, individuals' own sexuality, or the misfortunes awaiting those who left the movement. For example, UM apostate Scott McQuin told of the emotional conflict caused him by such techniques:

> I was happy inside the Church but not totally happy because I missed my wife. I was torn between my real family and my Moon family, and they told me that it was a choice between Satan and God. I would leave the church for a while and go home, but I never felt safe there because of sin. I was convinced that the only place that I would be really safe was the Unification Church [Schweikhart, 1976: 9].

Um apostate Larry Gumbiner, speaking to the Oklahoma Bar Association, recalled: "We were told that if we worked against the movement our grandchildren would dig up our bones and spit on them" (Anadarko News, [Okla.], Dec. 2, 1976). UM apostate Michael Englebert claimed even more pointedly: "I fear for my life. I was told repeatedly that if I left the Church I would be killed." He ominously recalled one anecdote:

> Allen, I can't remember his last name. He was starting to speak out against the church. For some strange reason he was killed a few days later. I had seen him three days before he died [The New Haven Register, July 30, 1976].

An additional, frequently indispensable, element included in apostates' accounts of how individual free will was "broken down" was physical deprivation—particularly, violations of values concerning proper nutrition, sufficient rest and sanitation, and physical safety. The implication was that such deprivations (undoubtedly having prima facie outrage value to a presumably well-read, rested, and secure reader) helped debilitate "cult" members or create in them a disorienting sense of insecurity, thereby contributing to suggestibility and an undermining of free will. In the article above, Alamo Foundation apostate Terry Sherven recounted:

> I was always compelled to sleep on the floor, including the winter. There were no adequate sanitation supplies. For instance, one or two toilets would periodically back up for as many as 100 200 males.

Ex-Moonie Diane Devine likewise produced a tale of unwholesome living conditions during an indoctrination seminar:

> Over a hundred girls were crowded into the basement of a recreation hall, some on bunkbeds covered with two-inch foam rubber pads, others on the floor. . . . All sharing two toilets, two showers, and four sinks [Columbus Evening Dispatch, Aug. 20, 1976].

The most extreme allegation of physical deprivation was that individual resistance was critically lowered by a lack of even minimally adequate nutrition. For example: "There was very little protein in the diet. The food was almost totally carbohydrates (cookies, ice cream, coke, peanut butter and jelly sandwiches). On Sunday you might get a drumstick" (The Patent Trader [Mount Kisco, N.Y.], Aug. 5, 1976). Likewise, UM apostate Reed Heller described a similar lack of proper nutrition: "We were kept busy 18 to 20 hours a day and restricted to two low-protein diet meals daily" (The Dallas Morning News, Dec. 4, 1975).[2]

The result of such deprivations left "cult" members, in the words of apostate Robert Buda (The Daily Argus [Mount Vernon, N.Y.), Oct. 4, 1975), "zonked out." Buda claimed: "I had lost 20 pounds, had a pneumonic cough and was staring strangely into space with a big smile." Ex-Moonie Christopher Edwards, in his book *Crazy For God* (1979: 51), portrayed a dramatic moment of horror when, during his indoctrination at the UM's Booneville ranch on the west coast, he suddenly realized the deleterious physical and psychological effects, including childlike regression, of such a lifestyle:

> I glanced into the mirror as I brushed my teeth. Back and forth, up and down. . . . Suddenly, my hand froze. Foamy Crest tooth-paste dribbled down my chin as I stared into the glass. I hardly recognized myself! My face was red and perfectly smooth. My eyes were wide as a child's as round as oranges. My eyelids, which normally partially hooded my eyes, were now glued to the skin above them. . . . I had the same glassy stare as all the others! I must be deeply spiritual after all, just like they'd said.
>
> Amazed and slightly frightened, I headed back to the Chicken Palace to retire. Slipping off my jeans, I climbed into my bag and zipped it up to my chin. . . . As I lay there drowsily, childhood dreams and fantasies mingled in my mind with images of chocolate-chip cookies and warm milk. I finally drifted off, carelessly running my fingers back and forth across the top of my bag, just as I used to do with my blanket as a child.

Not only did apostates claim that they themselves had been brainwashed, but they also reported that after conditioning by such processes the "brainwashed" individual went out in a vampire-like fashion and began infecting others in the same sinister, plague-like way. UM apostate Richard Greenwald offered a classic example of this pattern:

> I learned to hypnotize people and went out to witness, bring in new people. In Berkeley we were bringing 30 new people every day. And they were hooked by that first supper and lecture. . . . [Greenwald claimed he hypnotized them when he would] walk up to them, stare at their eyes, get their attention and hold their attention. Talk about things to form a common base with them. I would draw out from them things that they were interested in and then play on those. And I would suggest things to them that they wanted to hear so they

would want to come over and see what this is all about. We were
trained to do as our leaders did. It was very easy to pick up [The
Sun Messenger (Cleveland Heights, Oh.), Oct. 16, 1975].

ANECDOTAL EVIDENCE OF FRAUDULENT RELIGION

Three major themes employed to discredit new religious movements'
claims that they were in fact legitimate religions were deliberate disruption
of families, economically exploitive practices, and overtly political activities. One of the most common allegations maintained that new religions
deliberately sought to separate a convert from his or her biological family
in order to maximize their domination of the individual members. In
Chapter 2 we detailed the strains which arose in affected families; here it
suffices to point out that such strains and growing estrangement were
staple themes of atrocity stories. Thus Dennis Carper, UM apostate, told a
newspaper reporter:

[Upon joining] you . . . begin to cut off your other outside connec
tions. First of all, things are not so affected like your school or your
friends, then more and more you cut off your friends, your possessions, then your family.

It seems like the more you cut off, the cult becomes more and more
demanding and you become more dependent on this small group of
people inside the cult. They are the only ones that you have any
close relations with and they begin to control you more . . . until
you can't make your own decisions. . . . I cut myself off from all my
family [The Pioneer (Smith Center, Kan.), Dec. 4, 1975].

Others, such as UM apostate Michael Englebert, alleged deliberate attempts
to interrupt communications between parents and offspring:

They claim that parents are all Satanic because they don't approve
of the church. I wrote to my Dad and he never got one of the letters.
And when he sent me a message that he was coming to Yankee
Stadium I never received it [The New Haven Register, July 30,
1976].

The ultimate indices of alleged estrangement and a total reversal of filial
obedience can be found in the sensational claims by apostates that they
would have willingly committed murder, and particularly parricide, on
Moon's command. Dennis Carper proclaimed: "Had I been asked to kill
my parents I would not have hesitated" (The Sun [Colorado Springs,

Colo.], Nov. 23, 1975). Janis Feiden, also a Unification apostate, concurred: "I would have killed for him. I would have done anything Moon said" (The Dallas Morning News, Oct. 19, 1975).

"Cult" members' willingness to engage in fund-raising practices and behaviors which they formerly would have considered dishonest and reprehensible was also a standard value violation of honesty found in apostates' accounts of new religions' abilities to misdirect youthful idealism and use it for self-serving economic purposes. These stories generally reflected three subthemes: (1) the vast amounts of money flowing into the coffers of "cult" leaders via their duped followers, (2) the deception/exploitation of the public by "cult" members to obtain donations, and (3) the exploitation of members themselves by "cult" leaders. UM apostates' complaints that Reverend Moon and other UM leaders enjoyed a luxurious lifestyle at the expense of members who lived in spartan communal groups and knowingly manipulated them were common. On this theme ex-Moonie Michael Englebert stated:

> The average Moonie out fund-raising on the streets is not responsible for himself. . . . [But] regional directors and people above them, their senses are all right [The New Haven Register, July 30, 1976].

Such allegations were not exclusive to the UM, however. Terry Sherven, apostate of the Alamo Foundation, voiced a similar allegation of economic exploitation of members:

> The pay was $1 a week for the first month and after that members were asked to forego payment. For the last approximately four months that I worked there, I never saw any of the money that I made [The Spotlight (Washington, D.C.), Oct. 18, 1976].

Likewise, both Edwards (1979: 157-71) and Underwood and Underwood (1979: 75-95) reported in detail their rationales and deceptive activities as UM fundraisers, as did Ellen Rosemara and other UM apostates at the 1976 "Dole hearing" (CEFM, 1976a: Vol. I). Cynthia Slaughter told the various officials present at that hearing (p. 24):

> I fund-raised 18 hours a day. . . . I was kicked out of office buildings three times and came back bragging. And we really got a lot of reinforcement from our leaders. . . . I also fund-raised in bars at 11:00 at night. I was told to use my "fallen nature" to get money. I'm sorry if I sound this way, but I just feel I was exploited. And I did do deceitful things, which is against my general character.

Other apostates provided "seedy" testimonies that discredited the agencies presumably socializing and encouraging them to engage in such strategies. Dennis Carper told one reporter, in summarizing his fund-raising exploits: "I can't remember how many times I took the last dime from a bum." Likewise, Richard Greenwald reported:

> I pulled in $700 or $800 a week, selling flowers. You go to businesses, commercial places, industrial places. You sneak in. I was pretty good at it. . . . I could get money from anyone now. I know how. I got the last penny from a bum on the street [The Sun Messenger (Cleveland Heights, Oh.), Oct. 16, 1975].

Indeed, exploiting the poor for the millennium was a standard atrocity subtheme of apostates. For example, UM apostate Terry Murray recalled:

> We went door to door in the poorest section, telling the people we represented an organization called the World Crusade and were selling flowers to raise money to help rehabilitate people who were in trouble. The girl told me, "Any line you can use is a good line." So the line I adopted was "We're opening drug centers all over the United States and we're planning to open on in the Albany area and would appreciate your financial assistance."
>
> I was lying, of course, but I figured that if God wants me to lie, it's OK [The Knickerbocker News (Albany, N.Y.), June 16, 1976].

In the same vein, explaining how she was engaged in "heavenly deception" to earn between $80 and $200 a day for the UM as a street solicitor, apostate Ann Gordon said:

> I went door to door selling peanuts. . . . It was incredibly easy. I was told how to put ten cents worth of peanuts in a bag and sell them for a dollar. Later, we sold unshelled nuts because there were fewer to a bag. All I did was smile and say, "Hi, I'm with the Unification Church and we're raising money for a drug program!" Or, "We're trying to bring families together and people to God, won't you help us!" We'd say it real fast, and people never asked questions. Of course, we never *had* a drug program [Crittenden, 1976: 92].

Another theme in atrocity tales designed to discredit "cults" dealt with the alleged political aspirations of their leaders. This charge was leveled almost exclusively at the UM by apostates who claimed to have been involved in lobbying and/or other explicitly political activities on direct assignment from leaders of the movement. Such practices by religious dominations and other legally recognized religious groups, of course, were specifically prohibited by law. These allegations were often presented together with vitriolic excerpts from some of Moon's "insider" speeches (the *Master Speaks* series) to UM members in which he cavalierly spoke of his vision of a worldwide theocracy to be created in part by such lobbying activities. A particularly good illustration of such stories can be seen in 1976 at the first "Dole hearing," and again during 1976-1978 when U.S. Representative Donald Fraser chaired a House Subcommittee on International Organizations investigating the UM's possible role in the "Koreagate" scandal (see Chapter 7). In 1976, for example, UM apostate Ann Gordon gave a detailed personal statement before Senators Robert Dole, James Buckley, and others in which she named both prominent legislators and the respective UM members assigned to lobby their offices as part of an effort to promote pro-South Korean foreign policy (particularly American economic/military aid). She stated of her own activities:

> In August of 1975 I was sent to Washington, D.C., at Moon's personal request, to do public relations work on Capitol Hill for him and for South Korea. The Washington P.R. Center has approximately 20-25 young men and women working full-time in this capacity. I, like all the others, was assigned a list of Senators and Congressmen which were to be my own contacts exclusively. . . . P.R. members were to make gradual acquaintances and friendships with staff members and aides and eventually with the Congressmen and Senators themselves, inviting them to a suite in the Washington Hilton rented at $54/day (although the normal rate should have been around $120/day), where dinner and films or short lectures on Moon's ideas and "accomplishments" would be presented. All this effort is sort of an ongoing program by Moon to get political support for himself and the Park Chung Hee dictatorship in South Korea [CEFM, 1976a: Vol. II, 3-5].

In 1976, Allan Tate Wood, UM apostate and former president of Moon's anti-communist Freedom Leadership Foundation, testified to the Fraser committee as to the "true" political aims of Moon (see U.S. Government, 1976: 20-42, 1978: 338-48). Typical of his many discrediting anecdotes was his account of establishing American Youth for a Just Peace, a UM-based, pro-Vietnam war lobbying group:

> MR. WOOD. We set up the American Youth for Just Peace to be a legitimate partisan political lobby organization to carry out prowar

activities. . . . We used Unification Church members. I called up all the heads of the Unification Church in May 1970 and invited them to come to Washington and bring with them as many members as they could. We gathered about 70 to 80 people, and we lobbied for a week, going out in teams of three to all Congressmen's and Senator's offices.

MR. FRASER. I asked you earlier about American Youth for a Just Peace. I understand they lobbied to support the Cambodian invasion. When that took place, was the Unification Church asked to help in some fashion?

MR. WOOD. It was Unification Church members who carried out the lobbying. I was president of the Freedom Leadership Foundation, and I was co-chairman of the American Youth for a Just Peace. Every staff member in that office was a member of the Unification Church, except Charles Stevens.

MR. FRASER. Were there instructions on that particular lobbying effort coming from Church authorities?

MR. WOOD. Yes.

MR. FRASER. From whom?

Mr. WOOD. Again, coming ultimately from Mr. Moon [U.S. Government, 1976: 36-37].

Chris Elkins, another high-level apostate, recounted for the Fraser committee details of his own UM-assigned participation in (among other activities) work for congressional candidates perceived as favorable to pro-South Korean policies:

MR. FRASER. Now you referred to the fact that you were assigned to work in a political campaign. When did that take place?

MR. ELKINS. This was in October 1974. . . . I was sent up to New York to participate in campaigns.

MR. FRASER. Who gave you the instructions to go to New York?

MR. ELKINS. Neil Salonen [President of the UM in America].

MR. FRASER. Neil Salonen?

MR. ELKINS. Yes.

MR. FRASER. Did he give them to you directly?

MR. ELKINS. Yes [U.S. Government, 1976: 51].

Elkins also testified as to general lobbying activities of the UM:

MR. FRASER. Let me ask you about this. You say that you, yourself sat up at night working on the automatic typewriter typing letters?

MR. ELKINS. Yes.

MR. FRASER. These would be directed to members of Congress?

MR. ELKINS. Yes.

MR. FRASER. The subject matter was what?

MR. ELKINS. Was concerning military aid.

MR. FRASER. Military aid to—?

MR. ELKINS. South Korea, particularly Southeast Asia, particularly if there was a bill up.

MR. FRASER. Where were these typewriters located?

MR. ELKINS. 2025 "I" Street which were FLF headquarters at that time [U.S. Government, 1976: 53].

Other Consequences of Deprogramming

There were a number of other consequences of deprogramming tangential to the thrust of this chapter but which nevertheless deserve mention. First, the new religions were forced to expend considerable resources in combating deprogramming. The new religions could not allow such raw assertions of power as deprogrammings to go unchallenged, and because law enforcement agencies frequently were ambivalent about initiating a felony prosecution out of what appeared to be a family dispute, legal action often was contingent on the victim and/or religious group beginning it. Further, deprogrammings occurred all over the country, employed varying degrees of force, potentially involved federal and (50 sets of) state statutes, and resulted in victims variously willing to take legal action against deprogrammers (particularly if their parents were legally implicated). This constant monitoring of numerous possible cases for legal action and following up such cases through the appeals process not only was costly but also diverted the movements from their primary goals to coping with harassment by the larger society.

Second, because deprogramming frequently involved legal proceedings and/or considerable publicity, it brought the new religions and anti-cultists into direct confrontation in a forum where the relative merits of their respective positions were opened more fully to public scrutiny. In such proceedings, which ranged from civil or criminal trials to mental competency hearings to participation in television talk shows, the new religions often found that, despite apparent abrogation of their legal rights, juries and audiences frequently sympathized and sided with parents. Thus, deprogrammings stimulated public debate of a kind that ultimately had the effect of further denigrating new religious movements.

Third, and finally, deprogrammings had a disquieting effect within new religious movements. On one hand, even if many parents had made no overt threats to deprogram their offspring, the deprogrammings of fellow members in an unpredictable fashion increased everyone's wariness. In this sense deprogramming actually contributed to family estrangement which, in turn, for reasons that should be obvious, increased the likelihood of deprogramming. Moreover, members were suspicious of local officials seeking to enforce fund-raising ordinances (for example, demanding fund-raisers' identities) who might be in complicity with parents of anti-cult associations and deprogrammers. Evasiveness made officials more hostile, which further served to increase new religious groups' defensiveness. On the other hand, every "successful" deprogramming was a symbolic blow to morale in various groups. The specter of former members now allied with the ACM and condemning the new religion with equal vehemence was understandably disheartening. Members of new religions were forced to believe either that deprogramming really was effective (which increased defensive measures) or that one's fellow members were not nearly as committed as they had appeared. In either case deprogramming had a corrosive effect on movement morale.

Summary

In this chapter we examined the primary functions and impacts of coercive deprogramming as a raw exertion of power within the American family institution. Three major factors, until now ignored in any attempt to unravel systematically the dynamics of deprogramming, determined the outcome of such confrontations between parents and offspring: (1) both sides in the disagreement brought different motives and interests to the situation; (2) deprogrammings were not identical in terms of family histories and conflicts, extent of parental objectives to "cult" member-ships, and offspring's feelings and opinions about the given "cult" lifestyle; and (3) there were a variety of possible options which parents and offspring could settle on as ends to the confrontation. Contrary to the deprogrammers' own inflated claims, there was no reliable, standard "therapeutic" deprogramming procedure that invariably "restored free thought" and "returned" offspring to their families. Rather, so-called successful deprogrammings were the emergent products of parents communicating their sincere, heartfelt fears, concerns, and love to offspring; the offspring's empathetic reaction to parental emotion as well as to their preexisting doubts about various aspects of their particular new religions; and the deprogrammers' intuitive abilities to pick up on and exploit these factors within the volatile parent-child confrontation.

Coercive deprogrammings had a number of effects on the fortunes of the new religions. Foremost was their immediate discrediting through the media by the production of apostates of the new religions. A number of coercively deprogrammed ex-"cult" members engaged in face-saving attempts to account for their period of membership in these deviant groups, and, prompted by deprogrammers (who had an interest in portraying themselves as valid "liberators" of a pernicious captivity) as well as parents (who also sought an extraordinary explanation for their offspring's questing in unconventional groups, yet wanted to avoid marking them with any permanent stigma), they recounted a fairly standard litany of horrors ranging from claims that they were manipulatively recruited and brainwashed into "cults" to various tales of deliberate family estrangement, deceptive fund-raising, and political conspiracy or illegal lobbying. By telling such stories, apostates absolved their families as well as themselves for any responsibility for their errant behavior and paid the price of contrition, thereby reentering the previously rejected community. Thus, the stories not only resolved the families' problem of explaining offspring's deviance, but through their "smoking gun" quality as eye-witness evidence they seriously discredited many new religions. There were other ancillary consequences of deprogramming, such as the wariness which colored the relations and communications of many new religions' members with their families, the damage to morale within groups such as the UM when seeing formerly dedicated comrades viciously condemning the group, the time spent with lawyers and courts over lawsuits to end deprogrammers' harassment, and the credibility of brainwashing allegations lent by apparently successful deprogrammings. Overall, the single most important effect of deprogramming was the creation of the apostate role and accompanying atrocity stories.

NOTES

1. Deprogrammers frequently underscored their intransigence by asserting that they would hold the deprogrammee as long as was required to break the bonds of mind control. Unquestionably, the prospect of indefinite inprisonment had a potent psychological effect on the deprogrammee. In fact, however, deprogrammings rarely lasted more than a few hours—a few days at most—and only a small number of cases of which we are aware dragged on for a period of weeks. Time was on the side of the deprogrammee, as families and deprogrammers could not financially afford lengthy "treatment"; legal charges of kidnapping or false imprisonment increased the longer an individual was forcibly held; the chances increased that a given religious group might discover where their member was being detained; and the likelihood of escape increased.

2. Poor diet could also be interpreted as gastronomic overkill to suit the point of the writer. Contrast the above examples of nutritional atrocities with the following excerpt from a nonapostate reporter who attended a UM weekend workshop: "The food—both in its contents and amounts—was an aid to conversion . . . French toast and syrup, scrambled eggs, fresh fruit corrupted with sour cream, condensed tomato soup made with milk and cheese instead of water, tacos, pineapple. The array of food always looked like a round-up of all the calories in the West" (Backes, 1977).

Chapter 7

THE IMPACT OF THE
ANTI-CULT ASSOCIATIONS

The nature and extent of the anti-cult associations' impact on the UM and other new religions can be understood in terms of the relative balance of power between the two sets of protagonists. This relative balance of power was determined essentially by each side's ability to enlist the support of allies with a sanctioning capacity; and the viability and durability of alliances, in turn, hinged on two factors: (1) the degree of convergence of interests between the anti-cult associations and those other groups which they sought as allies, and (2) the amount of influence that the anti-cult associations were able to exert on those groups from which they sought the imposition of sanctions on the new religions. As we indicated in Chapter 2, the American family institution was made up of innumerable individual units which had no ready means of coordinating action and no collective sanctions at their disposal. Therefore, groups of families, which comprised the backbone of the anti-cult associations, pursued alliance with numerous other institutions possessing greater sanctioning capacity.

In this chapter we shall examine in detail the nature and degree of support which the anti-cult associations were able to elicit from a broad range of American institutions. Specifically, we shall consider the religions, political, educational, legal/medical, economic, and mass media institutions. In each case we shall demonstrate that, first, the more directly an institution's interests were threatened by the new religions, the greater the support that institution extended to the anti-cult associations. In many cases the assistance rendered the anti-cultists was a by-product of these other institutions' defense of their own interests; in other cases anti-cult association members constituted a sizable enough segment of the respective institutions' constituencies to mobilize them to action. Second, we shall argue that the greater the influence the anti-cult associations were able to marshal vis-á-vis any institution, the more responsive that institution was to their requests for support. In general this meant that anti-cultists were more effective at a local level where their small numbers were more impressive and their grass-roots organizations could be more easily mobilized. However, we should also note that the anti-cult associations frequently were the recipients of greater sympathy and indulgence than would be predicted from their absolute size and power, largely due to common cultural biases and tradition shared by all parties involved. That is, officials in these various institutions, like anti-cult parents, had children of their own, often were members of mainline Christian denominations, and possessed middle-class orientations, lifestyles, and morality—all of which led to common predispositions and values at a personal level.

Media Impact

The source of the anti-cult associations' greatest support ultimately proved to be the media (newspapers, magazines, radio and television). While the media never formally took sides in this controversy, by the mid-1970s coverage of new religions in general varied between the skeptical (at best) and the outright hostile. The media supported the anti-cultists for two major reasons: (1) The anti-cultists created precisely the kind of sensational stories that piqued reader interest, and (2) media representatives by and large shared the same set of cultural assumptions and biases as did the families of members of the new religions.

The "cult"-anti-cult conflict contained a number of compelling ingredients that made for dramatic articles and spectacular headlines. As we demonstrated in the previous chapter, these themes included the agony of distraught parents who had "lost" their children, intimations of sexual and economic exploitation of youth by megalomaniac leaders, charges of foreign conspiracy and political subversion, and allegations of mind control and kidnapping. Correspondingly, stories of deprogramming included cloak-and-dagger elements of carefully planned and executed rescues, high speed chases by night, sprinklings of violence, and tearfully reunited families. As time went on such stories built on this set of sensational themes also came to include linkages of these specific events to national and international controversies such as Watergate, "Koreagate," and Jonestown. Once the link between these local stories and larger issues was forged, it became possible to repeat these otherwise fairly standard accounts of "outrageous incidents" as part of a continuing saga that sustained reader interest indefinitely.

However, the stories' sensational aspects alone did not account for their overall negative flavor. Rather, the valence of media reports was determined by a number of interacting factors. First, in many cases the families did not actively seek out reporters with their plights. Instead, when journalists made contact with them and/or anti-cult associations, what they encountered frequently were reputable but distraught middle-class citizens with no apparent "crank" axes to grind. When families held press conferences or contacted reporters, their stated motives of wanting simply to rescue their offspring and to warn other parents, youth, and the public at large had great prima facie validity. It was difficult for media representatives to believe that such apparently ordinary middle-class citizens would go to the lengths of jeopardizing in many cases their own careers, expending great amounts of time and money traveling around the country, and risking legal prosecution by having their offspring kidnapped and deprogrammed were their allegations indeed groundless. Such people were simply not regarded as ordinarily given to radical or extreme behavior except in crises. It seemed obvious to reporters that such people had little to gain by seeking publicity for publicity's sake and that therefore they must be sincere.

Second, when families recounted anecdotes about the predominantly authoritarian types of groups about which they were concerned and/or when reporters visited the latter (surreptitiously or otherwise) and saw for themselves the groups' totalistic tactics and unfamiliar rituals, the reporters tended to concur with the parents' negative assessments. Because journalists also tended to share the parents' own middle-class values and lifestyle aspirations, it was not surprising that they reacted similarly to the radical changes in dress, attitudes, and behavior.

After a point in the "cult"-anti-cult conflict, internal pressures within various media contributed to the amount of negative coverage accorded the new religions. Several factors contributed to what became a wave of anti-cult-oriented articles. First, once "cults" became a "story," every major publication appealing to potentially interested reader markets (teenagers and homemakers, for example), felt competitively obliged to run at least one token exposé of "cults." For example, magazines such as *McCalls* (Rasmussen, 1976), *Seventeen* (Remsberg and Remsberg, 1976), *Good Housekeeping* (Crittenden, 1976), and *People* (1978b) ran articles with titles such as "How Sun Myung Moon Lures America's Children," "Why I Quit the Moon Cult," "The Incredible Story of Ann Gordon and Reverend Sun Myung Moon," "A California Teenager Goes Undercover to Investigate Life Among Moonies." Each sought to outdo the others in finding a sensational story usually recounted by an apostate or parents whose children were still ensnared in a "cult." These stories created a wave of events that left the impression that "cults" were growing rapidly in size and that innocent children were being plucked off the streets and college campuses at an alarmingly increasing rate.

Second, most of the "cult" stories were printed in small community newspapers, although a smaller proportion of major daily papers in the United States carried such articles. Local papers did not possess the financial resources to assign a reporter exclusively to any "cult beat" or to cover stories taking place outside the immediate locale. Therefore, the average journalist did not have the time, resources, or knowledge to cover an issue as complex and controversial as religious innovation. Further, these newspapers obtained many of their stories via national wire services and therefore lacked the ability to validate the allegations contained in such articles. The authors encountered numerous instances where a story appeared in one location and was subsequently reprinted verbatim in newspapers across the nation (as indicated by the repetition of even specific typographical errors). This sequence, of course, raised the distinct possibility that stories which were superficially researched and published initially assumed through widespread publication the quality of a national-level rumor (on this actual pattern in journalism, see Epstein, 1975).

Third, there was pressure on individual investigative journalists to produce dramatic and even lurid stories from producers (at least in the electronic media), and likely such pressures from editors in newspapers and particularly magazines. For example, a number of publications sent "undercover" reporters to the UM's Booneville center or to other weekend workshops from which the most atrocity-laden reports of psychological manipulation were based. It was clear from the accounts which ensued that journalists had sought to sensationalize their reports to produce a more saleable story (see People, 1978b; Backes, 1977).[1] It was also clear that cub reporters dared not return to their managing editors after spending several days at a notorious UM workshop and report that there was no real story there or that the atmosphere resembled simply an encounter group or church retreat. In fact, several authors/reporters informed us that when they did report back colorless stories their editors/producers found means of rendering them more newsworthy.

Despite the fact that many of the new religions maintained a high profile in their witnessing/fund-raising activities, few Americans had not knowingly encountered their members in any other context. Most of what the average citizen "knew" about "cults," therefore, was obtained through stories reported by the media. For this reason the overwhelmingly negative quality of such reporting had a noticeable impact on the public at large. In one national poll of teenagers (PRRC, 1979: 71-2), for example, 41 percent said they had heard of Reverend Sun Myung Moon and the UM and 32 percent reported holding an unfavorable opinion of the movement. Such media reports of atrocities and allegations also affected the attitudes of representatives of various institutions (discussed in the remainder of this chapter) with whom members of the new religions came in contact. Thus, when institutional leaders deliberated over setting policies that might affect new religions or were confronted with requests for various services by them, one critical source of "data" upon which they drew was the large volume of almost exclusively negative media reports. The sheer volume of these, coupled with the fact that they were virtually impossible to refute, meant that representatives of the new religions faced a serious handicap at the outset of any attempts to obtain legitimacy.

Religious Impact

Support for the anti-cult associations varied substantially among various groups and denominations, but overall the anti-cultists enjoyed great direct support from various segments of the religious institution. As we pointed out in Chapter 2, fundamentalist Christian churches were most threatened by the rise of new religions, and it was from this quarter that the ACM received the most support. A number of fundamentalists from different churches formed coalitions on the local level (the most notable being the Spiritual Counterfeits Project) to discredit various "cults'" pretentions of being Christian and/or of being religious at all. Jews also responded harshly, primarily to the UM, because they perceived that certain parts of its doctrines smacked of anti-Semitism and because they believed the sacrosanct Jewish tradition of a strong family was being jeopardized by a disproportionate recruitment of Jewish youth into the UM and several other groups. Mainline denominations experienced a much lower level of threat and hence limited their support largely to statements deploring characteristics allegedly associated with "cults."

THE FUNDAMENTALIST/CONSERVATIVE
PROTESTANT RESPONSE

Fundamentalist and conservative Protestants were quick to brand sectarian Christian groups such as the UM and other movements as either heretical or outright satanic. A copious literature stretching back through this century and earlier exists condemning heresies and "cults" such as the Jehovah's Witnesses, the Church of Jesus Christ of Latter-Day Saints, Unitarians, and Christian Scientists (see Davies, 1972; Martin, 1965), and it required no great effort to expand the net of criticism to include the newer movements of the 1970s. However, it was imperative that they remove any suggestion that they condemned the UM and other groups solely out of any sectarian invidiousness or within the context of intramural religious competition for souls. This they most frequently did by reaffirming their support for the freedom of religious belief and simultaneously decrying "cults" as "pseudo-religions" operated by egomaniac charlatans for personal gain. Thus, one typical clergyman, a Lutheran minister who publicly denounced "cults," took care to locate his complaints in terms other than religious disagreement. He said: "That's what we're fighting. Religion-for-profit groups that we feel are using mind control techniques to manipulate people" (Gazette [Redwood Falls, Minn.], Sept. 23, 1976).

Fundamentalist and mainline Protestant churches engaged in three different activities that directly or indirectly lent support to anti-cult associations: (1) They granted such groups use of church facilities, primarily for meetings; (2) they published their own religiously oriented anti-cult literature; and (3) they sermonized on the dangers of cult involvement. Churches not infrequently donated their buildings to local anti-cult associations for monthly meetings. A perusal of monthly newsletters of groups such as the Individual Freedom Foundation in Trenton, Michigan, during the late 1970s illustrates this point. Likewise, a variety of denominations and ecumenical associations prepared "cult" workbooks, pamphlets, packages, and public statements that not only criticized various groups such as the UM, the Children of God, and the Hare Krishna for heresies but also frequently impunged their leaders' motives and characterized members' states of mind as possibly unstable. For example, readers are referred to the Pennsylvania Conference on Interchurch Cooperation (PCIC, n.d.) representing the Pennsylvania Council of Churches and the Pennsylvania Catholic Conference (distributed by the Omaha, Nebraska, anti-cult association Love Our Children, Inc.); a blend of religious and brainwashing themes presented in a pamphlet issued by URC (1979), an interfaith group composed of B'nai B'rith, the YWCA, Luterans, Catholics, and Episcopalians, which offered standard ACM claims of mental manipulation, postulated widespread vulnerability to "cult" appeals, and referred readers to books such as *Snapping* (Conway and Siegelman, 1978) and Stoner and Parke's (1977) *All Gods Children*; LCUSA (1978), from the Lutheran Council in the United States, and LCMS (1978), representing the Lutheran Church Missouri Synod; and a widely reprinted statement by the Korean Council of Christian Churches (Christian Beacon [Collingswood, N.J.], Sept. 9, 1976), a branch of the International Council of Christian Churches led by right-wing president Carl McIntire. (The northern United Presbyterian Church Assembly considered a number of "cults" and "para-Churches" in a general public policy statement [see Ft. Worth Star-Telegram, May 31, 1979] but the latter was more moderate, no doubt reflecting the denomination's more overall liberal orientation.)

A striking example of the literature produced by this conservative reaction to the new religions was Langford (1977), representing the (southern) Presbyterian Church in America, which offered one of the most systematic and sophisticated religiously oriented anti-cult workbooks, designed for teenagers, of this genre. It featured eye-catching illustrations, short (and pejorative) capsule descriptions of the major "cults" and their ideologies, and study guide questions, all laced profusely with New Testament references and citations of evangelical anti-cult literature for further reading. Langford advocated that individual congregations should set up ongoing programs to educate youth as to the dangers of "cults," including assigning at least one church member to take on the responsibility to acquaint him or herself with ACM literature and who would not only serve as resident expert on "cults" for church families but also make annual or semi-annual reports to the congregation "on what the cults are up to." In addition to providing such information, workbook packets such as Langford's frequently referred teachers to anti-cult associations such as the International Foundation for Individual Freedom Educational Trust and the Personal Freedom Foundation for further information, thus explicitly endorsing the latter's ideology.

The Spiritual Counterfeits Project of Berkeley, California, was the outstanding example of a fundamentalist religious organization engaged in a full-time attempt to discredit "cults" and for this reason could even be considered itself an anti-cult association. Founded in 1974 by Brooks and Debbie Alexander, Bill Squires, and David Fetcho, all of whom had been involved in youth ministries in the Campus Crusade for Christ, SCP originated in a campaign to oppose the spread of Transcendental Meditation in California, particularly in schools. It was sponsored largely by the Berkeley Christian Coalition (itself an outgrowth of the Christian World Liberation Front, which in turn had spun off from the Campus Crusade for Christ) and by 1976 was dedicated to countering what it regarded as the satanically inspired wave of "counterfeit religions."[2] The SCP perceived its ministry as embracing two aspects of "spiritual warfare":

(1) Primarily, to educate the Church at large regarding the Eastern religious and occult philosophies gaining increasing credibility and prominence, so as to enable Christians to deal effectively in situations requiring this type of understanding;
(2) Secondarily, to present the Good News to adherents of these religions and philosophies from a position informed as to their depth and intricacy, and hence to the subtlety of their error [SCP, 1976b].

The SCP published undoubtedly the most sophisticated monthly anti-cult newsletter in the United States during the 1970s. Whereas other ACM newsletters simply reprinted newspaper articles sprinkled with homespun editorials, the SCP newsletter featured serious examinations of specific "cults" that applied not only an informed orthodox Christian perspective but also criticized "cult" doctrines on the "cults' " own theological terms—minus the vulgar ethnocentrisms so characteristic of the deprogrammers and many anti-cultists. SCP workers presented lectures across the country and published a number of pamphlets in addition to sponsoring in-depth research on religious movements (Yamamoto, 1977). Their critiques became reference materials which were used by other Christian groups wishing to "expose" marginal religions (for example, by the LCMS, 1978, in constructing their own anti-cult packet, according to a June 1978 communication to the authors by that group's Commission on Organizations' Executive Secretary).

The most important way in which fundamentalist attacks on the new religions served the interests of the anti-cult associations was by lending credibility to the contention that the new religions were not religions at all but rather were politically or economically inspired. Of course, the fact that the large total membership of fundamentalist churches shared the anti-cult associations' quest for investigation and exposure of the new religions as fraudulent provided anti-cultists with their largest single group of sympathizers. Although the fundamentalists explicitly rejected the deprogramming solution, the fact that the anti-cult associations and deprogrammers were at least nominally distinct allowed the preservation of the alliance. Each side essentially ignored its points of difference with the other.

THE JEWISH/ROMAN CATHOLIC RESPONSE

The strident condemnation of "cults," in particular the UM, by national and regional Jewish organizations (ordinarily the strongest defenders of religious pluralism) can be understood, first, in terms of a historical emphasis on defending strong familial values of Judaism itself and, second, with regard to perennial Jewish concerns about anti-Semitism. Thus, Jewish support of the ACM was indirect in the sense that it constituted defense of traditional but practical Jewish interests and not direct support of the ACM itself. Perceived threats to the solidarity and integrity of Jewish families constituted one of the few strains in which that religion's traditional support for civil liberties could be overridden. The conviction that Jews were disproportionately represented in "cults," specifically in the UM, was widespread among anti-cultists and became almost an obsession for some Jewish ACM spokespersons. Thus, long-time ACM activist Rabbi Maurice Davis was cited in Stoner and Parke (1977: 297) as indicating that Jews constituted 10 percent of "Moonies"; in other press reports he claimed 15 percent and higher. New York social worker William Goldberg estimated that 40 percent of UM members were Jewish (Fort Worth Star-Telegram, Feb. 10, 1979). Others, such as "Moonie" apostates Paul Engel (Patent Trader [Mt. Kisco, N.Y.], Aug. 5, 1976) and Chris Edwards (News Tribune [Woodbridge, N.Y.], Feb. 3, 1977), and Individual Freedom Foundation secretary Elaine Liberman (Jewish Post and Opinion, [Indianapolis], Jan. 7, 1977), freely provided figures of 20 to 40 percent, 50 percent, and 30 percent Jewish "Moonie" members, respectively.

However, actual surveys done by others, specifically Judah (personal communication, 1977) and ourselves (Bromley and Shupe, 1979b), found the proportion of Jews in the UM to be about the same as that minority's share of the total national population (around three percent). In 1976 the UM sponsored its own internal survey conducted by a social worker which found 5.3 percent of its 3000 members (many of whom were New Yorkers) to be former Jews, a figure slightly (but not outrageously) above Jews' actual proportion of the national American population. Nevertheless, the matter of realistic numbers of Jews involved in the UM aside, the perception by Jewish leaders of their youth being particularly "preyed" upon by "cult" recruiters and thereby threatening the continuity of Jewish families was sufficient to evoke denuciations of "cults" by Jewish groups. Jews for Jesus, an evangelical/fundamentalist ministry prevalent on major college campuses, was regarded as a particularly insidious, subversive group.

Charges of anti-Semitism were aimed almost exclusively against the UM. One of the most widely publicized attacks on the UM came in 1976 from Rabbis Marc Tanenbaum and James Rudin of the American Jewish Committee. Calling the UM's *Divine Principle* "a breeding ground for fostering anti-Semitism," Rudin claimed to have uncovered more than 125 examples of "anti-Jewish teachings" in its text. Wrote Rudin in a report to the AJC: "Because of his [Moon's] unrelieved hostility toward Jews and Judaism, a demonic picture emerges from the pages of his major work. One can only speculate on what negative and anti-Jewish impact *Divine Principle* may have upon a follower of Rev. Moon."

Rudin particularly bristled at the UM's doctrine that Jesus' crucifixion was the direct consequence of his rejection by the ancient Jews, an act which supposedly accounted for their dispersion and persecution for the past twenty centuries, including the Nazi holocaust (an anti-Semitic doctrine, he was quick to point out, currently repudiated by the National Council of Churches as well as Vatican II). Rudin noted 36 references to "faithless" Israelites, 65 references to Jewish hostility toward Jesus, and 26 "viciously anti-Jewish" references that cited Jewish suffering as atonement for rejecting Jesus. Tanenbaum, director of the AJC's interreligious affairs department, announced his intention to send the report to congressmen as well as the Justice Department so that they might be aware of its accusations during the "Koreagate" investigations of the House Subcommittee on International Organizations (see, for example, San Francisco Monitor, Dec. 9, 1976). This prompted UM public affairs personnel and even UM president Neil Salonen to issue statements claiming Rudin's report to be a misinterpretation of Moon's doctrines, a pamphlet "correcting" this "misinterpretation" (Moon, 1976), and even a full-page advertisement in the New York *Times* denying that Moon was anti-Semitic.

At times Jewish critics of the UM were joined by Catholic spokespersons and even Protestant leaders, although the attacks of the latter two groups were much milder in character because their interests were less directly threatened. In early 1977, one year after the Rudin-Tanenbaum press conference to announce the AJC report, Tanenbaum and Rudin met at news conference with the Reverend James J. LeBar, County Coordinator of the Office of Communication, Archdiocese of New York, and Dr. Jorge Lara-Braud, Executive Director of the Commission on Faith and Order, National Council of Churches of Christ, to denounce the UM as "anti-Jewish, anti-Christian and anti-democratic." Commented LeBar: "It is important to bear in mind that Rev. Moon's teachings are in direct conflict with Catholic theology and, therefore, render his movement suspect for Catholic participation" (The Catholic News [N.Y.], Jan. 6, 1977). Tanenbaum called for Moon to show his professed love for Jewish people and the Judeo-Christian tradition by a "comprehensive and systematic removal of negative and hostile references to Jews and Judaism and to Christians and Christianity which abound in the Divine Principle." In response, UM spokespersons again claimed that their doctrines were misconstrued. Herbert Richardson, a Canadian theologian and part-time faculty member at the Unification Theological Seminary, charged that such attacks by responsible mainline religious leaders lent respectability to the deprogrammers who illegally abducted and harassed UM members (The Catholic News [N.Y.], Jan. 6, 1977).

There were instances on the local level when church groups undertook stronger actions going beyond mere educational efforts in "combating cults." (AFT, 1977). In such cases local ministers, priests, or rabbis, for a variety of reasons, took strong personal positions on the "cult"-anti-cult conflict. In many church hierarchies, either formally or informally, it was possible for local leaders to exercise considerable autonomy. For example, the Council of Churches of Greater Bridgeport, Connecticut, released a unanimous resolution urging the State Government Administration and Policy Commission to investigate the UM's activities in that state, a move not paralleled by similar resolutions from the clergymen's respective national denominations (The Bridgeport Post, Feb. 10, 1977). Indeed, these more aggressive campaigns were not translated into similar national-level campaigns.

Governmental Impact

Efforts of anti-cult groups to enlist the support of public officials occurred at local, state, and federal levels. In general, the few legal/political sanctions which anti-cult associations successfully mobilized against the new religions were imposed at the local level where anti-cult organizations were strongest. A number of locally based initiatives against the "cults" were not supported by organizational counterparts at state or national level, and thus such initiatives never really assumed the quality of an orchestrated campaign against the new religions. The imposition of sanctions at the state and national levels was much less successful, because there never was any substantial imminent threat posed by the small, autonomous new religious groups to state and federal governments. Where there was a potential threat to the latter, as in the cases of "Koreagate" and Jonestown, they vigorously defended their own interests but offered only limited assistance to the anti-cultists. At the same time, however, state and federal governments did provide anti-cult associations with some symbolic support. This was largely in the form of linking government legitimacy with anti-cultists' values through use of public buildings for meetings, formal or informal hearings and investigations, and statements of support by prominent political leaders. This symbolic support should not be underestimated, as it performed an important reinforcement function for anti-cultists and undermined the legitimacy which new religious groups sought so desperately. Such symbolic support lent to the anti-cult associations also increased the difficulty of obtaining public donations upon which many new religions relied for financial resources. In essence, the indictments implicit in such hearings and investigations shifted the burden of proof from the anti-cult associations to demonstrate that new religions were unscrupulous pseudo-religions to the new religions to prove their innocence of such allegations.

LOCAL EFFORTS

Locally, anti-cultists managed to sustain intermittent harassment of "cult" fund-raising and proselytization teams and make life difficult for local centers or chapters of such groups as the Hare Krishna and the UM. Such "spot" harassment came in the form of anti-cultists goading town or city officials to apply solicitation statutes originally instituted to control peddlers and vagrants, convincing local municipal councils to pass new ordinances requiring more complicated charitable solicitation application procedures (such as having to supply organizational records, budget information, and so forth), and arranging for repeated zoning violation/public health "inspections." In the most extreme examples, which were relatively few in number, fund-raisers were temporarily jailed or escorted to the edge of town by police; rifle shots and damaging of nets and fishing lines even reportedly occurred in Gloucester, Massachusetts, when the UM began its entry into the fishing business (personal communication, 1979; see also later in this chapter).

The success anti-cult associations achieved at the local level was a product both of the stronger representation of their interests at this level and of backing by other affected community groups. In particular, local charities resented seeing local charitable dollars siphoned out of the community by national groups of dubious purpose and the increased difficulty in general fund-raising due to mistrust of public fund-raisers engendered by these groups. Thus, for example, the authors on numerous occasions encountered fundraisers from local fraternal and civic organizations wearing prominently displayed disclaimers that read "I am *not* a Moonie!" Local civil and fraternal fund-raisers could support the tightening of fund-raising ordinances, correctly perceiving that such ordinances would be selectively enforced by law officials and hence that their own interests would not be seriously threatened.

Nevertheless, efforts to mobilize public officials on a permanent or ongoing basis, particularly against fund-raisers, enjoyed only limited success for three basic reasons. First, many "cult" units, chapters, or teams were highly mobile, typically traveling cross-country with a minimum of personal possessions in buses or vans. When they temporarily stopped in motels (as did the UM International One World Crusade team which we studied for four weeks in the Dallas-Fort Worth Metroplex and then in Houston, Texas—see Bromley and Shupe, 1979b) or at their group's local center while soliciting funds and new members locally, the community usually could only begin to be aroused by ACM activists by the time the group had moved on. While some social contexts were frequently canvassed by fund-raisers and recruiters, usually areas of high potential donor/ recruit turnover such as urban city street corners, airports, and college campuses, many communities rarely saw the "cults" except on an irregular, impromptu basis. Second, despite ACM statistical claims to the contrary, the small absolute membership of most new religions coupled with their sporadic appearances meant that they posed more of a short-term nuisance to local magistrates than any permanent problem to be continually confronted. "Cults," in other words, were simply not that visible to authorities.

Finally, groups such as the UM and the Hare Krishna were not loathe to press for what they claimed were their First Amendment rights of religious expression: that is, that fund-raising was a fundamental sacramental activity. As we noted in our earlier study of the UM (see Bromley and Shupe, 1979a; also Bromley and Shupe, 1980a), restrictions on fund-raising that discriminated against new religious groups by excessively hampering their fund-raising activities were challenged in court, almost always to the advantage of the religious groups. As federal Judge Earl E. O'Connor in Kansas City ruled in such a case:

> It is a well established law that distribution of literature and solicitation of funds to support a religious organization are well within the protection of the First Amendment [The Kansas City Times, April 15, 1978].

Thus, it was the practice of the UM, for example, to select strategic municipalities which then became "test cases" or precedents for entire regions:

> Despite the fact that the UM consistently won such cases, municipal officials were likely to obstruct fund-raising activities until legal action was threatened. In order to avoid the prospect of countless suits against every local government, which would arouse continuing negative media coverage and involve substantial commitments of UM members' time and energy, the UM adopted a strategy of suing one municipality in an area as an example to its neighbors. If the municipality did not acquiesce it was threatened with suit for punitive or compensatory damages as well as legal fees incurred. . . . In general once the locality agreed to "reasonable" solicitation requirements the UM simply dropped the suit in order to avoid producing further ill will [Bromley and Shupe, 1979a: 233-234].

While fund-raisers were often required to carry or wear identification badges and refrain from touching passers-by or obstructing persons on sidewalks or cars at intersections, the courts invariably ruled that local municipalities could not arbitrarily decide on their own to prohibit new religions' members from fund-raising. That issue having been largely decided by the late 1970s, there was very little remaining leverage which local communities, at the anti-cult associations' behest, could bring to bear in seeking to restrain such groups' activities. The extent to which informal arrangements between anti-cultists and law enforcement/public officials continued is, of course, another matter.[3]

Although no single municipality was able to impede the UM's overall activities (or those of the Hare Krishna sect and other groups) because of its mobility and national-level organizational thrust, the sum of ongoing local anti-cult campaigns did have a significant cumulative impact. In the case of the UM, for example, it was forced to divert time, energy, and money away from movement goals in order to deal with the innumerable conflicts. Despite the fact that the UM was successful in appealing legal restrictions on its fund-raising/witnessing endeavors, the very fact that there were literally hundreds of communities attempting to so restrict their activities was a serious drain on resources. Further, top UM officials were forced to spend considerable time allaying public suspicion and fear about potential UM land or business purchases (see the business section of this chapter). Finally, UM officials had to be constantly on the alert for impending hearings, injunctions, lawsuits, or bills at the local or state levels and spend considerable time in defending themselves against a wide range of allegations in conjunction with many legal/political actions.

STATE EFFORTS

The anti-cult associations were less successful in mobilizing substantive sanctions at the state level than they had been locally, but they did manage to achieve a number of symbolic victories through which new religions were denigrated and discredited. Anti-cult organizations were able to exert influence on district representatives to the state legislatures in somewhat the same fashion as they influenced local officials. Usually, such local officials, in response to pressures from a broad range of interest groups or constituents, were willing to initiate special committees to hold public hearings on issues of concern, but these did not imply or involve any formal endorsement by the legislatures as a whole. Legislators thus allowed each other to respond to one anothers' respective constituents' interests and, as long as no formal legislation was involved, offered no opposition to initiatives that they could not have supported as legislative bills. (It should also be observed that very often hearings were initiated by legislators who were personal friends of parents who had "lost" their children to "cults," and hence committee initiatives really constituted personal favors.) While in one sense the foregoing observations constitute elementary political science, nevertheless, the fact that anti-cult leaders interpreted such actions as constituting real support suggests the true extent of their political naivete.

The first organized state response to anti-cult grievances of which we are aware occurred in August 1974 and was organized by the Volunteer

Parents of America (which shortly after was dissolved and reborn as the Citizens Freedom Foundation). Held in the Los Angeles area, the one-day hearing at which parents and apostates presented complaints against "cults" was chaired by State Senator Mervyn Dymally of the Senate Select Committee on Children and Youth in order "to determine whether legislation was needed to deal with alleged instances of teenagers being 'brainwashed' into joining some cults" (CFF, 1974a).

That same year the Charity Frauds Bureau of the state of New York issued its "Final Report on the Activities of the Children of God" to the state's attorney general Louis J. Lefkowitz. This report had resulted from a directive from Governor Nelson Rockefeller to the attorney general's office in February 1973 "to investigate and determine the extent of the various activities of an organization known as Children of God as its activities affect the public peace and safety" (New York, 1975: 1). Relying on 74 interviews with angry parents, former members of COG, various informed "experts," and half a dozen subpoenaed COG members as well as COG publications and communications concerning COG with attorney generals in the other 49 states, the report presented a highly critical account of the group's organization and finances, recruitment/indoctrination practices, and beliefs (referring to these as "twisted COG doctrines"). It charged COG with obstruction of justice, violation of earlier selective service laws (draft evasion), brainwashing ("tampering with personalities") and physical coercion of members, sexual improprieties, and anti-Semitism. Although no further formal action regarding COG was taken, there nevertheless was some impact from the issuance of such an official state report. The report was widely disseminated and became a standard reference source on the Children of God for anti-cultists as well as other officials contemplating investigations throughout the decade.

Such hearings and the consideration of resolution by state legislatures to either investigate the "cult" problem or more closely examine the statutes governing activities of vital importance to such groups (such as charitable fund-raising) became more frequent as the 1970s progressed. In the next chapter we will deal in greater detail with the flood of such legislative actions that followed in the aftermath of the People's Temple tragedy in Jonestown, Guyana. There were others, however, which antedated that reaction. Texas, for example, saw several (unsuccessful) attempts to form special committees to investigate "cults," inspired largely by an intense lobbying campaign by Dallas and San Antonio anti-cult activists (Texas, 1977). Vermont's Senate established a special Committee for the Investigation of Alleged Deceptive, Fraudulent and Criminal Practices of Various Organizations in the State in July 1976 and held five days of hearings. The committee focused on alleged "fraudulent fund raising activities . . . mental and emotional subjugation of citizens, and possible violations of tax laws providing preferential treatment to charitable organizations" (Vermont, 1977: 1). Its targets involved a familiar set of "cults"; the UM, the Hare Krishna, and the Children of God. Testimonies ranged from parents, apostates, and sympathetic professionals (including Harvard psychiatrist John G. Clark, Jr., whose widely reprinted testimony against new religions eventually became a staple in the anti-cult movement's brainwashing ideology) to a dozen UM members and officials.

Similar hearings followed elsewhere; in a few cases specific legislation was proposed and even occasionally passed. The Minnesota legislature (Minnesota, 1978), for example, passed an amendment to its laws on charitable solicitation to "tighten up" such requirements. This was the only area in which any legislation was ever produced, however, and even then it had virtually no "teeth" to affect "cults." The failure of the anti-cultists to achieve passage of bills outside of solicitation issues was classically illustrated by what was indisputably the most extreme attempt at legislating social constraints: proposed bill AB9566-A of the New York State Asembly. New York State, where the UM had its national headquarters, seminary, newspaper and printing houses, Reverend Moon's private residence, and many of its American members, witnessed undoubtedly an inordinate share of anti-cult activity. In 1977 New York Assemblyman Robert Wertz (a prominent example of an official who became involved in ACM activities through having a close friend's son join The Way) introduced bill AB9566-A to amend the state's penal law with a new section entitled "Promoting a Pseudo-Religious Cult." The bill aimed to make promoting such a "cult" a felony. The proposed amendment read as follows:

A person is guilty of promoting a pseudo-religious cult when he knowingly organizes or maintains an organization into which other persons are induced to join or participate in through the use of mind control methods, hypnosis, brainwashing techniques or other systematic forms of indoctrination and in which the members or participants of such organization engage in soliciting funds primarily for the benefit of such organization or its leaders and are not permitted to travel or communicate with anyone outside such organization unless another member or participant of such organization is present [New York, 1977].[4]

The bill failed in 1978 because of its obvious unworkability and dubious constitutionality, a fact driven home to legislators through a vigorous countercampaign against it led by persons associated with the American Civil Liberties Union and various new religious groups (predominant among these, of course, the UM). After Jonestown, however, the idea was to be revived by anti-cultists.[5]

FEDERAL EFFORTS

Since their earliest days, the anti-cult associations attempted to levy influence at the federal level; however, here even the achievement of symbolic victories largely eluded them (with the exceptions of the 1976 "Dole hearings" discussed in Chapter 4 and the 1979 "Dole hearings" examined in the following chapter).[6] In fact, the only instances in which the anti-cultists received any substantive assistance for their cause from the federal government occurred when congressional committees pursued investigations directed at defending specific governmental interests during the "Koreagate" scandal and after the Jonestown tragedy. Anti-cult associations were able to gain some entree to official forums; however, in each case their testimonies were limited to specific matters, and hence they could not voice their wider concerns. For example, as early as 1974, the Los Angeles Chapter of the Volunteer Parents of America instructed members to write Speaker of the House of Representatives Carl Albert and urge him to meet with deprogrammer Ted Patrick who was planning to visit the nation's capitol. (The meeting never took place, and Patrick subsequently served time in jail for an unsuccessful deprogramming.) VPA's January newsletter variously mentioned the coordination of signatures for petitions to be sent to Washington requesting congressional investigation of "cults" and a lobbying visit by one of its members, Robert Chalenor, to some congressmen presenting complaints that "cults" were abusing welfare and food stamp eligibility (VPA, 1974).

As we pointed out earlier, the 1976 "Dole hearings" raised the expectation of ACM supporters that at last concerted national-level action would be taken. Thereafter, their lobbying efforts increased, but their record was largely one of a succession of failures to obtain either substantive *or* symbolic victories. In 1976 Representative Robert Giaimo and 23 other congressional colleagues, at the prompting of anti-cult associations' petitioning activities, requested the Department of Justice to meet with Dr. Robert J. Lifton, internationally recognized psychiatric expert on brainwashing, and Richard Delgado, an outspoken anti-cult legal expert, in order to consider allegations that many new religions were holding members against their wills. The Department of Justice demurred.[7] Again, in 1977, 53 congressmen and a senator urged newly appointed U.S. Attorney General Griffin Bell to investigate charges of brainwashing by "cults" brought by parents' groups, but again the government refused to act (Ft. Worth Star-Telegram, Feb. 25, 1977).

As Chapter 6 stressed, anti-cult associations were to become frustrated at the lack of follow-up from the federal government. The civil liberties complications of moving against new religions could not be dismissed as easily as the anti-cult spokespersons might have wished. The realization that this was the case did not come about abruptly; indeed, at the start of the next decade, anti-cultists still held out hope that the government would eventually recognize the "cult menace" and act accordingly. This prolonged optimism can be explained not only by the vaguely sympathetic, courtesy audiences periodically extended to their ACM constituents by legislators, but also by two specific, highly publicized investigations by congressional committees which were not inspired by but which touched the concerns of the ACM: the "exposure" of UM activities in the context of the "Koreagate" scandal of 1977-1978, and the examination of factors contributing to the murder of Congressman Leo J. Ryan at Jonestown, Guyana in 1978. The latter investigation is discussed in the following chapter; here we consider only the former.

On February 3, 1977, the House Subcommittee on International Organizations, chaired by Rep. Donald M. Fraser, received authorization from the House Committee on International Relations to "conduct a full and complete investigation and study of . . . all aspects of the political, military, intelligence, economic, educational, and informational relationships between the Republic of Korea and . . . the United States" (U.S. Government, 1978: 3). Thus began the official congressional investigation of "Koreagate," an international scandal in which a number of South Korean agents and diplomats were accused or suspected of paying bribes to U.S. officials for continued support of economic/military aid to that Asian country. As became clear from media reports, the potential scope of the scandal was immense. Amid the various individuals and organizations caught up in the allegations appeared Sun Myung Moon and his UM. Moon's strident anti-communism and his past aggressive courting of congressional and even presidential good will—ostensibly to remind the nation's leaders of their moral obligations but also clearly to keep money, arms, and troops flowing into South Korea—and the UM's past ties to a number of persons and groups implicated in the bribery charges made Moon and his movement a logical target for congressional scrutiny.

The anti-cult associations were, of course, delighted at the UM's entanglement in "Koreagate." An official, well-publicized, bipartisan investigation by the nation's highest law-making body of the purportedly most influential, wealthiest "cult" had been set in motion without taxing the slim resources of the associations. The anti-cult associations attempted, however, to take a more active role in the investigation rather than simply sitting on the sidelines and cheering the government forward. They did this in two ways. First, they encouraged former UM members who claimed to have acted in specifically political roles (for example, those assigned to lobby congressmen for South Korean aid or to work for pro-Korean congressional candidates) while in the movement to testify before the Fraser committee. Apostates such as Chris Elkins came forward and offer their accounts of such experiences in sufficient detail to embarrass the UM.

The second active form of involvement for anti-cultists during the Fraser hearings came when UM official Dan Fefferman refused to cooperate in disclosing certain information about the UM to Fraser's House Subcommittee. Soon after, a new anti-cult association called the Ad Hoc Committee of Concerned Citizens surfaced in Lexington, Massachusetts, and coordinated a national effort funded by anti-cult groups to have Congress vote a citation of contempt for Fefferman. Such a move, they reasoned, would strike a devastating blow at the UM's public relations and encourage further investigation of the movement.

To this end, a Boston attorney with lobbying experience, Francis J. O'Rourke, was hired and assigned to contact personally 50 members of Congress, particularly those involved in the Fraser committee's investigations or those sympathetic to the ACM, urging prosecution for Fefferman. This lobbying effort was accomplished in three "waves," the first initiated in fall 1977 when O'Rourke briefed those congressmen's staff members on the progress and importance of the Fraser committee's actions. During the congressional recess that winter, a second "wave," consisting of follow-up calls and letters to those officials by individual anti-cultists nationwise, occurred. Finally, in February 1978, O'Rourke returned to Washington in order to push for support for a vote by the entire House of Representatives to cite Fefferman for contempt (O'Rourke, 1978; also participant observation notes, 1977).

Ultimately, such a vote of contempt never materialized, though the subcommittee (which included Leo J. Ryan) did recommend it to the full

House. During the entire length of the investigations, however, the anti-cult associations were absorbed (judging by conversations and the space in newsletters devoted to the subject) in following the progress of the subcommittee, positively gloating at the public embarrassment and defensiveness which the UM experienced, and struggling to achieve the symbolic victory of having Fefferman cited for contempt. Their failure on this last point is indicative of the anti-cult associations' general lack of success in dealing with the federal government. The Fraser committee's investigation was thorough: bank records were subpoenaed, for example, revealing Moon's intimate role in decision-making within the movement and "laundering" of large amounts of money. However, the focus of the investigation was narrower than the earlier "Dole hearing," and UM apostates who came forward to tell atrocity tales about their political roles and connections with the UM could not ramble over the standard long list of horror stories. What information they did give was discrediting, but only within a specific area of governmental interest. Moreover, those who testified were expected to produce evidence and/or concrete details of their experiences; the subcommittee's format was more critical than the "gripe session" atmosphere of the "Dole hearing." Most UM apostates did not previously have access to such politically sensitive information so as to be much use as witnesses in the investigation. In the end, after a long string of testimonies, subpoenaed records and documents, and discrediting facts had been amassed, little beyond continuing to monitor Moon's various organizations could be done officially. Despite talk of the "numerous violations" revealed by the committee, none seemed serious and certainly none moved any federal agency to prosecute or investigate the UM further.

Despite the meager returns for their efforts, the anti-cult associations did not abandon their lobbying efforts. For example, the American Family Foundation, a New England-based group whose primary function was to amass and disseminate information on legislative hearings, scientific research, and other pertinent news related to the anti-cult movement, announced in its September 1979 issue of its newsletter *The Advisor* that it had sent copies to over 1000 government officials, including all U.S. Senators and Representatives, all state governors, attornies-general and leaders of state assemblies and senates, and to over 200 mayors and selected professionals (AFF, 1979c). Likewise, the more recently formed Citizens Freedom Foundation—Information Service urged members in November 1979 to send 1000-word essays to the White House to request that the "cult problem" be addressed at the upcoming White House Conference on the Family to be held in Seattle, Washington, in January

1980. Clearly, the members of anti-cult association continued to hold out for an eventual stronger impact.

Educational Impact

Since most of the individuals joining new religions were young adults, anti-cult associations naturally attempted to deny these groups access to campuses and sought to impress educators in daily contact with young adults of the dangers of "cults." The anti-cult associations were relatively successful in excluding the new religions from gaining access to the educational system because their interests coincided at that point with the interests of educational administrators: Neither wished to see young adults diverted from conventional career trajectories into communal, world-transforming movements. Anti-cultists were less successful in influencing academic researchers, since the latter were so diverse in professional orientation. Nevertheless, they managed to amass enough academic allies to lend credibility to their brainwashing ideology and to serve as legitimating figures in the ACM.

Though the opportunity did not often present itself, anti-cult activists aggressively and fairly successfully resisted encroachment of the new religions into the educational system. One well-publicized example occurred when an intense lobbying effort during 1976-1977 directed at the New York State Board of Regents (and to state legislative politicians, who in turn put pressure on the Board of Regents) ultimately resulted in denial of a state charter for the UM's Unification Theological Seminary in Barrytown, New York (necessary for its accreditation). This denial was a serious setback for the UM in its campaign to achieve legitimacy. Without the state charter the seminary could not be accredited by professional associations, grant degrees or credits transferrable to other schools, obtain educational visas for foreign students, apply for various types of educational loans, or even make its faculty eligible for some pension plans (see Bromley and Shupe, 1979a: 234). In another case in 1977, the New Jersey Department of Education had disbursed over $40,000 in federal grants for Transcendental Meditation programs to be started in five New Jersey public schools. A number of individual Protestant and Catholic plaintiffs as well as several ACM groups (Americans United, the Coalition for Religious Integrity, and the Spiritual Counterfeits Project) which claimed TM was essentially Hinduism (and therefore religion), protested. On

October 19, the U.S. District Court for the District of New Jersey ruled that it was unconstitutional to use such monies for the advancement of religion, a clear victory for the anti-cult associations involved (personal interviews, 1977).

By the late 1970s anti-cultists began seeking to influence larger audiences. During much of the decade, most of such efforts had been focused at the local community level with anti-cult association spokespersons appearing before Parent Teacher Association groups and public school faculty meetings, protesting to college and university officials when various "cult" groups appeared on campus, and even contacting various academics whose research did not reflect ACM ideology (to which we and various of our colleagues can attest). After 1976, however, a national level perspective began to emerge. A resolution on "Pseudo-religious Cults" issued by the International Foundation for Individual Freedom in spring 1978 was sent to the National Parent Teacher Association's annual convention in Atlanta, Georgia, after extensive letter-writing and telephone calls to local, regional, and national PTA officials. The resolution called for the national PTA to establish seminar "workshops" and programs to educate young persons about new religious movements as well as to have them join in petitioning the federal government to investigate a number of religious groups (IFIF, 1978). That the PTA's 900 chapter delegates to the national convention approved the resolution can probably be attributed to the fact that the PTA is a family-based organization dominated by parents and thus was a natural ally for the ACM. Typical of the initial statewide response were the actions of the New York State PTA (300,000 members strong) which organized a campaign to warn school children about "negative influences" and "dangers" to family life from the UM (singled out as the primary nemesis). Local PTA groups were to organize workshops about the UM for parents and children and to coordinate statewise mailings of anti-cult material (CFF, 1977).

One strategy employed by various anti-cult spokespersons to "spread the word" was to seek out regional meetings of professional teacher associations and arrange to reserve a room or suite in a motel or hotel for a one-hour presentation on "cults." Such sections often drew large audiences which, because of their previous unfamiliarity with either "cults" or any "cult problems," were predictably shocked by what they heard. In the fall of 1979, one of the authors attended such a session (which began at 8 a.m. but played to a standing-room-only crowd) of home economics teachers from high schools, junior colleges, and colleges around the state of Texas. Before over 200 female teachers, a Dallas-Fort

Worth Metroplex panel that included Alan Tate Wood, author of the just-released anti-UM tract *Moonstruck* (Wood and Vitek, 1979), and several angry parents plus a psychologist sympathetic to the ACM first showed a print of an NBC report that originally appeared on the program "Weekend" and was hardly complementary to the UM. One of the parents stressed his estrangement from his daughter and the grief it had caused his family. A lawyer, he deplored the impotence of conventional legal channels to aid him in her recovery. Wood offered a discourse on his days as Moonie leader, titillating sexual innuendos about Moon, and the ominous intimation that he still might be the target of UM reprisals. The psychologist followed suit by presenting a series of statements legitimizing the mind-control argument. The aroused and horrified audience alternately sighed disapprovingly, moaned in sympathy for the parents, requested further information, and at the end flocked around Wood for his autograph and/or the address to write for his book.

Another gauge of the more widespread impact of the anti-cult associations on the new religions through the educational institution was the effectiveness with which ACM groups set the agenda for the discussion of new religions. Rather than focusing on new religions' concerns about moral decay and alternative visions of the future, the anti-cultists managed to shift the debate largely to questions of brainwashing, financial exploitation, and political conspiracy. For instance, after 1977, professional societies of academics clearly recognized the importance of the "cult" controversy. Many included as part of their annual conventions seminars, symposia, and even plenary sessions on the topics of new religions, conversions, and deprogramming. Among these societies were the American Sociological Association, the Religious Research Association, the Association for the Sociology of Religion, the Society for the Scientific Study of Religion, the American Academy of Religion, the American Psychological Association, and the American Psychiatric Association (plus a multitude of its state/regional affiliates). The plethora of scientific sociological and psychological studies by researchers in social and behavioral science disciplines, as exemplified by our bibliography in this volume alone, should also be evident. Moreover, awareness of the possible implications of the participation of academics in the UM's lavishly funded annual International Conferences on the Unity of Science (founded and presided over each year by Moon himself) became an issue to which they became sensitized, not only because of a polemic article on the subject by Horowitz (1977) in *The Atlantic Monthly* but also by the efforts of anti-cultists who attempted to obtain advance lists of past and future participants in order to personally dissuade the latter from attending (personal interviews, 1977).

Anti-cult associations' indirect impact could be seen elsewhere. In August 1979, we visited the book exhibit of the annual meeting of the Association for the Sociology of Religion and found displayed a mimeographed booklet authored by two academics and entitled "Kids in Cults" (Doress and Porter, 1977) with an anti-deprogramming bent. Likewise, *The Chronicle of Higher Education* (Middleton, 1979) contained an article on CARP (the Collegiate Association for the Research of Principles, the UM's college-level recruitment organization) which sensationally overestimated the extent of UM involvement in an "invasion" of campus communities. Such estimates reflected more the near-hysteria of large numbers characteristic of the anti-cult associations than they did CARP's own more modest figures (see Bromley and Shupe, 1979a: 128-129).

Perhaps the clearest sign that anti-cult associations had managed to legitimate their concerns and imagery of new religions came in commercial form in 1979 when Dell Books sent college and university faculty in sociology departments across the nations a flyer advertising the paperback edition of *Snapping* (Conway and Siegelman, 1979) and suggesting it for course adoption in such areas as social problems. ACM ideology was now being touted as social science, suitable for consumption in freshman sociology courses. Furthermore, a combination sound-slide package of 240 slides in three carousel trays, accompanied by cassette tapes and a teacher's guide, was advertised to faculty by mailed flyer and was available for $175 from a company specializing in educational media packets on a wide range of subjects (see Ibis, 1980).

What these various examples demonstrate, of course, is that the entire topics of "cult" influence became appropriated by the educational institution in various ways (and by those who serviced it) in the terms and according to the dimensions by which the anti-cult associations had defined the controversy.

Medical/Legal Impact

The medical profession's response to the "cult" controversy, as originally defined and later promoted by anti-cult groups, was through its psychiatric wing. Included here also would be the number of clinical psychologists who became involved either through their own research or through media accounts of their opinions and pronouncements. Many of these we have considered in earlier chapters (see particularly Chapter 3 on the secular possession metaphor of brainwashing). Anthony et al. (1979) conceptualized a continuum of psychiatric attitudes toward the viability of the whole mind-control-in-new-religions argument, ranging from the total rejection of brainwashing as a value-laden metaphor (a la the works of iconoclast psychiatrist Thomas Szasz, 1961, 1970a, 1970b), to a middle position acknowledging the existence (and efficacy) of a brainwashing procedure but only under extremely controlled, coercive, and rare conditions, to the opposite extreme where brainwashing was unquestioningly assumed not only to exist but also to be a staple operating procedure in new religions. The latter spoke freely in terms of "ego regression" and "mentacide" and among new religions' members threatened, in Anthony et al.'s view, to establish a "therapeutic state" based on a medical model that defined social deviance (in the most generic sociocultural sense) as inherently pathological. In terms of our earlier discussion of ACM ideology, the middle position on Anthony et al.'s continuum would be occupied by those psychiatrists and psychologists such as Ungerleider (1979), whom we placed under our secular deception rubric. Those on the extreme radical end of brainwashing-affirmation, such as Singer (1979) and Clark (1979), would fit under our secular possession label.

The array of attitudes toward the inherent viability of a concept of intensive personal influence termed brainwashing, as well as its relevance for those recruitment/indoctrination practices allegedly employed by various new religions, demonstrated a lack of consensus among mental health professionals toward acceptance of the ACM ideology proffered by anti-cult associations. This disagreement could not be attributed to first-hand clinical experience with "cult" members versus nonexperience. Singer (1979) and Clark (1979), for example, who were vocal proponents of the secular possession model, confronted sophisticated, challenging (even contradictory) evidence produced by professionals such as Ungerleider (1979; Ungerleider and Wellisch, 1979a, 1979b) and Galanter et al. (1978, 1979). However, once again, *the terms* of the controversy had been defined by anti-cult associations. Their psychiatric/psychological "champions' " participation on behalf of anti-cult associations at state and federal hearings as well as in the role of sympathetic consulting professionals at anti-cult conferences conferred some measure of legitimacy on anti-cult claims.

The proponents of ACM ideology had a greater impact on public opinion because the anti-cult associations widely publicized their writings and because these professionals' opinions lent themselves more readily to popular publication. That the medical establishment was influenced enough by ACM allegations to examine the whole controversy can be supported by two examples. First, in Ungerleider (1979), who related an interview with a psychiatrist on the subject of "cult" influence, a major drug manufacturer published a multicolor glossy booklet and distributed it without charge to psychiatric/medical practitioners. Second, in 1980, the Center for the Study of New Religious Movements of the Graduate Theological Seminary in Berkeley, California, obtained a three-year grant from the National Endowment for the Humanities and was a leading candidate for a grant from the National Institute of Mental Health to fund a multifaceted program of counseling, referral, and information accumulation/dissemination for members, ex-members, and families of those connected with the new religions as well as for policy makers (see Anthony, 1979). Earlier in 1979, after Jonestown had become a well-publicized event, the NIMH had debated funding an investigation into the area of new religions, but the proposal was at least temporarily shelved when the very meeting to deliberate the question was interrupted by protesting members of such groups (personal interviews, 1979).

If anything, the legal institution in contrast to others was even more divided on the issue of "cults" and deprogramming but, in the roles of defending and prosecuting attorneys, actively involved. For example, prosecuting attorneys were as likely to find themselves attempting to indict deprogrammers and assistants for kidnapping as they were to seek various restrictions on "cults."

However, the lack of legal consensus over the logic of deprogramming manifested itself not only in the obvious outright confrontations of lawyers in adversary courtroom situations, such as the numerous trials in which "cult" members sought to sue deprogrammers and parents for allegedly violating their civil rights, but also in the academic debates over law and religious liberties. The latter instances provided anti-cult associations with opportunities to put forth their viewpoint, if only indirectly, through lawyers who shared their views and/or represented ACM activists. Such occasions included the February 1979 "Dole hearing" (see Chapter 8), conferences such as the one on "Alternative Religions: Government Control and the First Amendment" sponsored by the New York University Review of Law and Social Change in November 1979 (which included as participants Richard Delgado, pro-ACM law professor, and Patrick Wall, long-time counsel for deprogrammer Ted Patrick; see GTU, 1979), and various publications which essentially argued that First Amendment rights extended without restriction to beliefs but not to specific actions of believers (Delgado, 1977, 1979; Woodruff, 1978).

The debate over the legitimacy of anti-cult associations' claims and deprogramming methods reached to the very heart of the legal institution. In 1977 and 1978, various committees and sections of the American Bar Association—notably, those on law and mental health and on family law—began considering the deprogramming phenomenon with the aim of preparing a recommendation to the general association as to legal ramification of religious "cult" conversions and deprogrammings affecting minors (Finney, 1977). However, the ABA's Individual Rights Section opposed the general association taking any stance, and none ultimately was taken. One official wrote the authors: "The whole matter is so controversial that there probably is no consensus in any A.B.A. Section or in the A.B.A. itself as to what, if anything, should be done" (Foster, 1978). The legal complexities of the controversy produced such a distinctive literature that by 1979 Robbins (1979b) compiled a 32-page annotated bibliography specifically dealing with the legal issues raised by deprogrammings, such as the use of conservatorship laws and involuntary servitude. Nevertheless, as in our previous discussions of other institutions, the fact that the legal profession felt it could take no formal action did not erase the stigma attached to "cults" during the debate, their civil liberties, and, ultimately, their public image.

Business Impact

The anti-cult associations were unable to attract any significant support from businesses except as local businessmen might exclude witnesses or fund-raisers from their premises. Other attempts to gain broader support were generally unsuccessful. In the early days of the ACM anti-cult associations had dispatched speakers to a number of local businessmen's civic organizational meetings, not to solicit contributions or members but rather simply to make contact with the large available groups of citizens and warn them of the "cult menace." One CFF chapter's newsletter, for example, mentioned speaking engagements for the past month at chapters of the Kiwanis, Optimist, Rotary, and Pro-America clubs (CFF, 1975d). By the late 1970s, however, they were able occasionally to arouse business interests in various communities with the specter of "cults" moving into given areas and investing their tax-free charitable funds in businesses and enterprises that would compete with local firms. Various other popularly known aspects of new religious groups like the UM and the Hare Krishna, such as the full-time voluntary labor of their members and the fact that such groups' profits would not be reduced by health or insurance benefits to "employees," made the prospect of their entry into local economies an alarming consideration.

The anti-cultists also were occasionally able to take advantage of disputes between UM-run businesses and their clientele or competitors. In one instance the UM's New York daily newspaper, *The News World,* ran free advertising for some local firms without their knowledge, creating precisely the kind of legitimate attack on "cults" which the anti-cultists delighted in pressing. However, the best and most publicized illustration involved a conflict between local fishing enterprises around the country and newly purchased UM fishing subsidiaries.

The prospect of "cults" moving into given areas, investing their tax-free (and, anti-cultists would contend, illicitly obtained) charitable donations, and using the voluntary labor of their members to compete with local businesses created yet another arena in which anti-cult allegations could be raised and receive some support from the course of events. It was also true, of course, that ACM allegations disseminated through the media had the effect of increasing local residents' alarm when "cults" moved into the area, thus feeding the dynamics of the conflict process.

The UM's purchase of various fishing fleets and canning facilities along the eastern and southern seacoasts of the United States (and even one in Kodiak, Alaska) in 1976-1979 illustrates the controversy resulting from the fears of local communities which extrapolated the conspiratorial picture of "cults" as fostered in the media by anti-cultists to construct a serious threat to their economic livelihood. Earlier we referred (Bromley and Shupe, 1979a: 132) to the UM's purchase through an interrelated network of subsidiary companies of fish, shipyards, land planned for fish-processing, ships, and marinas following Reverend Moon's inspiration "to turn to the sea" (for example, "Moon Sings New Tuna"—Fort Worth Star-Telegram, Oct. 31, 1976). Two of the better-publicized and more controversial purchases were made in Gloucester, Massachusetts, and Bayou La Batre, Alabama. In each community citizens reacted with fear and resentment at the UM's announced plans to expand its fishing operations locally, aware of the potential impact of a new competing group with cheap labor and virtually unlimited investment capital in an already fragile industry worked mainly by small, family-owned businesses. In Gloucester a number of heated town meetings were held, prompting a visit by UM president Neil Salonen to allay fears that the UM designed either to run other fishermen out of business or to become a dominant political force in the area. Salonen's apocryphal anecdotes of Moon's alleged ability to catch giant bluefin tuna on his hook without bait, however, and the past reluctance of the UM's various fishing subsidiaries (Tong-Il Fishing Company and International Oceanic Enterprises) to admit in a forthright manner their relation to the parent UM (see Bromley and Shupe, 1979a: 136-7; also U.S. Government, 1978: 372) did nothing of the kind.

In Bayou La Batre, Alabama, where the UM paid a reported $6 million for acreage and a boat-building company to erect a seafood plant, establish a maritime academy, and produce seagoing ships, citizens organized into ad hoc groups such as Concerned Citizens of the South and Concerned Mothers of the South, picketed the property where construction was planned, and even hired a law firm to block the proposed building. As one operator of a processing plant in Bayou La Batre, who claimed that Moon was willing to pay uncompetitively higher prices for fish in order to establish his business in the market, angrily complained:

> If a damn preacher can come in here and run me out of the seafood business with what I know about it, that's fine. Let him come in and compete. But don't come in here with free labor, tax-free status and those mind-bending techniques [New York Times, May 8, 1978].

Similar purchases by the UM, and anxieties on the part of local communities, occurred in Norfolk, Virginia, San Leander, California, and Kodiak, Alaska, and were monitored regularly in newsletters published by CFF, the American Family Foundation, and other groups. Moreover, members of anti-cult groups wrote congressmen in support of the fishermen's complaints of unfair encroachment by the UM. As a result, in December 1977, Senator Lowell Weicker, Jr., ranking Republican on the Senate Select Committee on Small Businesses, participated in hearings held by that committee (titled "Economic and Small Conditions in the Fishing Industry") to review the controversy. Weicker wrote the authors:

> Testimony given at those hearings indicated that foreign investments might have an adverse impact on the viability of American processors and fishermen.

> Since that time, the Committee's minority staff has been made aware of allegations that organizations associated with Sun Myung Moon have engaged in practices which might give them unfair competitive advantage over Small American businesses engaged in the fishing industries. I have direct [sic] the minority staff to conduct a [sic] inquiry limited to these allegations [Weicker, 1979].

The response of the business component of any community, however, was dependent on direct threats to specific economic interests. The overall lack of such threats, exceptions such as the fishing examples aside, meant that the business/economic institution in general never became seriously alarmed on any meaningful scale by the allegations of anti-cult associations and thus never constituted an important political ally of the ACM.

Alliances for the New Religions

The balance of power which finally emerged out of the conflict between the new religions and the anti-cultists could not be attributed to the adeptness of the latter at recognizing, seeking out, and forming alliances. As we detailed in Chapter 4, they were not even sufficiently successful at building a coalition among their own local and regional organizations to mount a viably coordinated, effective, nationwide movement. Further, their inability to agree on a definition of "cult" and their proclivity to expand constantly the list of "cults" to encompass more and more groups which the public at large hardly found threatening lost them potential allies. For example, a Christian Scientist wrote to a local newspaper (The Derry News, [Derry, N.H.] , Feb. 23, 1980):

It is always disappointing to find Christians of one denomination attacking other denominations with derogatory labels and, often, little genuine understanding of their beliefs. The inclusion of Christian Science in an upcoming course on "cults" is an unfortunate example of such mislabeling.

Nor did the anti-cult associations receive unqualified support from all of their allies; most groups rendered assistance largely as an extension of serving or defending their own interests. What gave the anti-cult associations the decided edge over the new religions in the balance of power was that the new religious movements were able to enlist few allies who would promote their causes or come to their defense. Indeed, the goals and organizations of many of these movements almost inevitably alienated significant power groups within American society from the outset. The UM clearly demonstrated this dilemma. On one hand, Moon's strident anti-communism and stalwart defense of the South Korean dictatorship alienated liberals; on the other hand, his socialistic leanings and dreams of a unified world political order offended the conservatives. His insensitivity to Jewish heritage in the United States drew allegations of anti-Semitism from Jews; his proclamation of a forthcoming Oriental messiah made him anathema to all but the most liberal Christians, and mainline Protestants were put off by his rejection of separation of church and state. Conservatives reacted to Moon's plan for a socialist utopia; liberals, to his linking of socialism and theocracy. His communistic lifestyle which removed UM members from conventional career trajectories aroused opposition from a broad range of institutions.

The UM attempted to influence public opinion through media representatives, academics, theologians, and government officials directly in order to forge alliances with what they considered critical audiences. The UM sponsored a number of conferences around the world through various of its affiliated organizations to promote discussion of its theology and the generic principles upon which it was constructed. The Unification Theological Seminary hosted a steady stream of theologians representing a wide range of religious persuasions to discuss contemporary theological issues and to discuss and evaluate the philosophical, religious, and ethical implications of Moon's *Divine Principle.* Scientists representing virtually all disciplines were invited to an annual conference sponsored by the International Cultural Foundation to examine the underlying commonality of religion and science. Individual groups of potentially sympathetic scholars were brought to special conferences where they were wined, dined, and familiarized with the UM, and cooperation was rendered in some of their research efforts which offered promise of redressing what the UM termed "negativity." After media coverage had become overwhelmingly negative, the UM launched in 1978 a public relations campaign dubbed Frontier '78, designed to alter local governmental officials' and media representatives' perception of the movement. A number of top UM leaders were dispatched to communities across the country in what appears to have been at least a marginally successful effort to stem the rising tide of hostility.

The first of such efforts, of course, were instituted by Moon himself when he headed a series of national tours during the early to mid-1970s. Large public gatherings preceded by intense public relations advance teams were organized in cities throughout the United States; local and national dignitaries were invited to and feted sumptuously at such occasions. However, rising fundamentalist Christian opposition (which took the form of sermonizing and alerts to the media prior to tour stops along with picketing of actual tour events) coupled with Moon's inability to speak English or inspire audiences with his message, meant that these tours fell far short of their intended effect.

Since the goals and interests of the UM and other new religions overlapped little with those of other major power groups within the society, few groups rose to their defense when the "cult"-anti-cult conflict ensued. A coalition of several new religions formed (principally Scientology and the UM, with considerably less participation by the Hare Krishna), calling itself the Alliance for the Preservation of Religious Liberty (APRL). APRL co-sponsored (with the American Civil Liberties Union) a major conference on deprogramming in February 1977 and circulated a collection of affidavits, testimonies, and articles entitled *Deprogramming: Documenting the Issue* (APRL, 1977). Throughout the late 1970s, its representatives were active across the country, seeking to enlist the sympathies of academics and civil libertarians. However, APRL was inescapably a weak coalition. Its members were united only by their persecution; indeed, in other instances they competed for roughly the same pool of converts, pursued the same supply of charitable dollars and/or discretionary income, and followed their distinct, mutually exclusive roads to salvation. As a result, each member religious group in APRL conducted its own lawsuits separately and on a day-to-day basis confronted a hostile society alone. Needless to say, no real attempt was made to gain support from earlier new religions (such as Jehovah's Witnesses and Christian Scientists) which might have sympathized with their plight.

The new religions were left, therefore, with very limited support from groups with a dedication to preservation of civil liberties. ACLU, for example, was steadfast in its opposition to deprogramming, going so far as to co-sponsor with APRL in 1977 the above-mentioned conference which sought to expose deprogramming as a naked, illigitimate assertion of power by parents over their adult offspring's religious and lifestyle preferences. One ACLU official called deprogramming "a hostile assault on freedom of association and liberty [that] represents one of the most serious challenges to civil liberties today" (Prichard, n.d.). From that conference the ACLU developed a special task force of legal experts that included several nationally known attorneys to serve as consultants "and give practical assistance" on matters concerning guardianship and conservatorship laws. More conferences at seminaries and on college campuses across the country followed in the same spirit. Two of the more important of these were the International Conference on Deprogramming held in Toronto, Canada, in November 1977, and the Graduate Theological Union Conference on New Religious Movements in America held in Berkeley, California, in June 1977.

The National Council of Churches, a champion of separation of church and state, saw a real danger in allowing even tacitly sanctioned violence to determine expression of religious preference and hence staunchly opposed deprogramming. Dean M. Kelley, who symbolically enough served both as Director for Civil and Religious Liberty of the National Council of Churches and Chairman of the ACLU Church-State Committee, unequivocally condemned deprogramming in language as vitriolic as any ever appearing in anti-cult newsletters:

> Let us not forget that the anguish of parents is not the only anguish involved here. Let us give equal consideration to the feelings—and rights—of young people who go about in daily dread of being physically seized and subjected to protracted spiritual gang-rape until they yield their most cherished religious commitments. *That is what's going on here.* That is the element that makes deprogramming the most serious violation of our religious liberty in this generation, and why it must clearly be seen as criminal. It should be prosecuted, not just as any other kidnapping, undertaken for mercenary motives would be, but even more vigorously, since it strikes at the most precious and vulnerable portion of the victim's life, religious convictions and commitments [Kelley, 1977: 32].

Liberal scholars attempted to demonstrate that the current deprogramming controversy was simply an old wrinkle in a historical pattern in this country of repression of new religious groups (as the Quakers and Mormons had earlier experienced). A spate of articles with titles such as "Even a Moonie has Civil Rights" (Robbins, 1977a), "Cult Phobia" (Robbins and Anthony, 1979), "Witches, Moonies and Accusations of Evil" (Shupe and Bromley, 1980b), "Deprogramming: the New Exorcism" (Shupe et al., 1977b), "Making Crime Seem Natural" (Testa, 1978), "Moonies, Mormons and Mennonites: Christian Heresy and Religious Toleration" (Sawatsky, 1978), and "Myths Sanctioning Religious Persecution" (Cox, 1978b) began to appear which were critical of deprogramming and which sought to locate the new religious movements in a context of cultural malaise and youth protest movements. Some of these articles appeared in quasi-popular publications such as *Psychology Today, Society,* and *The Nation* and hence may have had broader influence, but many others appeared in academic journals (such as *American Behavioral Scientist* and *Sociological Analysis*) which found few audiences outside educational/professional circles.

Finally, a few editorialists defended the civil rights of members of the new religions as they became aware of the complex, controversial issues involved in the "cult"-anti-cult controversy. The following headlines suggest the tenor of such essays which, while not representing any major backlash against deprogramming, nevertheless called for a more cautious approach:

- "Leave the Moonies Be" (White River Valley Herald, Jan. 27, 1977);
- "Whose Rights Next?" (Rockford Register-Republic, Aug. 26, 1976);
- "A Right to Be Wrong" (National Courier, April 16, 1976);
- "Who's Crazy Here—Moonies or Judges?" (Times-Picayune, April 3, 1977);
- "The Right to Be Brainwashed" (Berkshire Eagle, March 31, 1977);
- "The Right to Be Moonstruck" (Washington Star, April 17, 1977);
- "Defending Your Right to Be Weird in America" (Intelligencer Journal, March 31, 1977).

Indeed, one journalist sensitively wrote:

> The underlying tragedy in such cases is that many young people in our era are susceptible to pressure from their peers in exotic cults in part because they have rejected their parents and prevailing traditions of their community. But if we do indeed live in an age of hollow people, "leaning together, headpieces stuffed with straw," as poet T. S. Eliot put it, will stuffing another brand of straw have any lasting beneficial effect [The Atlanta Journal, March 30, 1977]?

Finally, when the attorney general of Kansas contemplated an investigation of the UM, an anonymous excerpt from an editorial in our files proclaimed:

> Given the choice between worshiping [sic] the preposterous Rev. Moon and the nearest parking meter, most of us would kneel before the latter. But we ought to be free to do it—without the Kansas Attorney General looking over our shoulders.

In the final analysis it must be remembered that the "bottom line" of the conditions for support from most of the above groups was simply the defense of constitutional rights and civil liberties. There was no explicit advocacy of the new religions' respective goals and values; rather, only a probing of the meaning of events (as with scholars) or a cautioning against hysteria and potential witchhunts (as with the civil liberties' advocates).

Thus, the new religions gained very little support from such groups, although the legal and ethical issues raised did have the effect of impeding coercive deprogramming. This was not an inconsequential victory for the new religions, but essentially it protected only their right to survive. It did not, we emphasize, advance their interests as social movements.

Summary

The anti-cult associations' component of the ACM had at best, as our review of six institutions with which the anti-cultists sought to form alliances illustrated, limited success in mobilizing other institutions against the new religions. That such alliances were mandatory for inhibiting or repressing "cults," of course, followed from the nature of the American family institution itself, a mass of individual units without ready means of exerting collective sanctions or coordinating actions for its common interests. We considered, in order of anti-cult groups' relative impact, the mass media, religion (fundamentalist/conservative Protestant and Jewish/Roman Catholic), government (local, state, and national), education, law/medicine, and business. In each case the viability and longevity of the alliance which anti-cult groups formed with a given institution depended on the degree of convergence of interests between that institution and the anti-cultists as well as on the amount of influence which anti-cult groups could bring to bear. That is why, for example, they were relatively more successful at stimulating local governments to act concretely against "cult" recruiters and fund-raisers than they were at mobilizing the federal government to "go after the cults" or why local clergymen were more likely to speak out vociferously against the UM and other religious groups than were their national denominational leaders. When anti-cult associations' constituencies overlapped considerably with those of the institution from which they solicited support (for example, the Parent Teacher Association in education or the American Jewish Committee in religion), their common interests led to greater mobilization.

Nevertheless, much of this support was symbolic and constrained, and the failure of anti-cultists to appreciate when they were effectively being "cooled out" by politicians and other officials undoubtedly exacerbated their later sense of frustration. In actuality, that a rather small number of poorly organized, inadequately financed families could go so far in discrediting new religions and harassing them as the anti-cultists did may be as much a function of the fact that newspaper reporters and editors, politicians, and religious leaders shared common values and biases of anti-cultists as it was a product of their intensive lobbying efforts. Still, the anti-cult associations did achieve an important effect in contributing to the generally pejorative public image of the new religions, even if for them this accomplishment fell far short of their stated purposes.

NOTES

1. See, for example, the *People* (1978b) article in which a teenage "undercover" journalist constructed an elaborate pseudo-identity complete with a false college I.D. to lend his story of experiencing a Berkeley UM center weekend workshop the flavor of an espionage adventure. Such pretentious, staged melodrama was particularly ludicrous in light of the Berkeley UM center's penchant for indiscriminately sweeping up any moving body in the 18-26-year range, no questions asked, to attend its weekend workshops.

2. The Spiritual Counterfeits Project also used the "front" name of the Committee of the Third Day. Explained co-founder Bill Squires:

> The Committee of the Third Day is a name we used on a few pieces of our literature in order to not turn people away from the content of the literature. The fact is that many people when handed a leaflet or tract will immediately look to see who it is from and then decide on that basis whether or not to read it. We wanted to avoid this and so chose the name Committee of the Third Day which would not give away, in just a glance at the name, our "Christian perspective" [personal correspondence to the authors, Nov. 23, 1976].

This tactic of utilizing "fronts" to minimize public resistance was, of course, famously employed by the UM, one of the SCP's primary opponents.

3. We know of two such examples from our own experience. First, one ACM informant regularly received reports from a municipal-level clerk responsible for issuing charitable solicitation permits as to the comings and goings (and registered names) of UM fund-raisers. On occasion, attempts were made by this ACM activist to contact the latters' families (practices which UM members suspected and which prompted them to respond by providing false identification). Second, one ACM activist arranged a "Good Old Boy" agreement with a local sheriff to stop and "shake down" Orientals passing through town on the chance they might be agents of Reverend Moon. We were contacted at one point with a request to help translate what was suspected to be the "secret sex manual" of the UM's inner leadership corps, rifled from one hapless Oriental's car trunk, used in their reputed orgaistic rite of *pikarume* (cleansing of the blood; that is ritual intercourse of leaders with female members) but which in reality turned out to be a best-selling sex advice manual from Japan.

4. For readers familiar with media atrocity tales told by UM apostates, particularly those derived from the Booneville, California, "ranch" where new members and potential recruits were never left alone even while telephoning "outsiders," it will be patently obvious that Wertz's bill was more than coincidentally tailor-made to attack the UM.

5. A drive to secure signatures for a petition urging the Michigan state legislature to make mind control a felony was undertaken in the summer of 1979 by the Individual Freedom Foundation (IFF, 1979e), though with little success.

6. The one major exception to this trend was action taken by the Immigration and Naturalization Service in 1974. In our previous volume on the UM (see Bromley and Shupe, 1979a: chap. 6) we presented evidence to show that Moon's insistence on defending President Nixon from critics during the Watergate investigations of 1974-1975, coupled with his aggressive publicity-seeking activities, drew the attention and suspicion of many public officials and political commentators. In 1974, the INS refused to extend visas of about 600 foreign UM "missionaries" (mostly Japanese, Koreans, and German nationals) when it became convinced that the UM missionary training program "has been designed primarily for fund raising rather than for training purposes. . . . We regard such extensive solicitations as productive employment both in violation of nonimmigrant visitor status and beyond the pale of . . . trainee classification" (quoted in the Wall Street Journal, Sept. 20, 1974). Many of these UM members were involved in working with Moon's cross-country "Day of Hope" speaking tours, and their geographically mobile, fast-paced lifestyle made them difficult to follow and locate, a fact which no doubt increased officials' suspicions about the UM's forthrightness in complying with the law. The INS finally met with 40 German UM members in Salt Lake City and ordered them deported. In February 1976, when Senator Robert Dole wrote the Justice Department concerning the visa status problem of UM members, Assistant Attorney General Michael M. Uhlmann replied in a letter that an additional 583 foreign UM members were being denied entry into the United States despite a suit filed by the UM against the attorney general, for the same reasons that the others had had their visas revoked. He gave Dole his assurances that the Department of Justice "will continue to monitor closely and respond to complaints of this nature" (Uhlmann, 1976). It is important to note, however, that these actions of the INS antedated any lobbying efforts of the anti-cult associations in this area of immigration and therefore cannot be interpreted as an anti-cult victory.

7. Assistant Attorney General Richard L. Thornburgh explained:

> Allegations that the victim was indeed persuaded, proselytized or brainwashed to continue his association with the cult would be insufficient. . . . In the case of a [federal] kidnapping investigation, there also would have to be information that the victim was being held for ransom, reward, or otherwise and that the jurisdictional element of interstate travel was present [Ft. Worth Star-Telegram, Feb. 25, 1977].

Chapter 8

JONESTOWN AND THE REVITALIZATION OF THE ACM

In one sense events at Jonestown, Guyana, in November 1978 appear to have only tangential relevance to the issues discussed in the preceding chapters, since the People's Temple had not been the target of ACM opposition. Yet, as we shall show, the tragic events surrounding the mass deaths at Jonestown rejuvenated a movement that was clearly foundering and, for a time at least, both revitalized its membership and boosted its credibility in American society. Indeed, we shall argue that Jonestown constituted a potent symbolic event which served as a catalyst in the ACM's broader attack on all of the controversial new religious movements.

As we detailed in Chapter 4, repeated attempts at centralization and reorganization by the regional anti-cult associations had foundered for a variety of identifiable reasons. By the late 1970s, the movement still lacked financial resources and the capacity for concerted, unified action. Further, there is evidence that groups such as the UM and the Hare Krishna were effectively coping with harassment (see Bromley and Shupe, 1979a: 229-241 on the UM). In addition to legal defenses by various "cults" which blunted the ACM's direct attacks, the extremism and heavy-handedness of deprogrammers brought the UM and other groups a certain amount of sympathy. Indeed, in some instances the UM in particular became identified as the underdog in this controversy, and some observers (as we saw in Chapter 5) began to ask if the deprogramming "cure" might not in fact be far worse in the long run than any alleged "cult menace." Increasingly, the ACM/"cultic" struggle took on the aura of fanatical opponents locked in mortal combat, neither of which any longer had untarnished credibility.

Jonestown had a number of serendipitous consequences for the ACM. Most importantly, Jonestown incorporated all of the ACM's worst fears and most dire predictions. Whereas the public previously had been confronted with individuals joining a plethora of religious groups characterized by varied ideologies and organizations and about which there was only speculation as to their "destructive potential," Jonestown seemed to provide dramatic confirming evidence for their claims in an undeniable, horrible event. Further, events at Jonestown made accessible once again to the ACM both the media and political institutions. With respect to the media, Jonestown, with its heaps of bodies and cups of cyanide-laced grape Kool-aid, provided precisely the kind of unitary catastrophic event that lent itself so well to sensational coverage. ACM channels to the government were also reopened or strengthened, especially since a United States Congressman had been assassinated, diplomatic and military personnel became involved in negotiating the removal of the victims' bodies from Jonestown, and congressional investigations of the People's Temple and Leo J. Ryan's death were launched. Finally, Jonestown provided the perfect opportunity for ACM spokespersons to convert their private family troubles into issues of public concern. No longer were they simply protesting the personal misfortunes of seeing their own sons and daughters join marginal religions; now they were able to base their allegations on the victimization of innocent bystanders with whom they had no prior contact or attachment. Thus, as we shall show, Jonestown took on importance as a potent symbol in the ACM/"cult" struggle that served to rekindle fears and apprehensions about "cults" in general.

The People's Temple and Events in Jonestown

BACKGROUND OF THE PEOPLE'S TEMPLE

Jim Jones founded his first church, the interdenominational Christian Assembly of God, in 1953 and later the Indianapolis People's Temple Full of Gospel Church which was affiliated with the Disciples of Christ denomination. Jones had been a fundamentalist preacher since at least 1950, and in 1964 he was ordained as a Disciples of Christ minister. In 1965 he and over 100 members of his Indianapolis People's Temple migrated to northern California as a result of his vision of an impending nuclear holocaust to occur in 1967 (California was apparently to be spared bombing and nuclear fallout.) In the years that followed he established churches in both Los Angeles and San Francisco while continuing to maintain his Indianapolis congregation. He attracted a large following of poor inner-city blacks and whites to whom his group's fundamentalist religion, liberal politics, and charitable services had great appeal. He also assiduously cultivated political influence in San Francisco. For example, he donated $4400 to twelve newspapers in 1973 as support for "defense of a free press" and contributed $6000 to the San Francisco Senior Assistance Program. San Francisco Mayor George Moscone appointed Jones to the city's Housing Authority in 1976 (Jones became chairman the following year). In 1975 Jones was named one of 100 "most outstanding" clergymen in America by one interfaith group, Humanitarian of the Year in January 1976, and recipient of the Martin Luther King, Jr. Humanitarian Award in 1977. It was during this period of aggressive expansion, in December 1973, that Jonestown was established as a foreign colony of the People's Temple in Guyana.

Jones, along with hundreds of his followers, moved to Guyana during summer 1977 after the controversial death of a defector and *New West* magazine published an investigative article critical of the authoritarian lifestyle in the People's Temple. Jones had known beforehand that *New West* intended to publish the article, but neither he nor friendly local politicians could prevent it. Soon after the article's publication, Jones resigned from the city's Housing Authority under threat of investigation from the City Supervisor and impending lawsuits by apostates and took up permanent residence in Jonestown. Jonestown was meant to be a community unto itself—self-sufficient and remote enough to discourage what Jones interpreted as persecution from officials and the media.

Although some families of individual members were concerned or angry with People's Temple over what was regarded as totalistic control over their relatives and banded together into a local opposition group, they were not integrated into the organization or network of communication of the national ACM. Indeed, prior to Jonestown, ACM leaders had never heard of Jones or his church. There are two salient reasons for this relative lack of controversy over the group. First, Jones maintained close ties with important civic and political leaders in San Francisco and was involved in a number of community service projects which offset negative publicity.

Second, Jones was an ordained minister of the Disciples of Christ denomination. Thus, the group was simply not defined as a cult, which, as Barbara Hargrove (1979) observed, explained the relative lack of attention to People's Temple by social scientists of religion and other professional observers prior to its spectacular demise.[1]

THE JONESTOWN TRAGEDY

It is beyond the scope and purpose of this chapter to attempt to explain the causes of events at Jonestown and the dynamics of the relationship between People's Temple and the larger society. Suffice it to say that the People's Temple became increasingly controversial in the months following the publication of the *New West* article, the publicized death of an outspoken apostate, and lawsuits even though much of this controversy was reported in only the regional media. Certain public officials and media representatives became increasingly disturbed about stories describing activities within the church, and Jones became increasingly convinced that his People's Temple was the object of a concerted campaign of harassment by state and federal officials.

It was in the context of this mutually perceived hostility that in November 1978 U.S. Representative Leo J. Ryan, his assistants, and a party of newspersons visited Jonestown to investigate reports (directed to Ryan by disgruntled family members of followers of Jones, 12 of whom were from his own congressional district) that residents of the settlement were subject to excessively authoritarian and sometimes brutal treatment and were even held against their will. After what at the time seemed a fairly upbeat visit and several positive testimonies by members on behalf of Jim Jones and the settlement's lifestyle, Ryan and a party that included a small number of disgruntled members made preparations to leave by private airplane. On November 18, while waiting at the Port Kaituma airfield to depart, a carload of heavily armed members pulled up to the plane and killed, among others, Ryan and well-known television reporter Don Harris in a sudden burst of gunfire. In all, five persons died and twelve were wounded in this ambush.

Meanwhile, in Jonestown proper a macabre ritual communion began. Convinced that their community was about to be "invaded" and "destroyed" by the outside world, People's Temple members, at Jones' orders and (up until the end) persistent encouragement, assembled to participate in a collective gesture of defiance by committing suicide. Following previously rehearsed drills, members queued up as Dr. Lawrence Schart, the settlement physician, and two nurses administered a potion of Kool-aid mixed with cyanide, first to infants and small children and then to adults. The extent to which this "suicide" was voluntary for residents has not been resolved. A tape recording made during the actual poisonings, widely reported in the media shortly after the tragedy, documented the chaotic din of loud sobbings by adults, children screaming, and Jones repeatedly pleading with parents to "die with dignity" and to "control your children." The dozen or so survivors told of armed guards ringing the settlement's central pavilion and forcing any and all to drink the deadly mixture, later arranging the corpses in concentric circles and posing them in fraternal embraces. However, whether the deaths were voluntary suicides or not, the fact remains that when the U.S. Defense Department flew approximately 200 troops to Guyana to search the camp and rescue survivors, they counted over 900 corpses. Only a handful of members, for idiosyncratic reasons, escaped or were overlooked.

Reaction of the ACM

It took some time for public reaction to Jonestown to merge due to the piecemeal process through which information trickled into the hands of the media. Reports on the extent of the tragedy (even on such basic parameters as the death count) were mixed, incomplete, and sometimes confusing. As Wiencek (1979: 2-3) noted, it was not until the following Tuesday (November 21) that even the broad outlines of the tragedy appeared in newspapers, largely dealing with background stories on Jones and the People's Temple. Quickly, more descriptive articles emerged, but Weincek's survey of the media found few interpretive or analytic articles before December 1, almost two weeks later. Weincek chronicled this sequence of reporting as

(1) this is what we know about Jim Jones and the People's Temple; (2) this is what happened in Guyana; (3) this is what people tell us about those who belonged to the People's Temple; and (4) this is why and how such a tragedy could occur.

After the immediate deluge of media attraction to the Jonestown phenomenon had subsided, there continued to be a steady flow of interpretive articles, editorials, reports, and books on the subject. These included a number of books by ex-People's Temple members and journalists (Mills, 1979; Thielmann, 1979; White, 1979; Krause, 1978; Kilduff and Javers,

1978), U.S. Government staff reports (U.S. Government, 1979a, 1979b), and papers and articles by academic scholars (Weincek, 1979; Melton, 1980).

Immediately after the tragic events at Jonestown, the ACM was as shocked as the public at large. The ACM's ideology portrayed "cult" leaders as egomaniac, manipulative charlatans who brainwashed their followers and reduced them to a position of servile disciples or zombies. However, the thrust of the ACM's accusations against "cults" had been that followers were duped or coerced into providing "cult" leaders with wealth, power, and even sexual favors. While there were occasional hints that such total devotion and subservience by followers might include fighting (and in this context dying) for the "cult," there was no indication that individual or mass suicides had been seriously contemplated by the ACM. Soon, however, the ACM was to assimilate the events of Jonestown into its ideological world view and inevitably a few spokespersons would even claim that they had expected it. Conway and Siegelman, for example, in a *People* magazine (1979: 87) interview, stated that they were not surprised at the "mass suicides" in Guyana, since "the people in this group were totally suggestible and they totally identified with their leader." There were also attempts to interpret retrospectively Jim Jones' personality and biographical details and make what was known of these compatible with reports of the People's Temple. For example, in a *People* (1979: 29) article it was written:

Anyone who cared to look further would have discovered that Jones' background was somewhat bizzare. The son of an invalid father and a mother who worked in a factory, he is recalled by childhood neighbors in Lynn, Ind. as a quiet and pious boy who delivered rousing sermons at funerals he held for neighborhood pets—and who was suspected of stealing cats for sacrificial rituals.

Yet, even before this long-standing crusade against "cults" incorporated Jonestown into its ideology, the combination of Leo J. Ryan's murder and the deaths of over 900 of the followers of Jim Jones regalvanized the ACM and increased its resolve. For some time Ryan had maintained close ties to the ACM as an outspoken critic of the "cults" in American society. In May 1977, he and Connecticut Representative Robert N. Giaimo had requested the Justice Department to investigate charges of brainwashing and physical abuse in certain religious groups (a request "rebuffed" by the Justice Department on the grounds that such investigations would violate those groups' First Amendment rights; see New York Times, Nov. 23, 1978), and Ryan had been instrumental in helping at least one ACM group (the Citizens Freedom Foundation, located in California) eventually obtain tax-exempt status as an educational foundation (personal interviews, 1978). Moreover, Ryan had been a member of the Fraser Committee (the House Subcommittee on International Organizations) which had extensively probed the UM's role in the scandal which became known as "Koreagate" (see U.S. Government, 1978). He was eulogized in their publications. For example, the Citizens Freedom Foundation announced in an issue of its newsletter that it was initiating a Leo J. Ryan Memorial Fund to be "dedicated to preventing another Guyana while preserving our unalienable [sic] rights to life, liberty and the pursuit of happiness" (CFF, 1978b). CFF's president pledged:

> Leo Ryan was our ally, friend and champion. CFF can and will continue his battle with courage and compassion for those who are unwilling victims through brainwashing by fanatical cult leaders.

The popular press also elevated Ryan to the status of a tragic but heroic man of action:

> "Leo was not content to sit behind his desk relying on information from bureaucrats," says Rep. Stephen Solarz, who served with him on the International Relations Committee. "He felt a responsibility to help people who couldn't help themselves" [People, 1979: 30].

Ryan's murder did more than rob the ACM of an influential voice. More important, it provided the ACM with its first major martyr figure. In ACM members' eyes, Ryan as their spokesperson had fallen victim to a ruthless religious cult's revenge (a possible consequence of such activism which, several ACM figures confided to us, never could be completely dismissed), and the obvious sacrificial theme in his death was not overlooked. Beyond Ryan and the other victims in his investigative party, moreover, the entire population of Jonestown became transformed into a legion of misdirected martyrs who represented a tangible and dramatic referent for the most extreme claims of ACM spokespersons. The presence of over 200 children, many preadolescents, and even some infants in the toll of the dead accentuated the image of Jones as the archetypical megalomaniac "cult" leader about whom ACM groups had been protesting for the better part of a decade.

More significant in terms of the ACM's impact on public opinion formation, however, was the former's linking of the tragic events at Jonestown to the ideology they had already constructed regarding the "cult menace." Jonestown both objectified the anticultists' own worst fears about the destructive potential of "cults" and provided a concrete referent to which they could point as evidence in their appeals to the public and political officials. Thus, conservative Christian sociologist Ronald Enroth (1979: 13), an outspoken ACM proponent, observed:

> Since Jonestown the word "cult" has assumed new significance on the American scene. In countless articles, interviews, and editorial pages, the public has been made aware of the reality and destrictive potential of religious-political groups that manipulate the mind, subvert the will, and vandalize the soul.

By early 1979, the ACM was engaged in a vigorous campaign to reinstill general concern over "cults." ACM proponents now felt vindicated by events in Jonestown and clearly adopted an "I told you so" posture in their new aggressive campaign. Enroth (1979: 13) claimed:

> The unprecedented media exposure given Jonestown has alerted Americans to the fact that seemingly beneficient religious groups can mask a hellish rot. . . . The People's Temple tragedy reminds us that religious evil is the worst form of evil, for it masquerades in a social form that we have come to associate with all that is good and decent and ennobling.

ACM spokespersons sounded the theme that the Jonestown tragedy could have been averted if governmental leaders had been responsive to long-standing ACM claims and less concerned with civil liberties, a theme to be repeated often in the year to come in public forums and in ACM publications. One ACM newsletter (IFF, 1979a) stated:

> News of the mass murder-suicide in Guyana has shocked the entire world and especially the American people. It is now obvious that groups such as IFF have not been exaggerating in our allegations as to the severe consequences of cult involvement. The tragedy in Jonestown is concrete evidence that large groups of people can be controlled by charismatic leaders who manipulate their lives even to the point of death. As you know, our purpose has been to reveal to the public the potentially destructive activities of groups such as

People's Temple and to urge our government to take the necessary steps to protect cult victims and to provide avenues for their rescue.

What in effect the ACM attempted to create was a perspective that can be termed a "Guyana Complex." This perspective centered on the preeminent conviction that events in Guyana could, without much difficulty or extension of the imagination, be recapitualted in other groups in the United States. It was a conviction grounded in a three-step syllogism: (1) Jim Jones, the charismatic and megalomaniac leader of the People's Temple communal settlement, exercised complete control over the wills and behaviors of his members through fear and other "mind control" techniques; (2) the mass suicide of over 900 persons in Jonestown was the result of his paranoid will, not theirs; and (3) similar cult leaders in the United States with similar control over their followers might, given the right provocation, order their followers to commit parallel acts of violence. This perspective was clearly articulated by Ted Patrick, the "father" of deprogramming, in an interview published in early 1979 in *Playboy* (Siegelman and Conway, 1979: 60). Patrick's statements summarized much of the fear of imminent disaster held by ACM members. In response to a query about the potential for future Jonestowns, Patrick emphatically stated that the potential for such destructive violence "unquestionably" existed for other new religious groups such as the UM, the Hare Krishna sect, and Scientology. In fact, he went on to predict that such incidents would begin occurring "like wildfire." He concluded by stating that Jonestown was nothing compared with the disasters which he foresaw involving thousands of people who would die right here in the United States.

Although Patrick's interview made mention of numerous groups, it was clear from the patterns in ACM rhetoric and activity that the UM had been singled out as a primary target. As early as January 1979, a link was constructed between the Jonestown "mass suicide" and the potential for similar extremism in the UM. In the *New West* of that month an article (Carroll and Bauer, 1979) entitled "Suicide Training in the Moon Cult" quoted five apostates of the UM, all of whom claimed to have participated in or attended lectures and discussion encouraging suicide as a last-resort resistance tactic taught systematically by the UM to cope with outsider harassment, particularly when members were kidnapped by deprogrammers. All five had joined the "Oakland Family" branch of the UM operating in the San Francisco Bay area in 1976 or thereafter. One apostate, Eve Eden, claimed to have been a member of the "initial staff that conceived of the suicide idea" in 1976, though she conceded that "we didn't exactly use that word." After Eden left, the article alleged, "instructions in suicide methods" began to be systematically given by December 1976. Apostate Virginia Mabry recounted how she had attended a lecture at that time in the San Francisco center that contained "anatomy lessons on where to cut with the razor if the time came." Mabry said that Moonies were encouraged to compete with each other in a sort of Kamikaze contest of loyalty by devising new suicide methods and described her own contributed idea: "I decided I would go to the bathroom where the deprogrammers were holding me, unscrew the light bulb, stand in the sink and stick my finger in the socket." In that same article another apostate, Pat O'Shea, alleged that she attended a 300-member meeting in the Berkeley center "where a Moonie nurse demonstrated how to slash a wrist."

Two other former members, one of whom eventually went on a nationally televised talk show to tell her story, also reported receiving similar instructions. Sensational, sacrificially relevant excerpts from one of Moon's more hyperbolic speeches printed in *Master Speaks,* the UM's insider collection of Moon's sermons, were presented later in the article to establish an affinity between Moon's calls for loyalty to the death if necessary (in fighting communism, Satan, and so forth) and Jim Jones' commands to drink cyanide-laced Kool-aid. Moon had once stated:

> Have you ever thought that you may die for the Unification Church? . . . Will you complain against me at the moment of death? Without me on earth everything will be nullified. So, who would you want to die, me or you?[2]

The article went on to offer other apostates' anecdotes and intimations that suicidal violence was a definite possibility in the movement as a whole.[3]

Thus, in early 1979, the UM suddenly became referred to by the media as a "suicide cult"; pictures of Sun Myung Moon were paired with those of Jim Jones when the motives of the Jonestown participants were mulled over by "experts" on television talk-shows; journalists compared quotes and excerpts from speeches of the two men to imply a common paranoia; and UM leaders found themselves on the defensive from reporters, politicians, and other government officials who were spurred to renew investigations of Moon's movement by such suicide stories. That suicide instructions were actually given in a specific locale at a specific time seems conceivable, though not definitely established. That such instructions were a movement-wide, systematic feature of the UM seems extremely dubious. Our own participant observation and study of the UM over a several-year period revealed no evidence of suicide training, the allegations of apostates notwithstanding. Further, in our own four years of researching the ACM and being exposed to the most vitriolic accusations imaginable made against the UM we never heard a single disgruntled defector claim he or she receiving suicide instructions *before* the Jonestown tragedy occurred. Finally, even outspoken ACM leader Rabbi Maurice Davis acknowledged in the *New West* article that "in his five years of working with Moonies, he has never heard of anyone being given specific suicide instructions." Irrespective of the accuracy of such reports, however, they served to anger and frighten an already unsympathetic press, a hostile countermovement, and a confused corps of public officials under pressure "to do something before it's too late."

Although, as we shall show, the ACM was successful in raising the specter of future Jonestown-like episodes of violence, at the same time there were some voices raised in opposition to attributing so simplistic a mass violence potential to all "new" religious groups. On December 1, for example, two weeks after the Jonestown tragedy, President Jimmy Carter publicly resisted requests to probe "cults" as unconstitutional government interference, stating:

> I don't think we ought to have an overreaction because of the Jonestown tragedy by injecting government into trying to control people's religious belief [sic] and I believe we also don't need to deplore on a nationwide basis the fact that the Jonestown cult—so called was typical of America because it's not [Ft. Worth Star-Telegram, Dec. 1, 1978].

Soon after, Dean M. Kelley (1978), liberal Protestant theologian and civil liberties advocate, likewise forewarned in an essay entitled "Beware 'Open Season' on Cults":

> The tragic suicides of over 900 Americans in Guyana may have even grimmer repercussions in this country if they cause people to declare "open season" on new and unconventional religious groups.

Nevertheless, the ACM made every attempt to capitalize on the shock value and public uncertainty over Jonestown, reiterating its standard atrocity claims both to the general public and governmental officials and in the mobilization of its members. Jonestown, Ryan's death, and the imminent possibility of such violence being repeated in the United States became dominant themes in anti-cult lobbying and public relations efforts.

ACM Influence in
the Aftermath of Jonestown

As we have already noted, prior to the tragedy at Jonestown the ACM had lost much of its momentum despite its sometimes effective harassment of the UM. The number of substantive victories the ACM had been able to achieve was limited, and some of the most important potential sanctions it sought to have imposed (such as large-scale abduction/deprogramming and revocation of the UM's tax-exempt status) proved elusive. Events at Jonestown did not significantly alter this state of affairs. Although there appears to have been an immediate but short-lived resurgence of the number of deprogrammings following Jonestown, for example, the basic lines of battle were unaltered (for example, suits and countersuits and appels to the media by both sides). There were powerful institutional interests committed to defending the states' monopoly on the legitimate use of force, separation of church and state, the rule of law, and preservation of constitutional rights which sharply constricted the substantive sanctions that could be imposed on cults. What had changed was a growing belief that perhaps the danger "cults" posed had been underestimated among a substantial segment of the public and some public officials.

Given the growing level of concern and anxiety over this previously unrecognized threat, political institutions were pressured to support stronger initiatives against the "cults" than had previously been the case. For example, pre-Jonestown governmental action had been strictly limited on the federal level to an informal hearing (the 1976 Dole hearing"). The Frazier Committee investigation did subpoena UM officials and records, but because it was technically concerned with "Koreagate" (charges of bribery and improper influence by the South Korean government), it was therefore limited in its ability to investigate other aspects of UM activity. The effect of the Jonestown tragedy was to create pressure on state and federal governments to move further toward more formal legal action. The most notable examples on the federal level were the full-fledged congressional investigation of the People's Temple organization (see U.S. Government, 1979a, 1979b) which ACM supporters wanted to extend to other marginal religions, a "trial balloon" proposal by the National Institute of Mental Health to consider funding of scientific/academic research into new religions (personal communications), and a recommendation included in the staff report on the People's Temple submitted to the House Committee on Foreign Affairs for further research on cults. The report (U.S. Government, 1979a: 37) stated:

We therefore recommend, on an urgent basis, that the professional scientific community undertake a concentrated program of research and training aimed at understanding fundamental questions in this area. Such a program, under the auspices of the National Institute of Mental Health, must be adequately funded and staffed and should be carried out by whatever mechanism will produce results as soon as possible.

They also recommended that

it would be appropriate to include on the agenda of an upcoming White House Conference on the Family a comprehensive and balanced discussion on the subject of cults with special reference to their mode of operation, the style and tactics of their leaders, and means and methods by which parents and their children can avoid becoming involved with such organizations.

On the state level, a number of legislatures actually established investigating commissions and/or held hearings to consider establishing such commissions. Although none, to our knowledge, had formally launched investigations through issuing subpoenas for religious leaders and organizational records by the end of the decade, in many cases these investigations nevertheless were ongoing and enjoyed broader public support than they would have had before the Jonestown tragedy. However, again, ACM efforts to mobilize governmental support ran into legal and constitutional strictures, and interest group opposition threw up barriers. As of 1980, what the ACM was able to achieve was another round of hearings at which their version of public morality was reasserted and reaffirmed, although the chances of further formal action remained higher than at any time in the previous decade.

In February 1976, Robert Dole, Republican Senator from Kansas and Vice-President during the administration of Gerald Ford, showed sympathy for the ACM and in the movement's eyes was firmly ensconced as an ally in the mold of Leo J. Ryan by holding hearings in the Senate Building at which ACM members are given the opportunity to voice complaints about the UM to various federal officials. Following the Guyana incident, Dole once again came to the forefront as he had in 1976 with public support for investigations of "new" religious movements and a thinly disguised suspicion of their legitimacy. In early December 1978, shortly after the first reports of the Jonestown massacre, Dole called for an examination of all "cults'" tax-exempt statuses. In a letter to Senator Russell B. Long, Chairman of the Senate Finance Committee, he explicitly linked this proposed investigation of "cults" (in particular, Moon's UM) to Jonestown:

The question surrounding the Jonestown incident and the continuing activity of the Unification Church require action. . . . The public

> needs protection from unscrupulous operations that flout the law
> for their own purposes. . . . The committee should review the criteria
> for determining if an organization is engaging in a bona fide pursuit
> and not a practice which undermines the laws and morals of the
> country [Dallas Times Herald, Dec. 2, 1978].

Though Senator Long's lack of response could hardly be taken as support for such an inquiry, Dole's request quickly took a back seat to his prominent role in presiding over a second major public hearing in Washington, D.C., this time with a departure from the format of the earlier 1976 hearings: On this second occasion, "cult" spokespersons were invited and permitted to speak.

The hearings to consider "The Cult Phenomenon in the United States" (technically a public information meeting) were held on Monday, February 5.[4] Late on Sunday afternoon, February 4, ACM leaders conducted a special pre-hearing memorial service for Leo J. Ryan at the First Baptist Church (the church of President Jimmy Carter and family) in Washington, D.C. Attended by several hundred ACM members from across the country (including the Ryan family), the service featured four different clergymen as speakers, among them CERF leaders Rabbi Maurice Davis and Reverend George Swope (IFF, 1979b). The sacrificial meaning of Ryan's death was reinforced for participants as well as the importance of recalling both the deaths of over 200 children at Jonestown and that 1979 was the International Year of the Child.

Thus regalvanized with determination, ACM representatives and supporters set out for the Russell Senate Office Building early the following morning to press their requests for government action against "cults" in a three-hour public forum. In the Senate Office Building the reserved caucus room was packed from wall to wall by 9 a.m. with partisans, government officials, and media reporters as well as the scheduled speakers. The audience was noisy (segments of it later loudly applauding or booing in sympathy with particular speakers) and doubtlessly excited by the presence of luminaries from both the UM (such as President Neil Salonen) and the ACM (such as deprogrammers Ted Patrick and Joe Alexander, Sr., and a veritable "who's who" of anti-cult association activists). "Moonies" and civil liberties advocates wore anti-Dole badges and buttons and held up placards. Many ACM members were unable to find standing room or even gain entry due to the size of the crowd. According to ACM reports (for example, 1979b), over 1000 members of the UM had spent much of the previous night braving subzero temperatures, singing, praying, and queuing up at the entrances to the building.

Dole, like many of the public officials who spoke, was careful to preface his remarks with a disclaimer as to the constitutional implications of this meeting: "This is not a hearing, not an inquisition, not a witch hunt, not a media event, but an effort to try to learn something" (AFF, 1979a: 8). However, individual statements quickly took on an accusatory tone. Commenting on the efforts of (among others) the UM, the American Civil Liberties Union, and various conventional denominational religious leaders to discourage the holding of the meeting, Dole said: "I can think of a couple of my colleagues who decided it was better not to show up here this morning" (AFF, 1979a: 20-21). Dole went on to speak of the government's obligation to investigate accusation of tax fraud and the possibility that the government "by granting a tax exemption for certain groups, actually is subsidizing activities prohibited under our tax laws" (AFF, 1979a: 23).

After opening statements by Dole and Senator Mark Hatfield (who alluded to experiencing deceptions in his own dealings with the UM), the Guyana theme surfaced repeatedly in subsequent presentations and gradually became dominant in discussions of other "cults." Representative Richard Ottinger, for example, stated:

> The Jonestown massacre I suppose illustrates the extremes of the dangers that can be presented by the cult phenomenon. But we have had accusations made by parents that their children have been coerced into entering cults, that once they were there they have been physically and mentally abused, subjected to drugs, they have been physically prevented from returning to society; that immigration laws have been violated; that the tax laws have been violated. These were all very serious matters that I don't think we can, as a government, ignore because *they are attempted to be cloaked in religious activity* [AFF, 1979a: 11-12; italics added].

Senator Edward Zorinsky mixed imputation with disclaimer when he noted: "There is a duty, too, it seems to me, to ask questions about the Unification Church, though I do not wish to imply that it and the People's Temple are in any way similar." Zorinsky went on to refer to some of Moon's followers ("the extreme cases") as "little more than automatons" and likened the idealistic civilization aspired to by Moon and to which Moon "has committed the massive financial resources of his diverse and far-flung business, political and religious enterprises" to the Roman Empire (AFF, 1979a: 13-14). Other officials made no overt connection between the UM and Jonestown, but they alluded to possible violations of laws that might remove them from First Amendment protection. Thus, Representative Robert Giaimo warned:

> I am convinced . . . that a distinction must be made between relig-
> ious beliefs and certain actions taken in the name of religion. Our
> society must tolerate unorthodox beliefs; that's a basic component
> of freedom; but society cannot tolerate all actions taken in the name
> of religion [AFF, 1979a: 16].

Subsequent speakers on behalf of the ACM showed little restraint in their accusations against American "cults." Others showed little compunction in lumping the UM and other religious groups together with the People's Temple as insidious, exploitive, and menacing to both members and larger society. Robert Boettcher, former staff director for the Fraser Committee[5] which had conducted an extensive investigation of the UM's role in recent controversies involving South Korea's relations with the United States, testified that "we are witnessing a perversion of freedom of religion by leaders of cults who think they have special license to violate laws" (AFF, 1979a: 31). Boettcher vehemently denounced the UM as a multinational "greedy business conglomerate" with subversive ties to the South Korean Central Intelligence Agency, "an army of brainwashed, obedient servants," and an "antidemocratic, brain-washed political party"; he went on to characterize Moon as a power-lusting "menace."

Dr. John Clark, the foremost psychiatric proponent of the brainwashing model, compared alleged "mind control" powers of the People's Temple leaders with similar alleged abilities of the Symbionese Liberation Army, the Manson cult, and the Nazi Party. Clark linked these allegations against current "cults" to Guyana ("our holocaust," in his words) and in his argument drew upon the favorite ACM atrocity tale themes of suicide and parricide. Similarly, Flo Conway and Jim Siegelman, whose "snapping" thesis we examined in our discussion of the brainwashing model in Chapter 3, reiterated their claims that mind-control techniques alleged to have been used by Jim Jones to hold sway over his followers were indeed utilized by other "cults"—in particular, the UM—in America at that time.

Most important, the theme that Jonestown could and would be repeated unless the federal government acted soon was reiterated by ACM speakers. For example, Jackie Speier, former legal counsel to Leo J. Ryan and one of those wounded in the Port Kaituma airstrip ambush, stated in her testimony that the "major religious cults in the United States show surprising similarities" to characteristics of the People's Temple group as she had observed it firsthand; for example, the presence of a charismatic figure "who had the ability to mesmerize his followers," behavior in members that is "devoid of normal emotion," and "monosyllabic, programmed" responses to questions. She gave the assembled officials an ominous warning:

> I am a victim of Guyana, but I am alive and very mindful of my responsibility to try and inform others about the tragedy. I hope this Committee, during the course of its investigation, will also be mindful of perhaps the singularly most important fact of Jonestown: *It can happen again* [AFF: 1979a: 24-29; italics added].

Likewise, Rabbi Maurice Davis explicitly linked the violence and destructiveness of the Nazi Youth Movement and the People's Temple with similar proclivities in the UM. He also asked the assembled congressmen a rhetorical question replete with some of the most vitriolic imagery ever offered in ACM literature:

> How many Jonestowns must there be before we begin to do something? Gentlemen of the Congress: I am not here to protest against religion, or against religions. I am here to protest against child molesters, for as surely as there are those who lure children with lollypops in order to rape their bodies, so, too, are there those who lure children with candy-coated lies in order to rape their minds [AFF, 1979a: 77].

Not surprisingly, there were those who not only predicted violence in this country similar to that in Jonestown but who also claimed to have anticipated the latter massacre. Daphne Greene, an outspoken west coast ACM activist and mother of an UM member, stated that events in Jonestown were no surprise to her. Indeed, she claimed, Jonestown was "highly predictable and was merely a harbinger of what is sure to happen as cults see themselves threatened by actions of an aroused populace" (AFF, 1979a: 56).

Unlike the 1976 "hearings," in 1979 Dole offered "equal time" to civil liberties advocates and to spokespersons representing the UM. The allegations we have sampled thus far did not pass unchallenged. In general, the rebuttals of the ACM's opponents followed a fairly standard argument firmly grounded in First Amendment rights and assumptions of cultural relativity. Dean Kelley, Director for Civil and Religious Liberty in the

National Council of Churches and appearing on behalf of the American
Civil Liberties Union, stated:

> We would be suspicious of an attempt to form a legal distinction
> between so-called "cults," a term that is usually used in a derogatory
> sense to apply to religions we don't understand and don't like, to
> distinguish them from what are thought to be more legitimate
> religons [AFF, 1979a: 37].

Likewise, Jeremiah S. Gutman, Director of the ACLU, stated:

> We have resorted and heard today resort to such words as pseudo
> religion. The first Amendment doesn't permit a distinction between
> religion and pseudo religion, because to do so would be to say that
> some religions are truthful and others are pseudo or false [AFF,
> 1979a: 68-69].

Later, he lashed out at the legitimacy of the meeting itself as part of a
"witchhunt" employing a "McCarthy-like catalog" of "cults." In response
to pro-ACM law professor Richard Delgado's proposed regulations for
"conversionist activities," which included, among other protections for the
"religious consumer," mandatory full disclosure of one's affiliation and
intent to proselytize, a required "cooling off period" for converts, and
governmental licensing of religious recruiters, Gutman bluntly commented: "I can't imagine how a lawyer could even suggest that such a
procedure could pass muster under a First Amendment test" (AFF,
1979a: 72). He referred to compulsory psychiatric treatment of "cult"
members, another Delgado suggestion, as "Sovietation of medicine."
      Others were equally hard on the core themes of ACM ideology running
through much of the earlier testimony. Reverend Barry Lynn, an ordained
United Church of Christ minister and denominational official, criticized
allegations of psychological harm resulting from "cult" involvement:

> To arrive at this conclusion they [the anti-cultists] engaged in
> unsystematic chronicling of terrifying anecdotes and quasi-scientific
> reports which lead them to believe in a theory of "mind control" at
> least as dubious and incomprehensible as the theologies of the
> religions groups they attack [AFF, 1979a: 97].

In response to statements such as that of a Catholic priest from the
Archdiocese of New York who proclaimed, "A true religious movement
will be able to withstand any investigation. It is the ones that are falsely

labeled that will fail" (AFF, 1979a: 97), Unification Church President Neil Salonen criticized the very holding of such a quasi-official meeting and predicted that it would have a "chilling effect on the free exercise of . . . beliefs" (AFF, 1979a: 118).

STATE HEARINGS AND INVESTIGATIONS

The ACM, as we have shown, did not lack for sympathetic public officials and legislators at the national level who were willing to use a promising wedge of attack against "cults." This was even more the case at the state level. The regional orientation of the various ACM groups as well as the opportunities for more frequent contact at the local level made it natural for them to focus heavily on influencing state officials such as attorney generals and legislators. By the summer of 1979, sympathetic allies in state houses had initiated bills to alter laws covering charitable solicitations, income tax exemptions, and property taxes (so as to curtail financial expansion by groups such as the UM) or called for investigations of "new" religions in such diverse states as Illinois, Wisconsin, New Jersey, Pennsylvania, Rhode Island, Texas, Minnesota, Connecticut, and Michigan. For example, the Connecticut General Law Committee conducted an informal investigation of only the UM's activities (and not those of other "new" religions) in that state. In Illinois, House Representative Betty Hoxsey, amid some controversy, sponsored House Resolution No. 121 to create a temporary six-member commission (three of whom were American Civil Liberties members) to investigate "illegal activities of religious cults who are coercing our children to join up with them." During the subsequent hearings, Hoxsey dismissed First Amendment considerations with her statement: "Any true religion doesn't have to worry about investigations into illegal activities . . . because they would not commit any illegal acts" (Illinois Times, June 21, 1979). The Minnesota House Judiciary Subcommittee, at the encouragement of Wallace Martin, President of Free Minds, Inc., held similar hearings at which anti-cult spokespersons such as lawyer/professor/deprogramming advocate Richard Delgado testified and then scheduled further hearings. In Pennsylvania, House Resolution No. 20 established yet another investigative committee to study groups which employed "improper mind control techniques in their re cruitment," techniques which presumably "undermine voluntary consent, employ duress, and interfere with free will." While regional ACM groups could and did continue to press for legislative/investigative action by federal officials (for example, a national petition coordinated by the Maryland chapter of the Individual Freedom Foundation, a widespread

ACM group, was distributed nationally within the ACM, its signers urging Congress to continue the investigations begun by the House Subcommittee on International Organizations into possible legal violations by the UM), they nevertheless put much energy into swaying state governments toward the ACM ideology (AFF, 1979b; IFF, 1979c, 1979d).

New York State, where the UM had its national headquarters, seminary, newspaper and printing houses, Moon's private residence, and many of its American members, witnessed perhaps an inordinate amount of such anti-cult activity and illustrates the range of repressive political action which ACM members and/or sympathetic legislators sought to implement and legitimate. The most extreme of these political attempts at social control occurred in late 1977, when New York Assemblyman Robert Wertz introduced bill AB9566-A to amend the state's penal code with a new section entitled "Promoting a Pseudo-Religious Cult." The bill aimed to make promoting such a "cult" a felony. (It is reproduced in toto in Chapter 7).

The bill failed in 1978, due in part to its dubious constitutionality and in part to a vigorous countercampaign against it by persons associated with the American Civil Liberties Union and various "new" religious groups. However, Jonestown suddenly made legislation calling for further social control measures seem more justified. Thus, in March 1979, Wertz sponsored a bill to allot $500,000 to form a committee to study the mental health aspects of "cults" and to print and disseminate booklets containing ACM ideology to adolescents on a statewide basis. The link between the events of Jonestown and Wertz's sponsorship was explicit:

> There is no mistaking the detrimental effects so-called "pseudo-religious cults" have on the youth of this country. In the wake of Guyana . . . it should be evident that such legislation is sorely needed [Wertz, 1979].

He added: "There is, of course, a concern that established and conventional religion not be jeopardized by a program to impede the growth of cults." The UM responded to this proposed legislation the following May with demonstrations in Albany led by the Ad Hoc Committee Against Nazism, its members dressed in Gestapo storm trooper uniforms and composed of students from the Unification Theological Seminary. The bill subsequently was postponed amid the usual concerns over constitutional issues.

However, a more serious legislative inquiry emerged in New York during the summer of 1979 and forced the UM—for a time at least—to take the defensive. In mid-1979, apostate Christopher Edwards, author of the ACM potboiler *Crazy For God* (1979), made public charges that child abuse was rampant in east- and west-coast branches of the UM. By mid-summer 1979, the child abuse allegations against the UM had come to the attention of Howard L. Lasher, a Brooklyn Assemblyman chairing the state assembly Committee on Child Care. With the incidents of Jonestown still fresh in mind, and generalizing from the latter to the UM and "cults" in general, Lasher began in July to solicit testimonies from both "cult" and anti-cult spokespersons on alleged "cult" child abuse. Typical of his solicitation for information was his letter of July 19 sent to the Church of Scientology of New York:

> In my capacity as Chairman of the New York State Assembly Child Care Committee, I have become increasingly concerned with the welfare of children living in communal situations. Although this matter was brought into focus last fall by the tragedy in Jonestown, I do not imply that every group is suspect of the extremes practiced by that one infamous organization. . . . I would like to make certain that groups located in our state offer safe environments for minors who are involved with them and that these children are protected from maltreatment or abuse [Lasher, 1979].

In Lasher's opening statement at the two-day hearings convened on August 10 at the World Trade Center in New York City, he again reiterated the Guyana Theme: "In the aftermath of the mass suicides last November in Jonestown where, of the 910 people who died, 260 were children, the existance of and practices of cults has become of deep concern to myself and other members of the assembly" (Stathos, 1979).

Edwards was the first substantive witness and made his charges in a straightforward manner:

> During my eight months in the Unification Church in Berkeley California, I had the opportunity to witness emotional torment to a number of members' children, a direct result of the practice of the secret documents of the group. Since the group teaches that children born of marriages outside the cult are children of satan's world, sons and daughters of members were generally treated with minimal care at best. Mothers were separated from their children who were kept in a small trailer on a farm in _____ California. If parents requested to visit their children too often or if they expressed much sorrow due to separation from their child, they were chastised as people who were too attached to their fallen life [New York, 1979: 11].

Edwards further charged that several of these children were of school age, yet were never sent to school and that they were supervised by a young girl who gave them minimal attention, herself allegedly suffering from frequent hallucinations. To Edwards, the children in the "hot trailer" appeared "scared and disorganized," living in isolation from the new recruits. Moreover, he charged that the overcrowded children's trailer adjoined a second trailer where adult UM members were housed without medical attention when they become ill:

> Children were constantly exposed to any illness from measles through a number of disorders caused [by] inadequate sanitary conditions. On at least one occasion when an epidemic on the farm was severe, adult members who were ill would be housed in the same trailer with these children [New York, 1979: 12].

Separated often from their biological parents, these children were, by Edwards' account, further abused and tormented by UM members who induced nightmares in the children and interpreted these dreams as satanic attacks. Perhaps just as significant, after his allegation about the Berkeley branch of the UM, Edwards repeated similar rumors of mistreatment of children heard from ex-UM members who allegedly saw such phenomena in Barrytown, New York, at the UM's seminary.

New York State officials, chaired by Lasher, closely cross-examined key witness Edwards and generally revealed the dubious foundation of much of his sensational accusations, particularly with regard to the New York UM. Edwards was only the first witness, however, and the symbolic importance of holding the hearing took precedence over whether or not his allegations passed muster as credible evidence under rigious examination. Of the more than 20 witnesses appearing during the hearings, the majority were hostile to the UM. In addition to Edwards, the latter critics included Rabbi Maurice Davis, Jean Merritt (a psychiatric social worker and founder of Return to Personal Choice, Inc.), and Galen Kelly, a private investigator-turned-deprogrammer. Among the witnesses for the UM were Michael Young Warder, publisher of *The News World* (the UM's daily newspaper), former president Farley Jones, Professor Warren Lewis of the UM's Unification Theological Seminary faculty, and representatives from the Alliance for the Preservation of Religious Liberty (APRL) and the American Civil Liberties Union. The questioning of UM representatives began on the subject of treatment of children in the UM. Committee members probed for details of the ages of UM children, provisions for their schooling and/or day care, and sanitation and health facilities available to them. Such questioning produced little but blunt denials that conditions such as Edwards had described existed anywhere in the New York UM.

(Interestingly, Farley Jones, himself a father of six children, took some pains to separate the east-coast "mainstream" UM from the Berkeley, California, wing—as did Professor Warren Lewis in no uncertain terms—reflecting a growing schism within the UM about which the public generally knew nothing but which was described in our earlier volume on the movement—see Bromley and Shupe, 1979a: 97-105, 138-142.) Soon the committee became sidetracked on the inevitably sensational questions concerning the larger operation and resources of the UM. In reply, UM witnesses such as Michael Young Warder berated the committee for its dubious constitutional appropriateness in the open-ended investigation of "cults" and not other religious groups, stating: "I feel that there has been too much emphasis on the government's concern with the new religions" (Stathos, 1979). Instead, Warder challenged the committee to put funds and "more teeth and a little more punch" into control of heroin and narcotics as well as into criminal justice in general.

The UM did not treat Lasher's hearings lightly, for in spite of popular stereotypes about celibate "Moonies" there were married members in the UM, some of whom had young children either being raised in conventional nuclear family settings or in special nurseries while their parents were dispatched elsewhere on assignments important to the movement. UM witnesses reported back to leaders their expectations of further trouble from the hearings. The special theological significance of the family for UM members, however unusual its appearance to outsiders, lent this particular issue extraordinary seriousness. On the final day of hearings, Farley Jones wrote UM President Neil Salonen:

> From the questions they asked, they had caught wind of the nurseries in Tarrytown. . . . The most dangerous point they are considering is to extend the conservatorship laws of New York to include the children of cult members. If the parents [members of cults] can be proven to be mentally incompetent then the children will be made wards of the state [Jones, 1979].

Likewise, Michael Young Warder, in a memorandum to various UM officials, expressed his uneasiness and urged their anticipation of further harassment from Albany:

> I believe it is reasonable to expect that the Tarrytown nursery will be visited by a New York State Agency of some sort in the near future. It may be an agency charged with supervicion [sic] of "foster care facilities" or perhaps the State Health Department. Evidently, our nursery is in the category of a "foster care facility." I would suppose the nursery staff should check the statutory limitations for foster care facilities as soon as possible [Warder, 1979].

Warder recommended the UM's public relations office to prepare a "basketful of literature" for each committee member including a demographic profile of UM membership. He also suggested that remarks made by Galen Kelly be preserved for a possible libel suit or other pending litigation. (Kelly had boasted to the committee that he had gotten into legal trouble only twice out of 130 deprogrammings—neither of which occurrences produced indictments—sometimes using admittedly questionable legal tactics).

Summary

The Jonestown tragedy occurred at a time when the ACM was foundering in its attempts to repress the new religious movements. While the ACM had succeeded in discrediting and occasionally harassing them it was not able to pose a serious threat to such groups as the UM through mobilizing mechanisms of social control through the political institution. Jonestown was an unexpected event which provided a scenario more hellishly gruesome and spectacular than ACM members had ever been able to construct in even their most virulent atrocity stores. In this sense Jonestown illustrates the impact which a single unanticipated event in the larger social environment can have on the course of a social movement. The ACM quickly seized the opportunity to trumpet anew its claims of a "cult menace," and for a moment the nation literally paused to consider "the cults" in precisely the terms which the ACM had for so long hoped. Numerous apostates from the UM came forward and claimed to have received suicide training, and once again the UM was identified as the ACM's primary target, this time as the "suicide cult."

From another perspective, Jonestown illustrates the problems countermovements face in attempting to institute formal legal repression. Just as quickly as public attention was riveted on Jonestown, it shifted away with the emergence of new crises. Soon thereafter political turmoil in the Middle East, the upcoming 1980 presidential political campaign, the Soviet invasion of Afghanistan, and domestic problems such as fuel shortages and rising inflation eclipsed public concern over possible future Jonestowns. It is significant, for example, that on the first anniversary of Jonestown there was only one-day, back-page coverage in most newspapers given to the incident, and these stories contained neither a sense of urgency nor links with the current activities of other "cults." Jonestown also demonstrated that even with such a spectacular event to mobilize public anxiety, the structural impediments to invoking repressive sanctions through legitimate channels proved well nigh insurmountable for the ACM. While major institutions were willing to offer sympathetic, symbolic support, the ACM was not powerful enough, and dominant institutional interests were not sufficiently threatened, to overcome the legal/constitutional ground rules under which disputes were resolved. Thus, the ACM was forced to settle for symbolic victories in which its values were reaffirmed as public morality by the media and religious and political institutions. This, of course, was no small victory, since the UM was substantially discredited, forced to be consistently on the defensive, and excluded from a number of legitimate institutional forums to which it sought access. Yet, at least for the more extreme ACM proponents, the final fruits of victory proved no less elusive than they had a decade before.

NOTES

1. J. Gordon Melton of the Institute for the Study of American Religion, Inc., apparently was collecting data on the group in the early 1970s as part of a larger survey of all American religious bodies, but not because the group had been defined as a new religious movement.

2. It was easy for opponents of the UM to cull Moon's speeches for "Armageddon rhetoric" and heady "last-days" imagery that spoke of confrontations with satanic communism and hinted at possible casualties among UM members. Such references to altruistic death hardly resembled detailed suicide instructions, however, as the following excerpt from the *120 Day Training Manual* (Sudo, 1975: 43), now out of use by the UM, illustrates:

> If the parents [the Moons] are alive, at the price of my own life all mankind can be born anew. But if I am alive and the Parent's life [sic] is lost, no mankind can be saved. The Parents' life must be more precious than the life of the children . . . a prayer: "Father, I can give my life. In the case of emergency please take my life first. If only you and Mother and Father's family can be saved, I am willing to die."

3. The truth of the allegations seems difficult to establish. Certainly, the "Oakland Family," a sectarian branch of the UM where suicide instructions allegedly were given, with its passionate reverence for its leaders Martin Irwin ("Mose") Durst and his wife almost eclipsing loyalty to Moon himself and its unwavering certainty in the moral superiority of its radically communal celibate lifestyle (see Bromley and Shupe 1979a: 138-142), was capable, under feelings of besiegement, of considering death in

preference to being forced to abandon a highly valued faith and lifestyle. Such sentiments are, after all, not unusual in the history of persecuted religious minorities. It is quite possible that such lectures, or at least a "don't let them take you alive" theme in lectures and discussions, occurred at some place, perhaps repeatedly.

4. The meeting was officially sponsored by five congressmen, several of whom had been previously involved either with the ACM or "cults": Kansas Senator Robert Dole, New York Representative Hamilton Fish (whose daughter had been a member of the UM), Connecticut Representative Robert Giaimo (who had advocated a federal "cult" investigation together with Leo J. Ryan two years earlier), Vermont Representative Richard Ottinger (another previous "cult" opponent), and Virginia Representative G. William Whitehurst.

5. Its official name was the Subcommittee on International Organizations of the Committee on International Relations, U.S. House of Representatives, chaired by Representative Donald E. Fraser (see U.S. Government, 1978).

Chapter 9

CONCLUSIONS

In one sense this book deals with a rather minor social movement, one which never achieved great organizational strength or even captured the public spotlight, with the exception of media coverage given to spectacular abduction/deprogrammings and occasional dramatic courtroom confrontations. Like the new religions which it so fervently sought to expose and repress, the ACM may well be destined to become simply part of another chapter in the history of sectarian conflicts and challenges by new religions to established denominations which has long characterized the American religious landscape. From another perspective, however, the new religions and the anti-cultists are revealing not just regarding religious and familial conflicts but also regarding the more generic process of attempting to create social order and to preserve established patterns of that social order in the face of what are perceived to be serious threats to it. It is this latter set of issues which lends the "cult"-anti-cult conflict major sociological significance.

Social Order and Social Movements

Here we proceed from the rather basic assumption that human beings operate so as to maximize gratification and minimize deprivation. As social

233

beings, humans construct social relationships which will yield a maximal gratification/deprivation balance. These human relationships are organized through social roles which involve reciprocal sets of normative rights and obligations. Since social order flows largely out of these normative expectations, humans are highly (although variably) dependent upon one another in their attempts to achieve their goals. Social organization, then, emanates from the creation of normative expectations based on actors' relative abilities to influence one another's resources and goal attainment.

For the purposes of the present analysis, we are interested in three specific aspects of social organization. First, organization involves an authority structure—that is, a legitimated differential capacity to exert influence in establishing and maintaining the normatively prescribed bases of social exchange. Second, organization involves a set of goals or interests which can be achieved only by control over the flow of certain sets of resources both within the organization and with other organizations. Third, organization involves symbolic interpretations of actions, resource distribution, and interests which are designed to legitimate these vis-à-vis appropriate audiences so as to avoid challenges to the organization's control of resources, authority structure, and ongoing operation. Each of these aspects of social organization is emergent in the sense that each is the product of ongoing exchanges among individuals and groups. Therefore, any challenge to the established social order is not a challenge to a static structure but to a continuous flow of social exchange which requires concerted effort for its maintenance.

Social movements can be viewed as emergent challenging organizations which have, as a consequence of their development, an interest in promoting change in the distribution of resources within and among at least some other organizations. While the nature and extent of the threats posed by social movements to established organizations vary enormously, some resistance and conflict is likely. Because the normative expectations out of which social order flows are ultimately based on control of resources, the social structure is essentially reshaped by the organizational development of social movements. This "new" social order, however minor the projected change, at least potentially alters the specific interdependencies of organizations and even institutions, which is then the source of resistance and conflict. In particular, we are interested here in challenges to existing organizations' authority structures, goals and interests, and legitimating ideologies.

The new religious movements of the 1970s posed a threat to the distribution of resources within and among established institutions in a number of ways. Social movements like the UM had as their stated goal the transformation of the entire social structure, and in fact they sought to construct an alternative social order in microcosm within the movement itself. We have termed these movements which seek rapid, total structural change as "world-transforming" movements. Because they often begin with few resources, they must rely on the larger society for resource mobilization. For example, the fact that these movements seek rapid change of major proportions but initially have only a small number of members makes it inevitable that members will be recruited from the larger society rather than through the lengthy process of procreation. Because they possess a low capacity to exercise selectivity in recruitment, new members are subjected to intensive socialization in order to achieve the desired behavioral orientation. Naturally, the new religions at issue sought to create normative expectations consistent with their vision of a new social order, but the resulting behavior orientations were patently inconsistent with the requisites of the established social order.

Similarly, such movements typically have limited economic resources with which to initiate and sustain broadly based change. And since they lack skills or commodities which can be utilized to marshall economic resources, those movements that reject coercive tactics are reliant on what are essentially voluntary contributions from the very societies which they condemn, reject, and seek to transform. Predictably, these financial mobilization tactics rely on pressure, deception, or public ignorance for their success and therefore evoke opposition from the larger society.

Further, in seeking to legitimate the change which they envision, social movements of the world-transforming type are compelled to present a reinterpretation of history which describes the sources and consequences of the corrupted present, links current problems of contemporary society to this reconstruction, and offers a vision of the future in which their alternative social order is realized. The movement's ideology thus constitutes a direct attack on the symbolic underpinnings of the established social order and hence exposes to public view problems, inconsistencies, and inequalities which are deliberately camouflaged by established institutions.

These movements exhibit a charismatic type of leadership. The "truths" discovered by or revealed to a movement's leader/founder accords him a special moral status: his unparalleled vision and understanding render him uniquely capable of interpreting past and present events as well as unfolding the future. Individuals recognizing this moral superiority assume the status of disciples in recognition of their lesser capacities. The result is virtual equality among members and enormous social/moral distance between them as a group and the charismatic leader. This, of course, yields the charismatic leader an enormous amount of influence over his followers, and he can be regarded by outsiders as dangerous when such qualities are not put in the service of conventional goals and values.

Finally, such movements seek out public visibility as a means of warning others of the danger of continuing to support the corrupted, decaying status quo, proclaiming their own vision of the future, and attracting members and economic resources. Again, if these movements rely on persuasive rather than coercive means for effecting change, they typically attempt to link the movement to cultural symbols already possessing high legitimacy. This high public profile and portrayal of the movement as promoting central cultural values (which established institutions vehemently dispute) makes it difficult to simply ignore the movement. Gatekeepers of established institutions therefore feel compelled to reveal the movement's "true" identity.

Communal organization is congruent with all of these requisites of world-transforming movements. Members commit virtually all their time, energy, and other resources to the group, and in turn most of the members' day-to-day needs can be met within the group itself. This makes it relatively easy to isolate members from what the ideology defines as a corrupt world. Hence, communal groups are able to achieve intensive socialization in the context of clearly defined role expectations and a high degree of control over sanctions; this produces the kind of rapid behavioral changes characteristic of conversions to the new religions. With no other demands on their time and energy, members are free to focus almost exclusively on proselytization, fund-raising, and proclaiming the movement's message. Perhaps most important, the communal group constitutes an actualized microcosm of the new social order which movement members envision and hence sustains the intense commitment and involvement requisite for communal organization.

From the standpoint of the status quo order, then, the foregoing argument suggests that if social movements are viewed as emergent organizations—that is, as attempts to create social order—then movements of the world-transforming type by their very nature create a social order which is incompatible with the established order. The fact that institutional boundaries are to be redrawn (for example, the UM's design for a socialist theocracy) means that control over resources vital to the pursuit of various established organizations' interests is placed in jeopardy. Not only are resources to be reallocated, but resources to support the movement's emerging alternative order (such as members or money) are drawn from the same society which opposes and resists this development. Further, the social movement seeks to institutionalize normative expectations which render members unresponsive to the incentives and sanctions through which the larger society maintains control over individuals. In addition to this detachment of individuals from conventional incentives, world-transforming movements exercise a high degree of control over members due to the charismatic leadership structure. Members, then, are highly involved and committed but to an organization incompatible with the established order. For purposes of the present analysis, we are concerned with the impact of social movements' emergent organizational structure on established institutions' control of vital resources, achievement of central goals and interests, maintenance of authority, and ability to legitimate its resource control, pursuit of interests, and exercise of authority.

Emergent Organization and Strain

As we documented in Chapter 2, the established institutions for which the strain between the emergent organizational forms of the new religions and their own structures were greatest were the familial and religious institutions. In the case of the family it was the family's interest in preparing offspring for successful entry into the economic system (a goal which had been pursued through commitment of its resources to maximizing educational opportunities) and preservation of parental authority to set normative expectations (which would ensure appropriate behavioral orientations that were jeopardized). By contrast, the new religions had an interest in disengaging individuals from participation in the economic order and creating and defending normative expectations which would yield behavioral orientations consistent with the requisites of communal organization. This clash of interests and struggle for control over what was to both organizations a vital resource (the offspring-converts' time, energy, and loyalty) brought on attempts by each side to exercise authority in order to maintain social control. In those instances where offspring proceeded to join a new religion, not only were familial interests violated, but parental authority was eroded. The communal group literally replaced the family (as in the case of the UM's fictive kinship system where Moon and his wife became "True Parents").

In addition, the family's public portrayal of its goals and exercise of authority were called into question. Parents typically depicted the family as concerned only with their offspring's happiness. Yet, when their *adult* offspring chose a course counter both to parental interests and to parental definitions of what their offspring's interests should be, parents' assertions of their own interests suddenly became highly visible. In addition, the more coercive aspects of parental control which parents hoped could remain implicit surfaced when they literally reasserted their control over their "children," in the most extreme instances through physical abduction and restraint. Finally, parents' pride in their offspring's achievements and developing careers and in their own performance as socializers was undermined. It was embarrassing and even humiliating to admit and attempt to explain this disastrous turn of events to friends and relatives and to have to reconcile the question of how offspring could have become so involved in such bizarre groups with their self-images of having effectively socialized their children.

In the case of the religious institution it was the fundamentalist churches which experienced the greatest strain as a result of the emergence of the new religions. Members of fundamentalist churches relied more heavily on religiously based norms for regulation of their day-to-day behavior than did members of mainline denominations where social control of members by churches was relatively minimal. The former churches therefore had a strong interest in preserving the normative context within which members acted and upon which their loyalty was based. This social control could be exercised, of course, only so long as members recognized the churches' authority. Thus, it was this issue of authority structure which was the primary source of contention.

It was clearly in the interest of the new religious movements to challenge the ideology of established institutions in order to legitimate the new social order which they sought to establish. Their reinterpretations of history and for new cosmologies were proffered as explanations for a range of contemporary social ills and set the stage for their visions of an imminently attainable utopian state. If individuals were to make extreme personal sacrifices to help usher in this new era, then such efforts had to be defined as spiritually indispensable. This motivation was provided in part by the constructions of charismatic leaders, a common commitment to whose respective discoveries of new absolute truth could mobilize members to action, and in part by belief that individual efforts were spiritual works which both enhanced their individual spiritual status and speeded the dawning of a new order. As we observed in Chapter 2, such organizational requisites of the UM in particular clashed with those of fundamentalist churches. In seeking to exert control over members' daily social relationships, fundamentalist churches required absolute spiritual authority. Important elements of this authority derived from Jesus' status as *the* messiah and redeemer, the Christian church as the only legitimate heir of Christ, and the church (through Christ) as the conferrer of salvation through faith. The interests of the fundamentalist churches were to regulate their members' conduct within the context of conventional institutions, while the new religions sought to mobilize individuals to action which involved abandoning pursuit of personal interests in conventional institutions. The symbolic constructions requisite to sustain these two different orientations and levels of commitment conflicted with one another.

As in the case of the family, however, there was also a challenge to the churches' public portrayal of their own mission and its success. Christian churches proclaimed theirs to be the absolute truth and the source of omnitemporal spiritual experience. It was therefore embarrassing to the churches, as it was to families, to acknowledge the attraction of Christians to these new religions and the new converts' apparently deep and satisfying spiritual experiences. Of course, explanations in terms of indirect satanic influence were readily available and invoked, but at the same time much of the fundamentalist literature admitted the failings of the churches to fulfill their spiritual responsibilities. While this recognition of shortcoming may have been viewed in some quarters as a necessary (even healthy) corrective, it was nevertheless humiliating to be forced into such public confessions by groups regarded as spiritual counterfeits.

The mainline denominations were less directly threatened by the rise of the new religions, although it was from these churches that the new religions drew a vast majority of their recruits. The major denominations sought limited control over their members, and hence revisions of the legitimating ideology had fewer organizational implications. These churches did have a major interest in accommodation with the political/economic order, however, and as a result they *were* threatened by the reformulation of institutional boundaries envisioned by the new religions. Churches were protected and assured control of necessary resources so long as the church-state boundaries were not breached. In fact, these churches ended up opposing action by the state against the new religions to avoid any precedent-setting repression by government. The mainline denominations would have faced a major dilemma had the new religions achieved sufficient power to mount a political challenge. This never became a significant issue simply because the new religions never effectively allied themselves and, taken individually, did not control sufficient resources to pose a threat. To the extent that the political institution did consider such action (through legislative hearings), it sought to remove the target groups from the category of religion, thereby preserving that critical but ambiguous boundary.

The dynamics of the conflict between the new religions and the familial and religious institutions initially were played out on an individual level. In the case of the fundamentalist churches, individual ministers spoke out against "cults," attempted to warn parishioners against the "cult menace," and confronted "cults" with biblical evidence of their heresy. In describing the conflict with the UM in Chapter 2 we noted, however, that such efforts were not totally successful. The UM pushed ahead aggressively with witnessing campaigns, conspicuously sought to cloak itself with the mantle of legitimate Christianity, and asserted the superiority of its own doctrines. The UM (like other new religions) was then seeking to shape normative expectations in a fashion consistent with its own organizational interests and was unresponsive to warnings and reactions when its resource mobilization efforts threatened the interests of established churches. It was not, however, merely the threat to resources, interests, and authority itself which ultimately provoked attempts to exert social control over the new religions; rather it was their inability and/or unwillingness to recognize their own deviance (in this case, heresy). Each of the new religions characteristically claimed superiority of "truth" over all other groups and rejected sectarian labels. Fundamentalists thus concluded that the new religions were incapable of orienting their behavior in accord with the dictates of "true," "legitimate" religion.

A similar sequence typically unfolded in encounters between members of the new religions and their families, as we detailed in Chapter 2. Challenges to parental interests and authority as well as what parents defined their offspring's interest were met first with efforts to reason with offspring and, later in the sequence, to sanction their aberrant conduct. However, these efforts were frequently unsuccessful because of the rapidity of the changes in offspring's role behavior (as a product of the intensive socialization and readily assumable roles in communal groups), the ineffectiveness of parental sanctions (as a result of the communal group's capacity to provide physical, emotional, and social support), and the offspring's integration of role behavior in terms of what was to parents an unintelligible symbolic system. This outcome was extremely anxiety-producing because, until recently (at least from the parents' perspective), there had been a common set of interests, mutual contributions to building of important career resources, and behavioral orientations based on shared normative expectations within the family. All of these seemed to have quite suddenly and inexplicably disappeared. Again, then, it was not merely the challenge to parental interests and authority which led parents to attempt to impose social control measures, but also the fact that they perceived their offspring to be incapable of responding in an appropriate way. That is, offspring were not responding as parents could imagine themselves having responded to a similar set of stimuli. Once offspring's behaviors were deemed unintelligible *and* uncontrollable, parents began to conclude that their offspring were no longer responsible for their own actions.

Conferral of Deviant Status

Once families and fundamentalist churches had concluded that the new religions, their leaders, and members were unable to develop appropriate lines of action, they initiated attempts to exert social control over the new religions. This exertion of social control was contingent upon the designation of the new religions as deviant—that is, outside the boundaries of and unresponsive to shared normative expectations. This designation of deviance in effect constituted a lowering of the status of the new religions and their members; due to their inability to respond appropriately, these groups and their members were allocated fewer rights and more obligations vis-à-vis the larger society. In other words, because they were unable or unwilling to align their actions in accord with what were defined as legitimate, shared expectations, these groups were obligated to allow representatives of conventional society to align their actions for them. If this imposition of deviant status were successful, the new religions would be compelled to accept a new set of normative expectations of their behavior, one which incorporated social exclusion from free access to and participation in the larger society as well as symbolic degradation of their actions, motives, and goals.

The imposition of deviant status was largely determined by the two sides' relative resource capacity (power). The balance of power was weighted heavily in favor of the familial and religious institutions because of their much greater capacity to form alliances with other institutions possessing symbolic and behavioral sanctioning capability. Individual families and churches lacked the capacity to take significant actions against the new religions (with the exception of families' individual vigilante attempts to "rescue" their own offspring). What emerged in both cases, therefore, were alliances of families (anti-cult associations) and coalitions of fundamentalist churches (for example, the Spiritual Counterfeits Project and various other interchurch groups) which were based on having experienced a common threat and mutual incapacity for adequately responding to that threat individually. That these alliances were very narrowly based, however, can be seen in the facts that (1) participants in the fundamentalist coalition at other times competed vigorously with one another for members and disputed one another's sectarian theological interpretations, and (2) that families which recovered their offspring from "cults" usually dropped out of anti-cult associations shortly thereafter.

There were, as we pointed out in Chapter 2, significant differences between even these two components of the ACM with respect to the nature and extent of threat posed by the new religions. The fundamentalist churches were primarily concerned that the new religions not gain access to the symbols of religious legitimacy through which they exercised authority. As churches, they had little interest in demonstrating coercive power over specific members, and they could expect no support from other institutions in attempting such control. For families, the loss of a single offspring was a devastating blow to familial interests; challenges to parental authority were a secondary concern. For obvious emotional reasons, families also had somewhat greater potential for tolerance of efforts to control their "children." The result of these differences between the familial and religious institutions resulted in very different methods of gaining behavioral and symbolic leverage on the new religions.

The attempt led by the ACM to confer deviant status on the new religions required symbolic degradation of those groups. The nature of the symbolic constructs the ACM sought to impose reflected the interests of the two components. As we discussed in Chapter 3, the religious and familial institutions chose the deception and possession imagery, respectively. Consistent with their quest for preservation of church authority based on biblical Christianity, fundamentalist supporters of the ACM argued that members of the new religions were spiritually naive, idealistic but misguided religious zealots unwittingly enlisted in a pseudo-religious crusade corrupted by satanic influence. This symbolic construction of new religions' converts' actions implied no direct, coercive control over them, as they retained their essential humanity/free will and were in a position to ultimately see the error of their ways and give themselves up to Christ. By contrast, many ACM families aimed to legitimate direct, physical control over their offspring. Consistent with this objective, the family-dominated anti-cult associations and family-supported deprogrammers portrayed members of the new religions as innocents possessed by coercive mind-control techniques which reduced them to zombie-like slaves in the service of egomaniac power-hungry religious charlatans. Once their minds had been captured and imprisoned, these individuals were incapable of reasserting their free will/former natural personality without the exorcism-like process of deprogramming.

Although these two ideologies differed in certain key respects, there also existed some important continuities. First, in both cases the ideologies emerged over time rather than being created full-blown. This process was much more rapid among the fundamentalist churches than it was among ACM families, since the former, despite the lack of organizational coordination, could react in historically erected Christian criteria for heresy. The brainwashing ideology employed by ACM families emerged simultaneously with parental efforts to defend family interests and authority and awaited inputs from sympathetic behavioral scientists for its elaborated, more sophisticated formulation. Second, in both cases the members of the new religions were portrayed as the unwitting victims of an evil, anti-social force (although different degrees of social control were called for in the two metaphors). Each model thus presented the deviance as accidental rather than deliberate, and hence the appropriate response was educational/therapeutic rather than punitive/repressive. Third, in both models the new religions as organizations and their leaders in particular were depicted in more anti-social terms, although the supporters of the brainwashing/possession metaphor went further in this direction. Finally, as we noted in Chapter 3, formulation of the anti-cult ideology at least partially neutralized blame directed at the respective institutions. In the case of the church, the rise of "cults" was simply another attempt by satanically inspired forces to take advantage of lapses in Christian faith and wariness and called for vigorous, forceful reassertion of Christian authority. In the case of the family, neither parents nor offspring could be blamed if the latter fell victim to mysterious, coercive mind-control techniques. Indeed, parental "rescue" could then be conceived of as an enormous risk taken in the service of sacrificial love.

These ideologies which developed in the various components of the ACM served as the basis for seeking behavioral controls over the new religions. Both the family-based anti-cult associations/deprogrammers and coalitions of predominantly fundamentalist churches sought alliances with other institutions that possessed the capacity to impose sanctions. In the case of the fundamentalists, the problems in forming alliances were less problematic for two reasons. On one hand, these churches sought few behavioral controls, and so the cost of support was considerably less for their allies. On the other hand, most of the controls they sought could be imposed by allies refraining from positive action (for example, rejecting bids for membership in groups of "legitimate" churches such as the National Council of Churches or not extending free, uncritical media coverage to the spokespersons for the new religions). The fundamentalist churches then were able to reassert their own authority in books and tracts which exposed the divergence of heretical "cult" doctrines from biblical Christianity.

The problems confronting the family-supported components of the ACM were more complex. They sought repressive action against "cults" as organizations through the lobbying efforts of the anti-cult associations as well as at least tacit support for deprogramming. This campaign encountered two major difficulties. First, the anti-cult associations were never able to mobilize the key resources (members and money) with which a strong organization could be built. They vacillated between federated and centralized organizational forms, but neither produced sufficient mobilization of resources to mount a serious lobbying effort before the federal government. They were sometimes successful in convincing local officials to impose sanctions (for example, ordinance restrictions on fund-raising teams), but these measures yielded occasional harassment rather than systematic repression.

Second, the punitive sanctions and legitimation for the use of force that the ACM sought constituted comprised a threat to the allies' own interests as well as those of other pressure groups. Allies were willing to absorb the costs associated with the use of coercion only where their own vital interests were involved. So, as we detailed in Chapter 7, while fundamentalists actively opposed "cults," they stopped short of advocating deprogramming, and mainline denominations adopted an even more equivocal position. Maintenance of the boundary was a more pressing concern to major denominations than was the "cult" crisis. While certain federal officials were willing to sponsor informal hearings, the federal government would neither pass laws which breached the church-state boundary nor abdicate its monopoly on the legitimate use of violence. It was only in those cases where governmental interests were potentially threatened (Jonestown and "Koreagate") that more aggressive actions were undertaken. In these and other cases, then, allies' actions reflected protection of their own interests as much as they did support of ACM interests.

What allies were willing to do was rebuff requests for actions favorable to the new religions. Such actions had little cost for these allies, offered limited support to the ACM, and operated to systematically exclude the new religions from access to conventional settings. As we documented in

Chapter 7, a wide variety of institutions contributed to these exclusionary actions. The combined impact of these exclusionary activities was devastating to the new religions, however, as they were reliant on a strategy of persuasion to achieve their goals and mobilize resources. Rather than concentrating their limited resources on goal attainment, they were forced to expend much of their resources on simple defensive actions designed to curtail harassment and ensure their survival.

While the ACM was unable to move the new religions or their members into a position where legitimated management or outright coercive repression was possible, they were nevertheless highly successful at achieving symbolic degradation of these movements. Affixing the label "cults" to the new religions (however imprecise from sociological and even theological viewpoints), along with all the stereotypical attributes we have described in foregoing chapters, was both more easily accomplished and also extremely effective in locating these movements beyond the pale of public morality. The reasons for the success at the imposition of ACM-inspired symbolic sanctions were many. Numerous institutions perceived a potential threat to themselves and the established social order in general and therefore were willing—at least rhetorically—to take a stand against them. In addition, institutional gatekeepers were much more likely to share the values and world view of the ACM than were the new religions and hence, at least through symbolic gestures, rallied to the formers' defense. Further, the family and church were allocated legitimacy for their respective roles within society; thus, their appeals for assistance were met with some measure of symbolic support when defined as being consistent with their socially defined roles. In addition, the new religions lacked allies who might resist the ACM's campaign of symbolic degradation. While a few groups defended these movements' legal/constitutional rights, virtually no powerful groups advocated their cause. Finally, the testimony of apostates from the new religions offered dramatic, powerful "proof" which the new religions found difficult to refute. To much of the public, parents and former members of the new religions had no reason to construct such stories aside from a desire to warn others of the dangers of cults. As a result, these stories gained widespread credibility and were the most significant factor in the symbolic degradation of the new religions.

Once it commenced, the symbolic discrediting of the new religions created a ripple effect through the entire society. Each group which engaged in exclusionary activity (which in turn became public knowledge) or denigrated the new religions as a group influenced the behavior of other similar groups acting at a later time. The fact that there was a constant barrage of accusations against the new religions exponentially impugned their credibility and led to the classic presumption that "where there is smoke, there is fire." This virtually complete discrediting of the new religions in turn helped to produce the self-fulfilling prophecy so well documented by labeling theorists. The new religions increased their norm-violating conduct (such as deceptive practices in fund-raising and misrepresentation in witnessing), became more defensive and secretive in their relations with outsiders (for example, toward parents and investigatory agencies), and began to develop stronger exclusionary subcultural beliefs which increased their isolation and rejection of the outside world (outsiders were seen as satanic). At this point, the process of social/symbolic exclusion had achieved a momentum and self-sustaining quality of its own that had the effect of conferring long-term, if not irrevocable, deviant status on the new religious movements.

Perhaps the best illustration of the self-sustaining nature of the deviance conferral process was to be found in the activities of the deprogrammers. Initially responding to a perceived lack of support from law enforcement officials and parental requests for assistance, deprogrammers informally undertook "rescue" missions. However, these new vigilantes quickly recognized the lucrative potential of their new-found enterprise and sought to transform it into an accepted occupation. Despite their relative lack of success in this regard, they did push the ACM as a whole toward a more extreme position. They were forced by their own developing organizational interests to insist that all new religious converts were brainwashed and that they alone possessed a unique set of skills and knowledge which was the sole means by which individuals could successfully and permanently be extricated from "cults." A similar scenario probably would have emerged if the anti-cult associations had achieved greater organizational success.

On a symbolic level, the self-sustaining quality of deviant status was observable in a series of unrelated incidents which were tied to the "cult menace." The tragedy at Jonestown was taken as evidence that all "cults" had a potential for suicide. The Hearst/SLA, Manson Family, and Synanon episodes were offered as evidence that "cultic" organization was much more prevalent and dangerous than even opponents of the new religions had feared. On each occasion, a religious, communal, or quasi-communal group came into conflict with the larger society after the middle of the 1970s, and each time the cult imagery was revitalized. Groups which bore no resemblance to the new religions and incidents which had few, if any, commonalities were linked together and treated as part of a hitherto unrecognized social problem—the "menace of cults." It seemed probable that only the passage of time and the emergence of new crises could dissipate the fear and rhetoric.

From one perspective, what all of this demonstrates is the enormous repressive power which exists in the social order. The ACM, even by its own standards, was not successful in attaining its goals. The anti-cult associations failed miserably in organizational development, the deprogrammers never obtained sufficient legal protection to operate freely, and ACM allies did not furnish the kind of behavioral sanctions the ACM had hoped for. Yet, taken collectively, the impact of the ACM campaign against the new religions was devastatingly effective. This analysis renders the ACM all the more instructive for our understanding of the dynamics of social movements, for it highlights, by the contrast between its limited organizational success and the impact of its campaign, the capacity for repression of social movements under less constrained circumstances.

The foregoing generic analysis, of course, represents a far cry from the subjective impressions of participants in the anti-cult movement. No doubt many parts of it also radically depart from the perspectives of new religions' exponents and sympathizers. What we have attempted to do, with some effort and to our own satisfaction at least, is to render the sensational and mysterious aspects of the "cult"-deprogramming controversy into terms more mundane and yet at the same time perhaps more useful to students of social behavior. Finally, insofar as our study mitigates rather than exacerbates the major parameters of this conflict, it will have performed a latent but certainly not an unimportant function.

REFERENCES

ACLU [American Civil Liberties Union] (1977) "News on conference on religious deprogramming." New York. (January 25)

AFF [American Family Foundation] (1979a) Transcript of Proceedings, Information Meeting on The Cult Phenomenon in the United States. Lexington, MA: American Family Foundation, Inc.

——— (1979b) The Advisor: Journal of the American Family Foundation. 1 (August).

——— (1979c) "Foundation news." Lexington, Massachusetts. (September)

AFT [Agenda for Tomorrow] (1977) "Baptists and Jews face the future." Three-day conference held at Southern Methodist University Campus, Dallas, Texas, December 5-7.

Anthony, D. (1979) Non-Traditional Religions and Mental Health: A Non-Ideological Prototype for Counseling, Community Education, and Technical Assistance. (Concept Paper for a Service, Demonstration, and Research Project Submitted to The National Institute of Mental Health). Berkeley, CA: Program for the Study of New Religious Movements in America, Graduate Theological Union. (March 2)

———, T. Robbins, and J. McCarthy (1979) "Legitimating repression." Society 17 (March/April): 39-42.

APRL [Alliance for the Preservation of Religious Liberties] (1977) Deprogramming: Documenting the Issue. New York: American Civil Liberties Union.

Aversa, R. (1976) "Psychologist deals with cultic 'brainwash.'" Los Angeles Herald Examiner (Sept. 11, 1976).

Backes, N. (1977) "Following Rev. Moon from Wisconsin." Post-Crescent (January 28). Appleton, Wisconsin.

Barker, E. (1980) "With enemies like that . . . some functions of deprogramming as an aid to sectarian membership," in J. T. Richardson (ed.) The Deprogramming Controversy: Sociological, Psychological, Legal, and Historical Perspectives. New Brunswick, NJ: Transaction Press.

Beckford, J. (1980) " 'Brainwashing' and 'deprogramming' in Britain: The social sources of anti-cult sentiment," in J. T. Richardson (ed.) The Deprogramming Controversy: Sociological, Psychological, Legal, and Historical Perspectives. New Brunswick, NJ: Transaction Press.

——— (1979) "Politics and the anti-cult movement." Annual Review of the Social Sciences of Religion 3: 169-190.

——— (1978a) "Through the looking-glass and out the other side: withdrawal from the Rev. Moon's Unification Church." Les Archives de Sciences Sociales des Religions 45(1): 95-116.

——— (1978b) "Cults and cures." Japanese Journal of Religious Studies 5(December): 225-257.

Bell, D. (1976) The Cultural Contradictions of Capitalism. New York: Basic Books.

Bellah, R. N. (1976) "New religious consciousness and the crisis in modernity," pp. 333-352 in C. Y. Glock and R. N. Bellah (eds.) The New Religious Consciousness. Berkeley: University of California Press.

Berry, H. J. (1976) Moon's Unification Church: Is It Biblical? Lincoln, NE: Back to the Bible Publications.

Bjornstad, J. (1979) Counterfeits at Your Door. Glendale, CA: Regal Books.

——— (1976) The Moon is Not the Son. Minneapolis: Bethany Fellowship, Inc.

Breese, D. (1979a) "How to witness to a cultist." Moody Monthly (July-August): 26-27.

——— (1979b) Know the Marks of Cults. Wheaton, IL: Victor Books.

Bromley, D. G. and A. D. Shupe, Jr. (1980a) "Financing the new religions: a resource mobilization perspective." Journal for the Scientific Study of Religion 19 (September).

——— (1980b) "Evolving foci in participant observation: research as an emerging process," pp. 191-203 in W. Shaffir, A. Turowitz, and R. Stebbins (eds.) The Social Experience of Field Work. New York: St. Martin's Press.

——— (1980c) "The Tnevnoc cult." Sociological Analysis 40 (Winter): 361-366.

——— (1979a) "Moonies" in America: Cult, Church, and Crusade. Beverly Hills, CA: Sage.

——— (1979b) " 'Just a few years seem like a lifetime': a role theory approach to participation in religious movements," pp. 159-185 in L. Kriesberg (ed.) Research in Social Movements, Conflict and Change, Greenwich, CT: JAI Press.

——— and J. C. Ventimiglia (1980) "The role of anecdotal atrocities in the social construction of evil," in J. T. Richardson (ed.), The Deprogramming Controversy: Sociological, Psychological, Legal, and Historical Perspectives. New Brunswick, NJ: Transaction Press.

——— (1979) "Atrocity tales, the Unification Church, and the social construction of evil." Journal of Communication 29(Summer): 42-53.

Carroll, J. and B. Bauer (1979) "Suicide training in the Moon cult." New West (January 29): 62-63.

Carter, B., M. Reese, and M. Kasindorf (1978) "Leaning on the press." Newsweek (November 20): 133-134.

CEFM [National Ad Hoc Committee Engaged in Freeing Minds] (1976a) A Special Report. The Unification Church: Its Activities and Practices, Vols. I and II. Arlington, TX: National Ad Hoc Committee, A Day of Affirmation and Protest.

——— (1976b) "Memorandum" (May 20). Arlington, Texas.

——— (1976c) "Memorandum #3" (June 14). Arlington, Texas.

——— (1976d) "Memorandum #4" (October 20). Arlington, Texas.

——— (1976e) "CEFM's objectives" (November 8). Arlington, Texas.

——— (1976f) "Memorandum #5 (Confidential: not for publication)" (November 30). Arlington, Texas.

——— (1976g) "Magnitude of the cult phenomenon." Arlington, Texas.

CERF [Citizens Engaged in Reuniting Families] (1976) Memorandum. (January 30). Scarsdale, New York.

CFF [Citizens Freedom Foundation] (1979a) "NEWS" 4(May). Redondo Beach, CA: Los Angeles Volunteer Parents Chapter.

——— (1979b) "News" 4(September). Redondo Beach, CA: Los Angeles Volunteer Parents Chapter.

——— (1978a) "Organization recommendations for CFF" 3(June). San Francisco, California.

——— (1978b) "NEWS" 3(December 15). Redondo Beach, CA: Los Angeles Volunteer Parents Chapter.

——— (1977) "News" 2(December). Redondo Beach, CA: Los Angeles Volunteer Parents Chapter.

——— (1976a) "NEWS" 1(January). Chula Vista, California.

——— (1976b) "NEWS" 2(February-March). Chula Vista, California.

——— (1976c) "NEWS" 3(April-May). Chula Vista, California.

——— (1973a) "NEWS" 2(March). Chula Vista, California.

——— (1975b) "NEWS" 4(July). Chula Vista, California.

——— (1975c) "NEWS" 5(October). Chula Vista, California.

——— (1975d) "NEWS" 2(May). Chula Vista, California.

——— (1974a) "NEWS" 1(November) Chula Vista, California

——— (1974b) "NEWS" 2(December). Chula Vista, California.

CFF-IS [Citizens Freedom Foundation–Information Services] (1980) Appeal for Money Letter. (January 21, 1980)

Chalenor, R. E. (1975) "Religion, Mind Control, Money and Power." Chula Vista, CA: Citizens Freedom Foundation. (pamphlet)

Clark, J. G., Jr. (1979) "Cults." Journal of the American Medical Association. 242(July 20): 279-281.

——— (1976) "Investigating the effects of some religious cults on the health welfare of their converts" (Testimony of John G. Clark, Jr., M.D. to the Special Investigating Committee of the Vermont Senate). Montpelier, Vermont.

Clements, R. D. (1975) God and the Gurus. Downers Grove, IL: Inter-Varsity Press.

Connecticut (1970) "An act concerning establishment of a commission to investigate activities in Connecticut of the Rev. Sun Myung Moon and the Unification Church of America" (Proposed Bill No. 7337, Referred to the Committee on General Law). Connecticut General Assembly. (January)

Conway, F. and J. Siegelman (1978) Snapping. New York: J.B. Lippincott.

Cox, H. (1978a) "Deep structures in the study of new religions," pp. 122-130 in J. Needleman and G. Baker (eds.) Understanding the New Religions. New York: Seabury Press.

——— (1978b) "Myths sanctioning religious persecution," pp. 3-19 in M. D. Bryant and H. W. Richardson (eds.) A Time for Consideration: A Scholarly Appraisal of the Unification Church. New York: Edwin Mellen Press.

Crittenden, A. (1976) "The incredible story of Ann Gordon and Reverend Sun Myung Moon." Good Housekeeping (October): 86ff.

Davies, H. (1972) Christian Deviations. Philadelphia: Westminster Press.

Davis, M. (1974) "The Moon people and our children." Jewish Community Center Bulletin 20(July 10). White Plains, New York.

Delgado, R. (1979) "Limits to proselytizing." Society 17(March/April): 25-33.

—— (1977) "Religious totalism: gentle and ungentle persuasion." Southern California Law Review 15(November)

Dell (1979) Advertisement. New York: Dell Education Department.

Dole, R. (1976) News release, February 18. Washington, D.C.

Doress, I. and J. N. Porter (1979) Kids in Cults. Brookline, MA: Reconciliation Associates.

Downton, J. V., Jr. (1979) Sacred Journeys: The Conversion of Young Americans to Divine Light Mission. New York: Columbia University Press.

Edwards, C. (1979) Crazy for God. Englewood Cliffs, NJ: Prentice-Hall.

Eister, A. W. (1967) "Toward a radical critique of church-sect typologizing." Journal for the Scientific Study of Religion 6(April): 85-90.

Enroth, R. (1979) The Lure of the Cults. Chappaqua, NY: Christian Herald Books.

—— (1977a) Youth, Brainwashing and the Extremist Cults. Kentwood, MI: Zondervan.

—— (1977b) "Cult/countercult." Eternity 27(November): 18-22, 32-35.

Epstein, E. J. (1975) Between Fact and Fiction: The Problem of Journalism. New York: Vintage Books.

Etzioni, A. (1961) A Comparative Analysis of Complex Organizations. New York: Free Press.

Finney, J. C. (1977) Personal Communication to the authors from Joseph C. Finney, Co-Chairman, American Bar Association Committee on Law and Mental Health. (November 7)

Fitzpatrick, T. (1978) Affidavit of Thomas Fitzpatrick, Attorney for the Holy Spirit Association for the Unification of World Christianity in a suit against Sequoia Elsevier Publishing Co., Inc., Theodore Roosevelt Patrick, and Tom Dulack. Supreme Court of the State of New York, County of New York. (June)

Foss, D. A. and R. W. Larkin (1979) "The roar of the lemming: youth, postmovement groups, and the life construction crisis," pp. 264-285 in H. M. Johnson (ed.) Religious Change and Continuity. San Francisco: Jossey-Bass.

Foster, H. H. (1978) Personal communication to the authors from Henry H. Foster, American Bar Association. (August 23)

Galanter, M., R. Rabkin, J. Rabkin, and A. Deutsch (1979) " 'The Moonies': a psychological study of conversion membership in a contemporary religious sect." American Journal of Psychiatry 136: 165-170.

—— (1978) "The 'Moonies,' a psychological study." Presented to 131st Annual Meeting of the American Psychiatric Association, Atlanta, Georgia.

Gamson, W. A. (1975) The Strategy of Social Protest. Homewood, IL: Dorsey Press.

Glock, C. Y. and R. Stark (1965) Religion and Society in Tension. Chicago: Rand McNally.

Goode, E. (1967) "Some critical observations of the church-sect dimension." Journal for the Scientific Study of Religion 6(April): 69-77.

Grant, J. (1973) The Enemy. Wheaton, IL: Tyndale House.

Greeley, A. M. (1972) The Denominational Society. Glenview, IL: Scott, Foresman.

GTU [Graduate Theological Union] (1979) "New religious movements newsletter" 1(December). Berkeley, California.

Hampshire, A. P. (1979) "Thomas Sharp and anti-Mormon sentiment in Illinois." Journal of the Illinois State Historical Society 72: 82-100.

Hargrove, B. (1979) "Informing the public: social scientists and reactions to Jonestown." (unpublished)

Harper, C. (1979) Religious Cults and the Anti-Cult Movement in the Omaha Area. Submitted to the Nebraska Committee for the Humanities. Omaha, Nebraska: Department of Sociology, Creighton University.

Horowitz, I. L. (1977) "Science, sin and scholarship." Atlantic Monthly 239(March): 98-102.

Hultquist, L. (1977) They Followed the Piper. Plainfield, NJ: LOGOS International.

Hunter, E. (1962) Brainwashing: From Pavlov to Powers. New York: The Bookmailer.

——— (1953) Brainwashing in Red China: The Calculated Destruction of Men's Minds. New York: Vanguard.

Ibis (1980) "Cults, charisma and mind control." Media slide/cassette packet. Pleasantville, NY: Ibis Media.

IFF [Individual Freedom Federation, Inc.] (1980) Newsletter (January). Trenton, Michigan.

——— (1979a) Newsletter (January). Trenton, Michigan.

——— (1979b) Newsletter (March). Trenton, Michigan.

——— (1979c) Newsletter (April). Trenton, Michigan.

——— (1979d) Newsletter (July). Trenton, Michigan.

——— (1979e) Newsletter (August). Trenton, Michigan.

——— (1979f) Newsletter (November). Trenton, Michigan.

(1978a) Newsletter (November). Trenton, Michigan.

——— (1978b) Newsletter (February). Trenton, Michigan.

IFIF [Internation Foundation for Individual Freedom] (1978) "Resolution of pseudo-religious cults under consideration by the National PTA Board." Princeton, West Virginia.

——— (1977a) "Announcement" (March 1). Ardmore, Pennsylvania.

——— (1977b) "Announcement" (April 18). Ardmore, Pennsylvania.

——— (1977c) "Memorandum" (April 22). Arlington, Texas.

——— (1977d) "Memo on national conference" (June 5). Ardmore, Pennsylvania.

IFFET [International Freedom Foundation Educational Trust] (1977) "Memorandum" (June 15). Arlington, Texas.

Illinois (1979) "House Resolution 121." Springfield: Illinois General Assembly.

IPH [The Institute of Pennsylvania Hospital] (1979) "Understanding religious cults." Physician Education Project presented in three separate cities (New York, Chicago, Atlanta) by Anthony J. Campolo.

Jones, F. (1979) Memo to Mr. Salomen RE: Hearings on Cults Held at the World Trade Center. New York. (August 10)

Judah, J. S. (1978) "New religions and religious liberty," pp. 201-208 in J. Needleman and G. Baker (eds.) Understanding the New Religions. New York: Seabury Press.

Kanter, R. M. (1972) Commitment and Community. Cambridge, MA: Harvard University Press.

Katz, J. (1975) "Essences as moral identities: verifiability and responsibility in imputations of deviance and charisma." American Journal of Sociology 80(May): 1369-1390.

Keller, E. B. (1974) "Glimpses of exorcism in religion," pp. 259-311 in S. E. Nauman, Jr. (ed.) Exorcism Through the Ages. New York: Philosophical Library.

Kelley, D. M. (1978) "Beware 'open season' on cults." Christian Science Monitor (December 18).

——— (1977) "Deprogramming and religious liberty." The Civil Liberties Review 4(July/August): 23-33.

——— (1972) Why Conservative Churches Are Growing. New York: Harper & Row.

Krause, C. A. (1978) Guyana Massacre. Berkeley, CA: Berkeley Publishing.

Kilduff, M. and R. Javers (1978) The Suicide Cult. New York: Bantam Books.

Lambert, R. D. (1967) "Current trends in religion: a summary," pp. 531-541 in R. D. Knudten (ed.) The Sociology of Religion: An Anthology. New York: Appleton-Century-Crofts.

Landis, B. Y. (1967) "Trends in church membership in the United States," pp. 523-530 in R. D. Knudten (ed.) The Sociology of Religion: An Anthology. New York: Appleton-Century-Crofts.

Lang, K. and G. E. Lang (1978) "The dynamics of social movements," pp. 96-117 in L. E. Genevie (ed.) Collective Behavior and Social Movements. Itasca, IL: F. E. Peacock.

Langford, H. (1977) Traps: A Probe of Those Strange New Cults. Montgomery, AL: Committee for Christian Education and Publications, Presbyterian Church in America.

Lasher, H. L. (1979) "Letter to the Church of Scientology of New York." Albany, New York. (July 19)

LCMS [The Lutheran Church—Missouri Synod] (1978) "Packet on 'new religions.' " St. Louis: The Lutheran Church—Missouri Synod, Commission on Organizations.

LCUSA [The Lutheran Council in the USA] (1978) The Cults: A Resource Packet. Chicago, IL: The Lutheran Council in the USA, Division of Campus Ministry and Education Services.

Levine, S. V. and N. E. Salter (1976) "Youth and contemporary religious movements: psychosocial findings." Canadian Psychiatric Association Journal 21(6): 411-420.

Levitt, Z. (1976) The Spirit of Sun Myung Moon. Irvine, CA: Harvest House.

Lifton, R. J. (1963) Thought Reform and the Psychology of Totalism. New York: W. W. Norton.

——— (1957) "Thought reform of Chinese intellectuals: a psychiatric evaluation." Journal of Social Issues 13: 5-20.

Lipsky, M. and D. J. Olson (1968) On the Politics of Riot Commissions (Discussion Paper, Institute for Research on Poverty). Madison: University of Wisconsin.

LOCI [Love Our Children, Inc.] (1979) Newsletter (December). Omaha, Nebraska.

——— (1976) "Memo" (September). Omaha, Nebraska.

Lofland, J. (1977) Doomsday Cult. New York: Irvington.

——— (1966) Doomsday Cult. Englewood Cliffs, NJ: Prentice-Hall.

McCarthy, J. D. and M. N. Zald (1977) "Resource mobilization and social movements: a partial theory." American Journal of Sociology 82(May): 1212-1241.

——— (1974) "Tactical considerations in social movement organizations." Presented at the annual meeting of the American Sociological Association, Montreal, Canada.

––– (1973) The Trend of Social Movements in America: Professionalization and Resource Mobilization. Morristown, NJ: General Learning Press.

MacCollum, J. (1978) The Way of Victor Paul Werwille. Madison, WI: Inter-Varsity Christian Fellowship.

McBeth, L. (1977) Strange New Religions. Nashville, TN: Broadman Press.

Martin, M. (1976) Hostage to the Devil. New York: Bantam Books.

Martin, R. (1979) Escape. Denver, CO: Accent Books.

Martin, W. (1965) The Kingdom of the Cults. Minneapolis: Bethany Fellowship.

Marty, M., S. Rosenberg, and A. Greeley (1968) What Do We Believe? The Stance of Religion in America. New York: Meredith Press.

Massachusetts (1979) Commonwealth of Massachusetts Public Hearing, Senator John G. King, Commerce and Labor. Transcribed by American Family Foundation, Inc. (March 21)

Means, P. (1976) The Mystical Maze. Campus Crusade for Christ.

Meerloo, J. (1956) The Rape of The Mind. New York: World.

Melton, J. G. (1980) "Deprogramming: a response to the rise of cults." (unpublished)

Merritt, J. (1975) "Open letter." Lincoln, MA: Return to Personal Choice, Inc. (pamphlet)

Middleton, L. (1979) "The Rev. Moon's Unification Church launches drive on college campuses." Chronicle of Higher Education November 13: 4-6.

Miller, D. E. (1980) "Deprogramming in historical perspective," in J. T. Richardson (ed.) Deprogramming: Sociological, Psychological, Legal, and Historical Perspectives. New Brunswick, NJ: Transaction Press.

Mills, C. W. (1959) The Sociological Imagination. New York: Oxford University Press.

Mills, J. (1979) Six Years with God. New York: A & W Publications.

Minnesota (1978) Section 309.50, Subdivision 10 of Minnesota Statutes 1976. Amendment of Chapter 601 (H.F. No. 1248), "Charitable funds–regulation of solicitation " 70th Minnesota Legislature.

Mook, J. D. (1974) "New growth on burnt-over ground. III: The Unification Church." A.D.(May): 30-35.

Moon, S. M. (1976) Statement on Jews and Israel. Tarrytown, New York: Holy Spirit Association for the Unification of World Christianity.

Morgan, R. E. (1968) The Politics of Religious Conflict. New York: Pegasus.

Nederhood, J. (1979) Cult Insurance. Palos Heights, IL: Christian Reformed Church. (pamphlet)

Needleman, Jacob (1972) The New Religions. New York: Pocketbooks.

New York (1979) Public Hearing on Treatment of Children By Cults. the State Assembly of New York. (August 9-10) Reprinted by American Family Foundation, Inc.

––– (1977) Proposed Bill AB9566-A (Section 240.46 "Promoting a pseudo-religious cult") to the New York State Assembly. Albany, New York. (October 5)

––– (1975) Final Report on the Activities of The Children of God to Hon. Louis J. Lefkowitz, Attorney General of the State of New York. Albany: Charity Frauds Bureau.

Nunn, C. Z., H. J. Crockett, Jr., and J. A. Williams, Jr. (1978) Tolerance for Nonconformity. San Francisco: Jossey-Bass.

Oesterreich, T. K. (1966) Possession, Demonical and Other (D. Ibberson, trans.). New York: University Books.

Orr, W. W. (1972) Are Demons for Real? Wheaton, IL: Scripture Press.

O'Rourke, F. J. (1978) Personal communication to the authors. (January 14)

Patrick, T. (1976) Lightning News (August). National City, California.

——— and Tom Dulack (1976) Let Our Children Go! New York: E. P. Dutton.

Pennsylvania (1979) House Resolution No. 20. Harrisburg: the General Assembly of Pennsylvania.

PCIC [Pennsylvania Conference on Interchurch Cooperation (n.d.) The Dangers of Pseudo-Religious Cults. Harrisburg. (pamphlet)

People (1979) "In their own words."

——— (1978a) "Why Leo Ryan and Jim Jones met on that day of death in the jungles of Guyana." December 4: 28-33.

——— (1978b) "A California teenager goes undercover to investigate life among the Moonies." July 24: 20-24.

Prichard, A. (n.d.) "Memo to ACLU affiliates re: response to kidnapping and efforts." New York: American Civil Liberties Union.

PRRC [Princeton Religion Center] (1979) Religion in America 1979-80. Princeton: Princeton Religion Research Center.

Rasmussen, M. (1976) "How Sun Myung Moon lures America's children." McCall's (September): 102ff.

Remsberg, C. and B. Remsberg (1976) "Why I quit the Moon cult." Seventeen (July): 107, 117, 127.

RFTCT [Recovery of Free Thought Charitable Trust] (1979) "Defense fund . . . for families and friends." Exeter, New Hampshire. (pamphlet)

Rice, B. (1976) "Honor thy father Moon." Psychology Today (January): 36-47.

Richardson, J. T. [ed.] (1978) Conversion Careers: In and Out of New Religious Groups. Beverly Hills, CA: Sage.

———, M. W. Stewart, and R. B. Simmonds (1979) Organized Miracles: A Study of a Contemporary, Youth, Communal, Fundamentalist Organization. New Brunswick, NJ: Transaction Press.

Robbins, R. H. (1974) "Exorcism," pp. 201-216 in S. E. Nauman, Jr. (ed.) Exorcism Through the Ages. New York: Philosophical Library.

Robbins, T. (1979a) Cults and the therapeutic state." Social Policy 10(May/June): 42-46.

——— (1979b) Civil Liberties, "Brainwashing," and "Cults." Berkeley, CA: Program for the Study of New Religious Movements, Graduate Theological Union.

——— (1977a) "Even a Moonie has civil rights." The Nation (February 26): 238-242.

——— (1977b) " 'Brainwashing' vs. religious freedom." The Nation (April 30): 518.

——— and D. Anthony (forthcoming) "Stop knocking cults." Psychology Today.

——— (1979) "Cult phobia." Inquiry Magazine (January 8): 2-3.

——— and J. McCarthy (1977) "The 'brainwashing' metaphor as a social weapon: a new conceptual tool for the therapeutic state." Presented at the annual meeting of the Society for the Scientific Study of Religion, Chicago, Illinois.

Rowen, C. T. (1979) "We can't ignore crimes done for 'religion.' " Fort Worth Star-Telegram (February 16).

——— (1978) " 'Religion' now sanctuary for scoundrels." Fort Worth Star-Telegram (December 30).

Rubington, E. and M. S. Weinberg (1971) The Study of Social Problems. New York: Oxford University Press.

Salisbury, B. (1979) "Cult-control faction wins hearing skirmish." St. Paul Pioneer Press (August 29).

Sargent, W. (1957) Battle for the Mind. New York: Doubleday.

Sawatsky, R. (1978) "Moonies, Mormons and Mennonites: Christian heresy and religious toleration," pp. 20-40 in M. D. Bryant and H. W. Richardson (eds.) A Time for Consideration: A Scholarly Appraisal of the Unification Church. New York: Edwin Mellen Press.

Schweikhart, G. (1976) "Moonstruck!" Omaha (September): 8-12.

SCP [Spiritual Counterfeits Project] (1976a) Newsletter 2(June/July). Berkeley, California.

——— (1976b) Newsletter 2(September). Berkeley, California.

Seth, R. (1969) Witches and Their Craft. New York: Award Books.

Shaffer, R. (1978) "Scientologists play rough to make church critics pay." Fort Worth Star-Telegram (November 26).

Shupe, A. D., Jr. (1978) Dual review of Ted Patrick-Tom Dulock's Let Our Children Go! and Carroll Stoner-Jo Anne Parke's All Gods Children. Journal for The Scientific Study of Religion 17(March): 83-85.

——— and D. G. Bromley (1980a) "Walking a tightrope: dilemmas of participant observation of groups in conflict." Qualitative Sociology 2(January): 3-21.

——— (1980b) "Witches, Moonies, and evil," in T. Robbins and D. Anthony (eds.) In Gods We Trust: Patterns in American Religious Pluralism. New Brunswick, NJ: Transaction Books.

——— (1979) "The Moonies and the Anti-cultists: movement and movement in conflict." Sociological Analysis 40(Winter): 325-334.

Shupe, A. D., Jr., D. G. Bromley, and D. Oliver (forthcoming) The American Anti-Cult Movement: A Bibliographic History. New York: Garland Press.

Shupe, A. D., Jr., R. Spielmann, and S. Stigall (1980) "Cults of anti-cultism." Society 17(March/April): 43-46.

——— (1977a) "Deprogramming and the emerging American anti-cult movement." Presented at the annual meeting of the Society of the Scientific Study of Religion, Chicago.

——— (1977b) "Deprogramming: the new exorcism." American Behavioral Scientist 20: 941-956.

Siegelman, J. and F. Conway (1979) "Playboy interview: Ted Patrick." Playboy (March): 53ff.

Simons, G. L. (1974) The Witchcraft World. New York: Barnes and Noble.

Singer, M. T. (1979) "Coming out of the cults." Psychology Today 12(January): 72-82.

Sklar, D. (1977) Gods and Beasts: The Nazis and the Occult. New York: Thomas Y. Crowell.

Sparks, J. (1977) The Mind Benders. New York: Thomas Nelson.

Spurgin, N. M. (1976) Unification Church Membership Profile. New York: Holy Spirit Association for the Unification of World Christianity. (June)

Stathos, H. (1979) "Unification Church stresses family in 'cult' child hearings." the News World (August 11).

Stoner, C. and J. Parke (1977) All Gods Children. Radnor, PA: Chilton.

Sudo, K. (1975) 120 Day Training Manual. Belvedere, NY: HSA-UWC.

Szasz, T. S. (1970a) The Manufacture of Madness: A Comparative Study of the Inquisition and the Mental Health Movement. New York: Harper & Row.

——— (1970b) Ideology and Insanity: Essays on the Psychiatric Dehumanization of Man. Garden City, NY: Doubleday/Anchor.

——— (1961) The Myth of Mental Illness: Foundations of a Theory of Personal Conduct. New York: Hoeber-Harper.

Testa, B. (1978) "Making crime seem natural: news and deprogramming," pp. 41-81 in M. D. Bryant and H. W. Richardson (eds.) A Time for Consideration. New York: Edwin Mellen Press.

Texas (1979) Resolution (S.R. No. 485) passed by the Senate Committee on State Affairs, State of Texas.

——— (1977) Resolution (H.S.R. No. 35) passed by the House of Representatives Committee on Criminal Jurisprudence, State of Texas. (May 10)

Thielmann, B. (1979) The Broken God. Elgin, IL: David C. Cook.

Tuchman, G. (1978) Making News. New York: Free Press.

——— (1972) "Objectivity as strategic ritual: an examination of newsmen's notions of objectivity." American Journal of Sociology 77(January): 660-679.

Uhlmann, M. M. (1976) Letter of Michael M. Uhlmann, Assistant Attorney General, to Honorable Robert Dole, Senator (Copy provided by Senator Dole in personal correspondence with authors). (February 17)

Underwood, B. and B. Underwood (1979) Hostage to Heaven. New York: Clarkson N. Potter.

Ungerleider, J. T. (1979) The New Religions: Insights into the Cult Phenomenon. New York: Merck, Sharp and Dohme.

——— and D. K. Wellisch (1979a) "Coercive pervasion (brainwashing), religious cults, and deprogramming." American Journal of Psychiatry 136(M..rch): 279-282.

——— and D. K. Wellisch (1979b) "Cultism, thought control and deprogramming: observations on a phenomenon." Psychiatric Opinion 16(January): 10-15.

URC [University Religious Council] (1979) Understanding Cult Involvement: For Counselors, Clergy, and Group Workers. Berkeley: University Religious Council at the University of California. (pamphlet)

U.S. Government (1979a) The Assassination of Representatives Leo J. Ryan and the Jonestown, Guyana Tragedy (Report of a Staff Investigative Group to the Committee on Foreign Affairs, U.S. House of Representatives). Washington, DC: U.S. Government Printing Office.

——— (1979b) The Death of Representative Leo J. Ryan, People's Temple, and Jonestown: Understanding a Tragedy (Hearing Before the Committee on Foreign Affairs, U.S. House of Representatives). Washington, DC: U.S. Government Printing Office.

——— (1978) Investigation of Korean-American Relations (Report of the Subcommittee on International Organizations of the Committee on International Relations, U.S. House of Representatives). Washington, DC: U.S. Government Printing Office.

——— (1976) Activities of the Korean Central Intelligence Agency in the United States" (Hearings before the Subcommittee on International Organizations of the Committee on International Relations. U.S. House of Representatives. Part II). Washington, DC: U.S. Government Printing Office.

Verdier, P. A. (1977) Brainwashing and the Cults. Hollywood, CA: Institute of Behavioral Conditioning.

Vermont (1977) Report of the Senate Committee for the Investigation of Alleged Deceptive, Fraudulent and Criminal Practices of Various Organizations in the State. Montpelier. (January)

VPA [Volunteer Parents of America] (1974) Newsletter No. 2 (January 1). Redondo Beach, California.

Wallis, R. (1977) The Road to Total Freedom: A Sociological Analysis of Scientology. New York: Columbia University Press.

Warder, M. Y. (1979) Memorandum to Col. Pak et al. New York. (August 13)

Washington Post (1978) "Deprogrammer upheld in appeal by Moon convert." December 29.

Weatherly, N. (1977) "Anti-cult group folds." Fort Worth Star Telegram (August 13).

Weber, M. (1964) The Theory of Social and Economic Organization (T. Parsons, trans.). New York: The Free Press.

Weicker, L., Jr. (1979) Personal communication to the authors from Senator Lowell Weicker, Jr. (April 30)

Weincek, D. (1979) "A demographic profile of Jonestown." Presented at the annual meeting of the association for the Sociology of Religion, Boston

Wertz, R. (1979) "Memorandum in Support of Legislation #6085." Albany: New York State Assembly.

West, W. (1975) "In defense of deprogramming." Arlington, TX: International Foundation for Individual Freedom. (pamphlet)

White, M. (1979) Deceived. Old Tappan, NJ: Fleming H. Revell.

Wilson, J. (1978) Religion in American Society: The Effective Presence. Englewood Cliffs, NJ: Prentice-Hall.

––– (1973) Introduction to Social Movements. New York: Basic Books.

Wood, A. T. and J. Vitek (1979) Moonstruck. New York: William Morrow.

Woodruff, M. (1978) "Religious freedom and the new religions." International Review of Missions (October): 468-473.

Wuthnow, R. (1976) "The new religions in social context," pp. 26-293 in C. Y. Glock and R. N. Bellah (eds.) The New Religious Consciousness. Berkeley: University of California Press.

X., Grant, T. Grant, B. Grant, X. Grant, and J. Grant (1973) The Enemy. Wheaton, IL: Tyndale House.

Yamamoto, J. I. (1977) The Puppet Master. Downer's Grove, IL: Inter-Varsity Press.

Zald, M. N. and R. Ash (1973) "Social movement organizations: growth, decoy, and change," pp. 80-101 in R. R. Evans (ed.) Social Movements: A Reader and Source Book. Chicago: Rand McNally.

Zald, M. N. and M. A. Berger (1978) "Social movements in organizations: coup d'etat, insurgency, and mass movements." American Journal of Sociology 83(January): 823-861.

INDEX

Ad Hoc Committee Against Nazism, 226
Albert, Carl, 186
Alexander, Brooks, 176
Alexander, Debbie, 176
Alexander, E., 140
Alexander, Joe, Jr., 138, 142
Alexander, Joe, Sr., 125, 136, 138-141, 144, 220
Alliance for the Preservation of Religious Liberties, 22-23, 88, 119, 123, 126, 201
American Academy of Religion, 192
American Bar Association, 196
American Civil Liberties Union, 119, 123, 186, 201-202, 221, 224, 226, 228
American Jewish Committee, 20, 114, 178-179
American Psychiatric Association, 192
American Psychological Association, 192
American Religiosity Patterns, 25-29
American Sociological Association, 192
Anderson, John, 26
Anthony, Dick, 23, 194, 202
Anti-cult associations
  financial limitations, 109-112
  ideological limitations, 112-116
  impact on economic institution, 196-199
  impact on educational institution, 190-193
  impact on medical/legal institutions, 193-196

impact on mass media, 170-173, 154-162, 203
impact on political institution, 94-100, 180-190
impact on religious institution, 173-179
membership/organizational limitations, 106-109
national coalitions, 88-94, 101-106
origins in family strains, 38-47, 88-94
problems in gaining allies, 114-115, 199-204
revitalization effect of Jonestown, 207-232
separation from deprogrammers, 13, 87, 126-130
sociocultural background, 25-29, 78-84
Anti-Cult Movement (ACM)
  ideology (religious), 63-70
  ideology (secular), 70-85
  origins, 88-94, 122-127
  See Anti-cult associations, Deprogramming
Armstrong, Herbert and Ted. See Worldwide Church of God.
Ash, Roberts, 24
Association for the Sociology of Religion, 192
Atrocity stories about "cults," 153-164, 167, 170-173
Aversa, R., 70, 127

Backes, N., 167, 172
Baptist Joint Committee on Public
    Affairs, 26
Barker, Eileen, 24, 151
Bauer, B., 113, 215
Beckford, James, 24, 146
Bell, Daniel, 25
Bellah, Robert N., 25, 27
Berger, M. A., 24
Berkeley Christian Coalition
    See Spiritual Counterfeits Project.
Berry, H.J., 49
Bjornstad, James, 52, 66, 68
Body, The, 139
Boone, Pat, 26
Booneville, 23, 205
Boettcher, Robert, 222
Brainwashing ideology
    See Deprogramming.
Breese, David, 48-49, 54, 65, 69
British Anti-Cult Movement
    See Barker, E., and Beckford, J.
Bromley, David G., 14, 19, 22, 24, 27,
    31, 43, 56-57, 61, 72, 120, 134, 147,
    154, 177, 182, 190, 193, 197, 202,
    206-207, 229, 231
Buckley, James, 93, 162
Bude, Robert, 158
Bugliosi, Victor, 139
Busching, Bruce C., 12, 61

Campus Crusade for Christ
    See Spiritual Counterfeits Project.
Cappelini, Gifford, 131, 142
Carper, Dennis, 155, 159, 161
Carroll, Gov. John, 26
Carroll, J., 113, 215
Carter, Jimmy, 26, 217, 220
Center for the Study of New Religious
    Movements, 195
Chalenor, Robert, 100, 186
Children of God, 27-28, 49, 58, 88-92,
    106-107, 113, 123-125, 174,
    184-185
Christian Science Monitor, 26
Christian Scientists, 115, 120, 174, 201
Christian World Liberation Front
    See Spiritual Counterfeits Project.

Church of Jesus Christ of Latter-Day
    Saints, 174, 115
Citizens Engaged in Reuniting Families,
    Inc. (CERF), 93, 97, 102, 123, 220
Citizens Freedom Foundation (CFF),
    90, 92-93, 95-96, 99-100, 102,
    105-106, 108, 111, 127-129, 196,
    213
Citizens Freedom Foundation—Informa-
    tion Services (CFF-IS), 101, 105-106,
    112, 189
Citizens Organized for the Public Aware-
    ness of Cults, Inc. (COPAC), 93, 102,
    105
Clark, John G., Jr., 73, 127, 137, 185,
    194, 222
Clements, R.D., 50, 66, 69
Cleaver, E., 26-27
Collins, Pam, 76
Colson, Charles, 27
Committee of the Third Day, 205
Conway, Flo, 23, 70-75, 77-78, 84, 113,
    120, 125, 135-136, 175, 193, 215,
    222
Council of Churches of Greater Bridge-
    port, Connecticut, 179
Cox, Harvey, 86, 202
"Cult" apostasy, 150-166
    allegations of child abuse in the Uni-
        ficationist Movement, 227-230
    allegations of suicide instructions in
        the Unificationist Movement,
        215-217
Crampton, Henrietta, 92-93, 103
Crittenden, Ann, 161, 172

Davies, Horton, 174
Davis, R., 27
Davis, Rabbi Maurice, 123, 177, 220,
    223, 228
Delgado, Richard, 186, 195, 224-225
Deprogramming
    attempts to find legal basis for,
        130-134
    brainwashing ideology of, 70-78
    conservatorship. See attempts to find
        legal basis for.
    definition of, 122-123

dynamics of, 145-150
facilities for, 138-142
financial underpinnings of, 135-136
occupational identity of deprogrammers, 136-138
origins in family strains, 38-47
reevaluation, 122-123
separation from anti-cult associations, 127-130
Deviance perspective, 241-247
Devine, D., 157
Dianetics
See Scientology.
Dini, R.F. and Associates, 103
Divine Light Mission, 27, 52, 91, 114
Dixon, Mitch, 142
Dole, Robert N., 96-99, 101, 119-120, 137, 160, 162, 186, 189, 195, 206, 218-221, 223, 232
Doress, I., 193
Dulack, Tom, 23, 71-72, 75, 77, 88, 123, 143
Durst, Martin Irwin "Moss," 231
Dymally, M., 184

Eckhardt, Jack, 103
Eden, Eve, 215-216
Edwards, Christopher, 158, 160, 227-230
Elkins, Chris, 163-164, 188
Engel, Paul, 177
Englebert, M., 157, 159-160
Enroth, Ronald, 22, 214
Epstein, Jay, 172
Erhardt Seminars Training, 113
Etzioni, Amitai, 51
Exorcism, 64-65, 75-78
See also Deprogramming.

"Faithful Five" trial, 132-133

Fefferman, Dan, 118-119
Feiden, Janis, 160
Fetcho, David, 176
Finney, Joseph C., 196
Fish, Hamilton, 232
Fitzpatrick, T., 135-136
Flynt, Larry, 27

Ford, Gerald R., 219
Foss, Daniel A., 27
Foster, H.H., 196
Fraser, Donald, 162-164, 187-189, 213, 218, 222, 232
FREECOG, 90-92, 106, 116
Free Minds, Inc., 102
Freedom of Mind, Inc.
See Freedom of Mind Rehabilitation Center.
Freedom of Mind Rehabilitation Center, 131, 142
Freedom of Thought Foundation ranch, 125, 133, 136, 139-141, 144

Galanter, M., 80-81, 194
Galper, Marvin, 137
Gamson, William, 24
Garbage-Eaters, The
See Body, The.
Geisler, D., 156
Giaimo, Robert, 186, 212, 222, 232
Gilmartin, Kevin, 137, 139-140
Glock, Charles Y., 63
Goldberg, W., 177
Gordon, Ann, 161-162
Graham, Billy, 27
Grant, J., 63
Greeley, Andrew, 39
Greene, Daphne, 223
Greene, Ford, 137
Greenwald, Richard, 155, 158-159, 161
Griffin, A., 26
Gumbiner, Larry, 156-157
Gutman, Jeremiah, 131, 224
Guyana
See Jonestown.
Guyana Complex, 215, 221, 227

Happy-Healthy-Holy, 27
Hare Krishna, 27-28, 70, 73, 91, 113-114, 142, 174, 180, 182-183, 185, 196, 201, 207
Hargrove, Barbara, 210
Harper, Charles, 22, 110, 114-115
Harris, Don, 210
Hatfield, Mark, 26, 221
Hearst, Patty, 30, 246

Heller, Reed, 157-158
Hopkins, Matthew, 135
Horowitz, Irving L., 192
Howard, Wayne, 139, 141
Hoxsey, Betty, 225
Hultquist, Lee, 89
Humbard, Rex, 115
Hunt, Nelson, 26
Hunter, Evan, 29, 71

Immigration and Naturalization Service, U.S., 206
Individual Freedom Foundation Educational Trust (IFFET)
    See International Foundation for Individual Freedom.
Institute for the Study of American Religion, Inc., 231
    See also Melton, J. Gordon.
International Council for Christian Churches, 175
International Foundation for Individual Freedom (IFIF), 101, 103-105, 108-109, 191
International Freedom Foundation (IFF), 103, 174, 177, 214-215, 220, 226
International Society for Krishna Consciousness
    See Hare Krishna.

Javers, R., 211
Jehovah's Witnesses, 113, 115, 174, 201
Jesus Movement, 27, 88
Jews for Jesus, 28, 114-115
Ji, Maharaj
    See Divine Light Mission.
Johnson, Billy "White Shoes," 26
Jones, Rev. Jim, 208-216, 222
Jones, Farley, 228-229
Jonestown, 17, 111-112, 117, 171, 180, 186-187, 195
    See also Chapter 8.
Judah, Stillson, 177

Katz, J., 51
Keller, E.B., 63
Kelley, Dean M., 26, 202, 217, 223-224

Kelly, Galen, 136, 228, 230
Killduff, M., 211
King, Martin Luther, Jr., 209
Klein, A., 131
Knight, Kathy, 155
Koreagate, 117, 162, 171, 178, 180, 187, 213, 218
Korean Council of Christian Churches, 175
Korean War, 29, 31
Krause, C.A., 211

Lambert, R.D., 120
Landis, B.Y., 120
Langford, H., 64, 68, 175
Lara-Braud, J., 179
Larkin, R.W., 27
Larsen, Barbara, 131
Lasher, Howard L., 227-229
LeBar, J.J., 179
Lefkowitz, Louis J., 184
Levine, Saul Y., 79-81
Levitt, Zola, 66
Lewis, Warren, 228
Liberman, E., 177
Lifton, Robert J., 29, 71, 186
Lipsky, M., 97
Lofland, John, 22, 32
Long, Russell B., 219-220
Love Israel, 92
Love Our Children, Inc., 93, 95, 105, 108, 110, 114-115, 175
lutheran Church—Missouri Synod, 175-176
Lutheran Council in the USA, 175
Lynn, Barry, 224

Mabry, Virginia, 216
McBeth, L., 69-70
McCarthy, John, 24, 111, 120
MacCollam, Joel, 68
McIntire, Carl, 175
McQuin, S., 156
Manson, Charles, 27, 30, 139, 246
Martin, M., 65
Martin, Rachel, 52
Martin, Wallace, 225
Martin, Walter, 174

Mascone, George, 209
Means, P., 113
Meerloo, J., 71
Melton, J. Gordon, 23, 212, 231
Morritt, J., 71, 228
Middleton, Lorenzo, 193
Mills, C. Wright, 79, 95
Mills, J., 211
Moon, Rev. Sun Myung
    See Unification Church.
Murray, Terry, 161

National Ad Hoc Committee Engaged in
    Freeing Minds (CEFM), 18-19, 21,
    101-120, 129
    See also Slaughter, George.
National Council of Churches, 57, 178,
    202, 224
National Council of Churches of Christ,
    179
National Endowment for the Humani-
    ties, 195
National Institute of Mental Health, 195,
    218-219
Nederhood, J., 52, 119
Needleman, Jacob, 27
New Jersey Department of Education,
    190
New York Council of Churches, 57
New York State Board of Regents, 190
Nixon, Richard M., 36, 57, 206
Nunn, C.Z., 63

O'Connor, E.E., 182
Oesterreich, T.K., 64
Old Catholic Church, 113
Oliver, Donna, 12
Olson, D.J., 97
O'Rourke, Francis J., 188
Orr, W.W., 63
Ottinger, Richard, 221
O'Shea, P., 216

Parent Teacher Associations, 191
Park, Chung Hee, 162
Parke, J.A., 22, 73, 79-82, 84, 114, 175
Patrick, Ted, 23, 71-78, 88, 90, 113-114,
    119-120, 122-125, 127-137, 143,
    186, 195, 215, 220

Pennsylvania Catholic Conferences, 175
Pennsylvania Conference on Interchurch
    Cooperation, 175
Pennsylvania Council of Churches, 175
People's Temple
    See Jonestown.
Porter, J.N., 193
Presbyterian Church in America, 175
Prichard, A., 201

Rambur, William, 89-95, 99-100, 103,
    111-112, 127-128
Rasmussen, M., 172
Reagan, Ronald, 123
Recovery of Thought Charitable Trust,
    142
Religious Research Association, 192
Remsberg, B., 172
Remsberg, C., 172
Resource Mobilization Theory, 11,
    14-15, 24
Return to Personal Choice, Inc., 71, 93
Richardson, Herbert, 179
Robbins, R.H., 64
Robbins, Thomas, 29, 196, 202
Roberts, Oral, 115
Robertson, Pat, 115
Robinson, James, 26, 115
Rockefeller, Nelson, 184
Roeshman, Ben, 103
Rosemara, Ellen, 160
Rubin, Jerry, 27
Rubington, Earl, 78
Rudin, James, 178-179
Ryan, Leo J., 187-188, 208, 210-213,
    219-220, 222, 232

Salonen, Neil A., 163, 197-198, 220,
    225, 229
Salter, Nancy E., 79-81
Sargent, William, 29, 71
Sawatsky, Rodney, 202
Scharff, Gary M., 113, 153
Schart, Lawrence, 210-211
Schumacher, Marti, 134
Schweikert, G., 157
Scientology, 27, 113, 201
Seth, Ronald, 135
Shervan, T., 156-157, 160

Shupe, Anson D., Jr., 14, 19, 22, 24, 27, 31, 43, 56-57, 61, 72, 76, 90, 102, 119-120, 147, 177, 182, 190, 193, 197, 202, 206-207, 229, 231
Siegelman, Jim, 23, 70-75, 77-78, 84, 113, 120, 125, 135-136, 175, 193, 215, 222
Simons, G.L., 135
Singer, Margaret, 194
Slaughter, Cynthia, 101, 160
Slaughter, George M. III, 101-104, 110-112
See also National Ad Hoc Committee Engaged in Freeing Minds.
Smith, Stan, 26
Society for the Scientific Study of Religion, 192
Southern Baptist Convention
See Baptist Joint Committee on Public Affairs.
Sparks, Jack   48-50, 52-53, 66, 68
Speier, Jackie, 222
Spielmann, Roger, 19
Spiritual Counterfeits Project, 65, 173, 176, 205
Squires, Bill, 176, 205
Stapleton, Ruth Carter, 113-114
Stark, Rodney, 63
Stathos, Harry, 227, 229
Stigall, Sam, 19
Stoner, C., 22, 73, 79-82, 84, 114, 175
Stookey, Paul, 26
Sudo, Ken, 231
Summer, Donna, 26
Swaggert, Jimmy, 115
Sweeney, John, 105, 112
Swope, George, 97, 103, 220
Symbionese Liberation Army, 222
Szasz, Thomas, 194

Tanenbaum, M., 178-179
Testa, Bart, 126, 137, 202
Thielmann, Bonnie, 211
Thornburgh, Richard L., 206
Transcendental Meditation, 27, 113, 176, 190
Trauscht, Michael, 136, 139-141

Uhlmann, Michael M., 206

Underwood, Barbara, 153, 160
Ungerleider, J. Thomas, 79, 80-84, 194
Unification Church
as archetypal world-transforming movement and "cult," 30-31
as heresy, 47-57
as primary target of the anti-cult movement, 97
effects of Jonestown on, 215-232
fishing fleets, 197-199
history, 27, 31-32
ideology, 32-34
International Conferences on the Unity of Science, 192
Rev. Sun Myung Moon's charisma, 34
organization, 34-36
Unification Theological Seminary, 35, 190
Unitarians, 174
United Presbyterian Church Assembly, 175

Vavuris, Lee, 133
Verdier, Paul, 70-71, 73
Vitek, T. 153, 192

Wall, P. 195
Warder, Michael Y., 228-229
Watergate, 57, 171, 206
See also Nixon, Richard M.
Watson, Tex, 27
Way International, The, 134
Weatherly, Nancy, 104
Weber, Max, 39
Weicker, Lowell, Jr., 198
Weinberg, Martin, 78
Weincek, David, 211
Wellisch, David, 80, 194
Wertz, Robert, 185, 226
West, William, 75
White, M., 211
Whitehurst, G. William, 232
Wilson, John, 16
Witch-pricking
See Hopkins, Matthew.
Witness Lee, 52
Wood, Allan Tate, 153, 163, 192
Woodruff, M., 195
Worldwide Church of God, 113, 115

Wuthnow, Robert, 28

Volunteer Parents of America (VPA), 92-93, 101, 104-105, 108-109

Yamamoto, J., 55, 65-69, 176

Zald, Mayer, 24, 111, 120
Zorinsky, Edward, 221

ABOUT THE AUTHORS

Anson D. Shupe, Jr., received his Ph.D. in 1975 from Indiana University, specializing in comparative political sociology. After teaching one year at Alfred University, he moved to the University of Texas at Arlington where he is currently Associate Professor of Sociology. His primary research interests are in the areas of social movements, sociology of religion, and political sociology. Professor Shupe has authored numerous articles which have appeared in such journals as *Social Forces, The Journal for the Scientific Study of Religion, Comparative Political Studies,* and *The Journal of Communication.* He is currently engaging in long-range study of social movements and societal response with co-author David Bromley.

David G. Bromley received his Ph.D. in 1971 from Duke University, specializing in political and urban sociology. After serving on the faculties of the University of Virginia and the University of Texas at Arlington, he is currently Associate Professor and Chairman of Sociology at the University of Hartford, Connecticut. His primary research interests are in the areas of social movements, deviance, and political and urban sociology. Professor Bromley has authored numerous articles which have appeared in *Journal of Health and Social Behavior, Phi Delta Kappan, Social Forces, Society,* and *The Canadian Review of Sociology and Anthropology.* He also co-edited *White Racism and Black Americans.*